To Dr. Robert S.
Hamilton
—

Best regards
from the author
—
S.D 3.13-477
Phannkonvials
—

Pham Kim Vinh

San Diego,   California

First Edition

Library of Congress No. 77-70369

The Politics of Selfishness:
VIETNAM—The Past as Prologue

PHAM KIM VINH

1977

By the same author

In Vietnamese

—Vietnam between War and Peace

—Toward an Effective Defense Policy for South Vietnam

—A new New Pattern of Development

—A New Pattern of Democracy for Developing Nations in the 1970s

—Farewell to Saigon

In English

—Super Media, Democracy and Ideological Warfare

—Political Warfare in Nuclear Age

—Law and Human Rights

In French

—L'Amerique Decouverte par un Refugie

—Detente et L'avenir du Monde Libre

This book is dedicated to those who believe in free and open human societies and who fight to defend and to preserve these societies.

CONTENTS

ACKNOWLEDGEMENTS

In writing this book, I have only myself to blame but many honorable people to thank.

I owe a particular debt of gratitude to Mr. and Mrs. James Turner, U.S. Navy Commander (ret.) because without them, this book might never have been completed.

I also owe a particular debt of gratitude to pastors Robert H. Mayo and Paul R. Pulliam, First Presbyterian Church, San Diego California. Their advice was both wise and valuable.

I am very pleased to acknowledge the Holy Spirit assistance of all members of the First Presbyterian Church, San Diego, California. Without their moral and physical support, I might never have had enough courage to accomplish this work.

I acknowledge the generous assistance of Mr. Bert Shephard, Chairman of the Relocation Committee of that Church for Indochinese refugees.

Special mention must be made as well of the assistance of Mr. Browning E. Marean, Attorney-at-Law; Mr. Kenneth O. All, Professor of Public Relations; Mr. Eric Pulliam and Miss Kerry Pulliam. All are residents of San Diego.

Some of the themes contained in this book and related to the U.S. policy on Vietnam were first explored by Mr. Bernard Fall ("The Two Vietnams," revised edition); Mr. Jerry Voorhis ("The Strange Case of Richard M. Nixon"); Mr. M. Stanton Evans ("The Politics of Surrender"); Mr. Chester L. Cooper ("The Lost Crusade"); and Mr. David Halberstam ("The Best and the Brightest"). To them, I owe many helpful suggestions and ideas.

To the famous magazines Time and Newsweek (issues of March, April and May 1975), I owe many precious details and information on the agony of South Vietnam.

To the Pentagon Papers published by The New York Times and written by Neil Sheehan, Hedrick Smith, E.W. Kenworthy and Fox Butterfield, I owe much data regarding the secret history of the Vietnam War.

My family has been extremely loving and supportive throughout this enterprise for which I am most grateful.

Finally, I should like to acknowledge my debt to my dear parents who greatly shaped my life and my ideas. It is my deepest regret neither is alive to see their son's modest work accomplished.

PHAM KIM VINH
San Diego
California, U.S.A.
January, 1977

PREFACE

The war in Vietnam was suddenly over. The last United States Ambassador in Saigon, Mr. Graham Martin, and his "bodyguards" had been lifted from the roof of the American Embassy on Thong Nhat Grand Boulevard* only five hours before communist tanks arrived at Saigon's Presidential Palace.

While there is still a wide range of opinion in the United States about America's unhappy participation in the Vietnam War, most Americans appeared to be relieved that the bloodshed was finally over. Senator Hubert Humphrey, a former Vice-President and a one-time presidential candidate, urged Americans to avoid feelings of guilt about the outcome. "We should not feel that we've let anyone down," he said. "No outside force can save a country that lacks the will or political leadership." Other thoughtful Americans urged that the nation begin a period of national self-examination to diminish the likelihood of future Vietnams.

The tragic exodus of thousands of Vietnamese had begun the last days of April 1975, shortly before the collapse of Saigon. By the end of June, the official number of refugees was 139,000. This number did not include thousands of others who were temporarily housed at various refugee camps in some non-communist countries in Southeast Asia. Had the Vietnamese been given more time, that number might have been increased many times.

Some Americans begrudged the fact that with this exodus, the United States would have to take on another Vietnam—at a time when the United States economy was in its worst recession since the 1930s. Others suggested that the refugees would be better off in their own country. But responsible public leaders tended to recognize that there was an obligation to the new arrivals. "Their situation is not voluntary," said Harvard professor Nathan Glazer. "They worked with us in a policy that we are at least equally responsible for." Interviewed by a Time Magazine correspondent, Senator Hubert Humphrey said: "What we've learned is that there aren't American answers for every problem in the world . . . It's clear that there's blame enough for all of us. I include myself."

These responsible statements have encouraged me to write this book. Much remains to be said about responsibilities for the collapse of South Vietnam, but right now, it is clear that at least there is blame enough for both Americans and South Vietnamese.

America can't escape responsibility for Vietnam. Nor can Saigon's own fatal weakness escape recognition. The United States has paid for Vietnam many times over but the people of Vietnam have paid much more. It was a tragedy.

It has been a lesson, an extremely costly lesson, in terms of thousands of human lives. Therefore, it deserves to be recorded. It must be remembered.

This book is only an attempt to bring some understanding to the plight of a peace-loving people that found itself, against its will, at one of the focal points of a worldwide struggle. Caught between two warring systems, most of the Vietnamese people would have certainly preferred to avoid both.

PHAM KIM VINH

*"Thong Nhat" means unified.

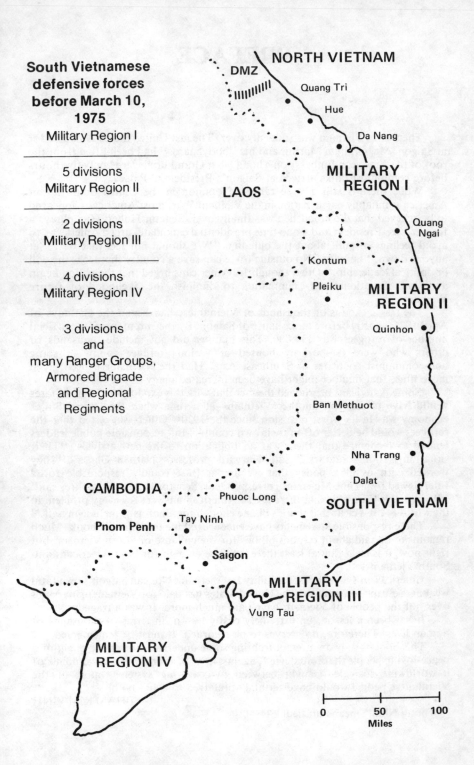

South Vietnamese defensive forces before March 10, 1975

Military Region I

---

5 divisions
Military Region II

---

2 divisions
Military Region III

---

4 divisions
Military Region IV

---

3 divisions
and
many Ranger Groups,
Armored Brigade
and Regional
Regiments

NORTH VIETNAM

DMZ

Quang Tri

Hue

Da Nang

MILITARY REGION I

LAOS

Quang Ngai

Kontum

Pleiku

MILITARY REGION II

Quinhon

Ban Methuot

Nha Trang

Dalat

CAMBODIA

Phuoc Long

Tay Ninh

Pnom Penh

Saigon

SOUTH VIETNAM

MILITARY REGION III

Vung Tau

MILITARY REGION IV

0   50   100
Miles

PART I
Chapter One
BIRTH OF A FOREIGN POLICY

When the guns of World War II fell silent, the United States was the only Western nation capable of conceiving a global foreign policy designed primarily upon lessons learned from the tragic mistakes of the democratic nations in the 1930s. During that decade, the United States and its European Allies watched but failed to act as Japan, Italy and Nazi Germany expanded their realms.

The result was aggression-fed agression. There were successive occupations of Manchuria, China, Ethiopia, the Rhine, Austria, Czechoslovakia. Finally, the assault on Poland set off World War II.

The Lesson seemed clear. One must stop small aggressions before they become large aggressions.

When Mainland China fell to Communism, Dean Acheson hardened American anti-communist attitude. He declared in 1949 that the U.S. did not intend "to permit further expansion of Communist domination on the continent of Asia or in the Southeast Asia area." (1)

So was born the U.S. foreign policy of containment. It remained in effect for over two decades, involved the U.S. in two unpopular wars on the Asian continent and brought it to the brink of war with China on many occasions.

The descent of the Iron Curtain across the frontiers of Eastern Europe was a stimulus to the Truman Doctrine. By Western standards, the nations behind the curtain were police states. They were controlled by Moscow in order to advance Communism at the expense of human freedom. In 1946, Russia attempted to frighten Turkey into ceding military bases and refused to evacuate northern Iran until faced with strong pressures in the United Nations.

What did that mean for American policy? What did that mean for the great faith in the United Nations as a guarantor of peace?

1

Early in 1947, President Harry Truman and his advisors made an important decision after the losing struggle of the Greek Government against Communist guerillas. The decision was that the U.S. recognized the existence of the Cold War and would respond appropriately. If the U.S. did not take Britain's place to help Greece (the British announced the end of aid to Greece because Britain was almost bankrupt), Greece might fall behind the Iron Curtain. Discouraged by such events, other nations might lose the will to resist Communism and Europe might fall under Russian domination.

President Truman made such hard decisions without hesitating. In March 1947, he went to Congress and asked for funds to provide military aid for Greece and Turkey. In a broad and unprecedented statement of American purpose, he postulated: "... It must be the policy of the United States to support free peoples who are resisting attempted subjugation by armed minorities or by outside pressures ..." This was the Truman Doctrine.

Many American officials thought that the Truman Doctrine by itself was too negative and too military. It did not do enough to eradicate the basic condition of human suffering which gave Communism its opportunity.

The Marshall Plan went into operation in 1948 for countries west of the Iron Curtain. Moscow had denounced the plan as a capitalist plot and had prevented her satellites from joining.

In February 1948, nine years after falling victim to Germany, Czechoslovakia was controlled by the Communists. In June 1948, Russia imposed a land blockade on the western sectors of Berlin. Russia's purpose was to force the U.S., Britain and France out of Berlin and to convince the people of all West Germany that the Western nations lacked means and will to defend them.

It seemed that Europe might collapse psychologically in the face of the Russian military threat before economic recovery under the Marshall Plan could be achieved. American and European leaders agreed that a North Atlantic defense organization linking Western Europe with the U.S. and Canada had to be created to deter the Russians.

Principal alliances like NATO and CENTO were bolstered by a series of bilateral U.S. alliances and agreements that held off Communist efforts to push into Iran, Turkey and Greece and to take over Berlin and Taiwan.

In 1949, President Truman had good reasons to be satisfied with America's accomplishments in Europe: security against Russia for Greece and Turkey, economic recovery for Europe. NATO was a tangible symbol of American military commitment and an effective deterrent to Soviet aggression.

Even Moscow appeared to acknowledge America's success. In Congress, the leaders and most members of both Democratic and Republican parties were behind the Administration. The bipartisan foreign policy was triumphant. Unfortunately, unhappy events were taking place in Asia soon after this constructive achievement.

Since 1945, China had been low priority for American policy. When the Chinese Nationalists and Communists resumed their civil war after the defeat of Japan, the U.S. tried to act as mediator. Some U.S. aid was wastefully used and although the Nationalist Government started with vastly more troops and weapons than the Communists, the latter grew steadily stronger. In 1949, the Nationalist regime collapsed. The remnant of that regime established itself on the island of Taiwan.

Many Americans were shocked and bewildered. Although the Truman

Administration published a full documentary record of its China policy, it was unable to silence the critics or win public support. American people even blamed treachery within the U.S. Government as the cause.

In June 1950, the Army of North Korea invaded South Korea. The American Government interpreted the invasion as a signal that Moscow intended to use military force to achieve its objectives. North Korea was a Russian satellite and if the aggression was not stopped, Russia might be tempted to attack in other places.

A United Nations Command under General Douglas MacArthur was established to fight the war. The North Koreans were stopped and in September and October 1950, they were driven back into North Korea.

At that time, the American Government did not think the Chinese Communists would enter the war. In November 1950, Red China did enter in force.

When Red China entered the Korean war, there was a serious conflict between President Truman and General MacArthur about America's primary objective. Truman and his advisors believed that the defense of western Europe was America's primary objective. For MacArthur, the destiny of the world would be decided by American action in Asia.

A Senate Committee began to investigate the circumstances of the MacArthur dismissal and in a larger sense, it began to investigate the entire Asian policy of the Truman Administration since the end of World War II. After many Senate hearings, the nation came to understand and support the Truman Administration policy.

Truce talks began in July 1951. The talks were to drag on for two years but the Korean War was over.

General Dwight D. Eisenhower won the Republican nomination and the presidential election in 1952. He was a strong supporter of the main lines of Truman foreign policy. With President Eisenhower and Secretary of State J.F. Dulles in charge (Dulles had been under President Truman), there was not likely to be any radical change in American foreign policy.

The fighting in Korea finally stopped in 1953 on the basis worked out by the Truman Administration. Stalin died in 1953 and his successors appeared to be reasonable men.

But there was still another war, the French Indochina War. How the U.S. got there . . . what they did there . . . are questions of mainly historical interest. The U.S. stake in Vietnam may have been self-created but it has become real.

Looking back over the period of World War II, it is difficult to find any precise American policy toward Indochina.

President Roosevelt brooded about and raised the possibility of some form of international arrangement as an alternative to the re-establishment of French colonial rule. But he never put his idea forward in detail and never incorporated it in any official White House document.

One official who was working on the Indochina desk during this period described Roosevelt's trusteeship issue as an idea or aspiration rather than a policy. No one privy to Roosevelt's idea felt interested enough to push it after there was strong French and British opposition. Finally, trusteeship for Indochina died shortly after Roosevelt's death(2).

When General De Gaulle visited Washington in late August 1945, President Harry Truman told him that the U.S. "offers no opposition to the return of the

French Army and authority in Indochina.''(3) According to De Gaulle's view, the collapse of Japan removed "the American veto which has kept us out of the Pacific. Indochina from one day to the next became accessible to us once again.''(4)

During his visit in Washington, De Gaulle had received a dramatic and prophetic appeal from Bao Dai, ex-Emperor of Vietnam. De Gaulle did not reveal the content of that letter to President Truman: ''. . . I beg you to understand that the only way to safeguard French interests and the spiritual influence of France in Indochina is to openly recognize the independence of Vietnam and renounce all ideas of re-establishing sovereignty or any form of French Administration.''(5)

On August 20, 1945, Bao Dai sent another message to President Truman in the knowledge that De Gaulle and Truman were to meet:

''. . . Knowing that the head of the provisional government of France is going to confer with you on the future of Indochina, I have the honor to inform you that the various states of Indochina have already proclaimed their independence and are determined to preserve it . . .

''The French people must yield to the principle of equity which the powerful American nation has proclaimed and defends. France must recognize this with good grace in order to avoid the disorder of a war breaking out on the territory of our country.

''I beseech you, Mr. President, to kindly accept my thanks and those of my people for the assistance which, for the sake of justice and humanity, you will be able to kindly furnish to us.''(6)

Bao Dai's two appeals were simply ignored.

Preoccupied with problems of postwar Japan and European recovery, Soviet troublemaking and reconversion of the U.S. economy, the United States could hardly concern itself with events in Southeast Asia. Indochina was a forgotten area. The fall of mainland China was later to remind the U.S. of its existence. At no time did the desires of the Vietnamese Nationalists themselves assume a role in the shaping of U.S. policy.

Meanwhile in Indochina, the Japanese occupation and capitulation lay open Vietnamese society to virtually any form of social protest. This situation bred a maturation among the Vietnamese revolutionaries. It was that change—most pronounced among the Vietnamese Communists—that had fundamental consequences for the Revolution of August 1945.

In the absence of any stronger power, the Communists were able to take advantage of the Japanese capitulation. Within this gap of authority, they staged a scenario which dramatically reflected the character of Vietnamese society and the politics of revolution.

The Viet Minh was able to pave the way for the coup d'etat which occurred on August 21, 1945 with effective propaganda techniques. They succeeded because there was no force to oppose a revolutionary seizure of power.

On September 2, 1945, Ho Chi Minh, descending from the Communist guerilla bases in the mountainous areas of North VN delivered the Declaration of Independence of the Republic Democratic of Vietnam. In addition to quoting from the American Declaration of Independence, Ho further identified himself with the mainstream of western democratic liberalism by referring to the French Declaration of the Rights of Man.

In retrospect, it was a lost opportunity to the U.S. America entered the postwar era with considerable influence over the future of Vietnam. Moreover, the U.S. had the goodwill of the leaders of Viet Minh. On the Vietnam Independence Day (September 2, 1945), Vo nguyen Giap, then commander of the Viet Minh armed forces, paid tribute to the intimate relations with China and the U.S.(7) The Viet Minh was counting on the U.S. to come to its support—at least by putting pressure on France to grant Vietnam's independence.

At the urging of some OSS officers and some American journalists, the Vietnamese Communist leaders sent formal letters to President Truman. These letters were ignored.

By the end of 1945, all American liaison and military groups had been removed from Hanoi. The only American representative was a solitary vice-consul. To the Vietnamese, the return of French soldiers signaled a major change in American policy. The brave words contained in Roosevelt's Four Freedoms clearly did not apply to them. General MacArthur was quoted by Edgar Snow as saying: "If there is anything that makes my blood boil, it is to see our allies in Indochina and Java deploying Japanese troops to reconquer the little people we promised to liberate. It is the most ignoble kind of betrayal."(8)

The American attitude toward the emerging Indochina can probably be best explained by considering the developments in Europe rather than in Southeast Asia. The Soviet Union was threatening the democratic Western Europe that had been the goal of American postwar planning. In the American concept of a new postwar Europe, France with American assistance began to assume a major strategic role in Europe. Because the U.S. needed France's support for American policy in regard to NATO and Germany, French attempts to preserve their empire in Asia were of little concern to politicians in Washington. The choice seemed to be between the evils of Communism and colonialism.

American efforts to induce the French to give ex-Emperior Bao Dai enough independence to establish himself as a counterweight to Ho Chi Minh were resented by the French. In an interview in 1949, Dean Acheson described the dilemma of the Truman Administration: "We came to the aid of the French in Indochina not because we approved of what they were doing but because we needed their support for our policies in regard to NATO and Germany. The French blackmailed us. At every meeting when we asked them for greater effort in Europe, they brought up Indochina and later, North Africa. They asked for our aid for Indochina but refused to tell us what they hoped to accomplish or how . . ."(9)

So, Washington was reluctant to influence French policy in Indochina. Besides, the French assured that steps were being taken that would lead to the eventual independence of Indochina. Simply stated, the U.S. was duped by the French Government.

Later when agreement between the French and the Viet Minh became less and less likely, Paris began to court Bao Dai. The need for developing a strong non-communist alternative to the Viet Minh became increasingly urgent to France. A series of intensive negotiations culminated on March 8, 1949 in the "Elysee Agreement" to bring Vietnam into the French Union. The U.S. State Department welcomed the new arrangement.(10) Again, the course of affairs in Asia worried Washington.

The Communist takeover in mainland China was the catalyst for a reconsideration of Vietnam's significance to the U.S. In light of the defeat of the Kouomintang, the State Department authorized in July 1949 a secret reassessment of American policy in Asia. Ambassador-At-Large Philip Jessup was appointed chairman of a special committee.

Jessup received a memo on July 18 from Dean Acheson, defining the limits of the inquiry as " . . . it is a fundamental decision of American policy that the U.S. does not intend to permit further extension of Communist domination on the continent of Asia or on the Southeast Asia area."(11)

At the end of 1949, the State Department was still convinced the future of world power remained in Europe, implying a French victory in Vietnam. It appears to have been the consensus that Bao Dai had only a poor chance for creating an effective alternative to Ho Chi Minh in Vietnam.

So, Jessup predicted an imminent crisis in Asia following the Communist takeover in China. It was determined to stop revolution in Asia along the Chinese border and to fortify Europe, the central arena of the Cold War. A western victory had to terminate small colonial wars. From that U.S. viewpoint at the end of 1949, an American intervention in Vietnam was inevitable.

1950-1953

By late 1949, Vietnamese Communist troops were trained and equipped in the Chinese southern provinces bordering North Vietnam. By 1950, the Viet Minh had a regular army of 60,000 men, organized into five divisions equipped with Chinese and Russian weapons.

In January 1950, China recognized the government of Ho Chi Minh, and was quickly followed by the Soviet Union. This event moved the French-Vietnam war into a confrontation between the Free World and the Communist World.

Secretary of State Acheson viewed this action as removing "any illusion as to the nationalist nature of Ho Chi Minh aims and revealing Ho in his true colors as the mortal enemy of native independence in Indochina."(12). But the French had to provide at least some form of independence to the Bao Dai government. After ten months of delay, France ratified the Agreements to provide nominal independence for Laos, Cambodia and Vietnam.

American recognition of Bao Dai Government on Feb. 7, 1950 followed the French ratification. Several weeks later, ambassador Loy W. Henderson clarified the U.S. position in a speech to the Indian Council of World Affairs: "The U.S. is convinced that the Bao Dai government reflects more accurately than any rival claimants to power in Vietnam the nationalist aspirations of the people of that country."(13)

In the years that followed, there was an agonizing struggle between Saigon, Paris and Washington to make progress in the "evolution toward self-government and independence." American recognition was accompanied by military and economic aid.

The U.S. did not appreciate French political direction. However, no serious pressures were put on the French until 1954. Dulles was aware of Bao Dai's political inability to create an alternative to the Viet Minh. In the middle of 1951, Dulles discovered in Ngo Dinh Diem, Bao Dai's former premier, the political solution for Vietnam.

Regarding a rationale for U.S. aid to Vietnam, at least three arguments were advanced. First, the Truman Administration insisted on regarding Vietnam as essentially an extension of a European affair. Therefore, the U.S. wished to bring France back to Europe via victory in Vietnam.

6

Second, the U.S. was always convinced that the domino theory would operate should Vietnam remain with the Vietnamese people. U.S. Ambassador to France, David Bruce, told a Senate Committee: "There is no question that if Indochina went, the fall of Burma and the fall of Thailand would be absolutely inevitable." And Bruce suggested, "If the French left, someone would have to replace them."(14)

Third, the political character of the regime in Vietnam was less consequential than the larger U.S. design for the area. A larger American conception of the importance of the war to its self-interest has been a constant basis of U.S. policy in Vietnam since 1951.

The Eisenhower Administration took office at a time Communist influence abroad seemed to be expanding everywhere, particularly in Asia. Eisenhower felt the need to demonstrate a posture of firmness toward Communism in Asia. To contain Red China, arms, weapons and equipment poured into Indochina even before the Korean Armistice.

Two years before Eisenhower took office, John F. Dulles advanced the intention of a Republican Administration: "There is a civil war in Indochina, in which we have, for better or for worse, involved our prestige. Since that is so, we must help the government we back. Its defeat, coming after the reverses suffered by the Nationalist Government of China would have further serious repercussions on the whole situation in Asia and the Pacific. It would make even more people in the East feel that friendship with the U.S. is a liability rather than an asset."(15)

In the meantime, the war in Vietnam had taken a definite turn. The armistice of Korea signed in July 1953 relieved Red China of its military burden there. Heavier and more sophisticated weapons and equipment were now in the hands of the Vietnamese Communists. The dilemma faced by the French prophecised the American dilemma a decade later. Nothing the French could do would redress the balance.

By early 1952, almost all North Vietnam outside the Tonkin Delta was under Communist control. In April 1953, the Communists launched a major offensive in Laos and occupied about 20,000 square miles of Laotian territories. This invasion dramatized French military weakness in three countries of Indochina.

The disaster caused by the French devaluation of the piaster (Indochinese money) in May 1953 reminded the three governments in Indochina how little independence they had. They asked for a major review of relationships between the three Associated States and France.

Their hard-line policy provided a rationale for a change of mood in France. French opinion held that France yielded too many concessions to Bao Dai and in addition, the war in Indochina had changed. From the French attempt to reassert its former control in Indochina, it became a war in which France was carrying the major burden against Communist aggression. However, the French government was reluctant to turn to the United Nations or to other countries for assistance for fear of losing prestige and influence in Asia.

The French tried to work out the best arrangement they could with the Communists in Indochina when they saw the Americans making terms with the Communists in Korea. Before Parliament in October 1953, French Premier Laniel said: "I must repeat in the clearest and most categorical fashion that the French Government does not consider the Indochinese problem as necessarily requiring a military solution . . . No more than the U.S. does France make war for the sake of war, and if an honorable solution were in view, either on the local level or on the international level, France, I repeat, like the U.S. in Korea, would be happy to welcome a diplomatic solution of the conflict."(16)

By the summer of 1953, U.S. policy remained to keep the French fighting on any basis and to convince them to do what seemed necessary to engage the loyalty and support of the Vietnamese. But, it was too late for the French to obtain popular support from the Vietnamese population in either North or South Vietnam.

The State Department confided to Eisenhower: "Failure of important elements of the local population to give a full measure of support to the war effort remained one of the chief negative factors."(17) Later, Eisenhower wrote: "It was almost impossible to make the average Vietnamese peasant realize that the French, under whose rule his people had lived for some eighty years, were really fighting in the cause of freedom, while the Viet Minh, people of their own ethnic origins, were fighting on the side of slavery."(18)

In September 1953, the U.S. agreed to give the French a grant of $85 million to implement the "Plan de Navarre," a scheme to build French and local troops to a level which was supposed to destroy Viet Minh regular forces by the end of 1955.

With that concept in mind, the U.S. was determined to make Vietnam a testing ground for a larger global strategy of which the French would be the instrument. The difficulty for the U.S. was that there was no military solution for Vietnam. The Navarre Plan failed and French troops were obviously marching to defeat.

Facing that desperate situation, Dulles delivered a speech on January 12, 1954, talking vaguely about "Massive retaliation." The vital problem for the U.S. at that time was how to apply its formidable military power to avoid a land war in Southeast Asia that the Americans might not win.

In February 1954, when the French posed the question of the direction of U.S. commitments, Dulles refused to answer the question. However, he did state that if the U.S. entered the war with its own manpower, it would demand a much greater share of the political and executive direction of the future of the area.(19)

Dulles then suggested that President Eisenhower intervene with Churchill to induce Great Britain to join the U.S., France and others in a military effort to prevent the Communists from overrunning Indochina. But London quickly reversed Dulle's position.

In March 1954, on his way back after an investigation of the situation in Indochina, France's Chief of Staff, General Paul Ely visited Washington. He made it clear that the French were in desperate military position.

A major American intervention seemed necessary if it was to save the situation in Indochina. But the Eisenhower Administration decided not to take unilateral action. In these anxious days, there were rumors that the U.S. might use atomic weapons to save the French in Dien-bien-Phu.

But despite Dulles' views on massive retaliation and despite Nixon's reference to 'troops,' the Eisenhower Administration remained reluctant to use U.S. ground forces in Indochina.

Finally, after another meeting between Dulles and Eden, Winston Churchill decided that no unified action could be taken until every effort had been made to resolve the Indochina situation through negotiation.

The Geneva conference began under severe conditions.

On May 7, 1954, the day before the Geneva Conference turned to the question of Indochina, Dien-bien-Phu fell to the Communists. That same evening, Dulles went on the radio and said Vietnam could not fall into hostile hands, for then, the Communists could move into all of Southeast Asia. "The present conditions there do not provide a suitable basis for the U.S. to participate with its armed forces. But we would be gravely concerned if an armistice or cease-fire were reached at Geneva which would provide a road to a Communist takeover and further aggression."(20)

The beginning of the Indochina phase of the Conference was accompanied by growing American suspicion and anxiety. But the American position as the New York Times described it during these weeks was "driving the U.S. deeper into diplomatic isolation on Southeast Asian questions . . . though the U.S. opposes . . . these agreements, there appears to be little the U.S. can do to stop them."(21)

And on May 11, 1954, Dulles seemed resigned to an unfavorable resolution of the Indochina conflict when he said at a press conference: "It is true that at Geneva, we have so far not achieved the unification of Korea, nor does it seem likely that we will achieve the unification of Korea, nor does it seem likely that we will achieve the unification of Indochina under the conditions of freedom and peace. We never thought that there was a good chance of accomplishing those results."(22)

The Geneva Agreements were hasty and unattractive. They had a predictably short life expectancy. The U.S. attached grave reservations to the Geneva Conference. The Wall Street Journal was correct when on July 23, 1954, it reported that "the U.S. is in no hurry for elections to unite Vietnam. We fear Red leaders would win. So Dulles plans first to make the southern half a showplace with American aid."(23)

When Ho Chi Minh established himself in North Vietnam, Dulles decided that the rest of Vietnam below the 17th parallel would be a western bastion against the Communists. He said: "Now, we enter Vietnam without the taint of colonialism."

A policy for South Vietnam was born.

Facing the ingenious and tricky preparations of the Vietnamese Communists to take over South Vietnam, what was American strategy? What weapons could Americans use to preserve a non-communist South Vietnam? The answers depended on the response to this more fundamental question: was the U.S. treating the Vietnamese as an end or as means to its own objectives?

If the South Vietnamese were ends, there might be at least an important principle to the American participation: the U.S. could not indoctrinate a South Vietnamese peasant or a Vietnamese intellectual with an ideology that was worth fighting for. American aid to South Vietnam had to help South Vietnamese build a strong and democratic non-communist government to compete with the alternative that North Vietnam proposed through a Communist-led Nationalism.

At the departure point of the Vietnam War, the Nationalists were not as strong as the Communists. So the Nationalists must understand that changing the course of their revolution required the liquidation of the Viet Minh and the re-education of the majority of the population that supported the movement. It would be a formidable task for any nationalist regime in South Vietnam. From the dying, corrupt and feudal society of South Vietnam, the Nationalists would have to build an attractive and new society to the Vietnamese peasants . . . which could compete with the new, modern North Vietnam born of a colonial war with the French.

But Americans would find it diffuclt to accept a radical changing of the hierarchical structure of the classical Vietnamese society. And yet, that radical changing would be the vital condition to the success of a non-communist alternative for South Vietnam.

And it would be more difficult to the Americans not to impose an American-style democracy on South Vietnam. Americans were overconfident in the 1950s and in the 1960s that there was an American solution for any international problem.

On the contrary, if South Vietnam was considered essentially and absolutely as a creation of the United States, it would not need to be a good alternative to compete with the Communists.

If the American leaders believed they had to fight fire with fire to ward off a communist success in South Vietnam, they would surely hire agents, spies, generals and presidents where they could find them in Vietnam and in Indochina. They would think and write of them almost in proprietary terms as instruments of the American policy. In that case, one could say in advance that the Communists would win in South Vietnam and the agony of a non-communist South Vietnam would begin the day the Americans hired agents, spies, generals and presidents.

Not only the freedom of South Vietnamese people was at stake. The contest was between the Free World and the Communists. Each side would try to persuade the human race that its system had the superior merit.

10

Chapter Two
NATURE OF A VIETNAM WAR

After the American setbacks in Cuba and in Laos in 1961, the United States discovered that insurgency warfare is a different and far more complicated art than guerilla warfare. As a result, there were hasty books and studies. Most were based on insufficient field data or on unwarranted comparisons. It was quite an overcompensation phenomenon. This new concern with insurgency warfare even embraced agencies whose normal functions did not include any relationship with that kind of warfare.

Those who develop hasty conclusions about special warfare in developing nations can easily be confused by subtle differences in jungle warfare, guerilla warfare, revolutionary warfare.

What kind of war was the one in Vietnam beginning in 1954? From the onset, the Vietminh knew that this was a political war fought for political objectives. In his book entitled *People's War, People's Army,* Vo Nguyen Giap, commander of North Vietnam Armed Forces wrote " . . . The People's Army is the instrument of the Party and of the revolutionary State for the accomplishment, in armed form, of the tasks of the revolution . . . Therefore, the political work in its ranks is of the first importance. It is the soul of the Army."

Among the leaders of developing nations and the scholars who were interested in studying special warfare, there was an easy tendency to compare the situation in Vietnam to the situation of some other country. For example, a comparison between British victories in Malaya and the situation in South Vietnam in the 1960s was not only a dangerous self-delusion but worse, it induced people into a deliberate over-simplification of the whole problem. The war in Vietnam combined the worst features of all the other theaters in which the West has had to fight Communism thus far. Moreover, the enemy in Vietnam is

11

one who has not only read all the classics of guerilla warfare, but has also added a few chapters of his own.

Political warfare is not a monopoly of Communism. But the Communists had the initiative to invent a scientific approach to apply war to every field of social activities in order to win and to take power. Therefore, political warfare has its special features. It has to rely upon fundamental principles: a solid ideology and an attractive philosophy.

Political warfare is not limited by time and space. It is extended to the rear area of the enemy and beyond national boundaries. It must have unified command and action.

There is a common pattern about Communist political warfare. That pattern was invented by the Russians and it has been applied since the Revolution of 1917. It continues to be the precious pattern used by Russian satellites. The pattern has been applied in China, East Europe and in Vietnam with many flexible variations.

For instance, when the Communists want to take over a country of the Free World, Moscow infiltrates through local Communist parties, Communist elements in organizations, services, and associations of the target country—as well as the allies of the most powerful country (the United States). These elements have a mission: To try to use local media and local mass communications to stimulate the surrender of target countries by destroying the fighting potentiality of local populations.

Each Communist party is an element of the organization of International Communism, of which, the Supreme head is Moscow. At the World Second Congress of Communist Parties, Lenin himself established twenty-one conditions. Every Communist party must accept these conditions if it wants integration with the Russian Communist Party. The most important condition for that integration is to absolutely obey to orders of the Third International.

In political warfare, however, the Russian leadership has met competition from the Chinese. The Chinese Communist Party wants to prove that it deserves to be the leader of all Communist parties in Africa and in Asia. Up to now, Red China has succeeded in organizing pro-Chinese elements in many local Communist parties. The pattern of Red China's struggle is the same as the pattern of International Communism. But remember one important point: the competition between Russia and Red China did not lessen the threat of Communism in the Vietnam War. On the contrary, it increased the threat. Each of these two giant Communist countries has tried to give the Vietnamese Communists its most sophisticated weapons and tactics to help North Vietnam to take over South Vietnam.

Given the unified command and action of International Communism . . . given the statement of Soviet Premier Secretary Khrushchev in January 1961 in his report on a party conference entitled 'For New victories of the World Communist Movement' in which he said the liberation war like the Vietnam war is a sacred war . . . South Vietnam not only faced the insurgency and later, the overt invasion of North Vietnamese Armed Forces. No, South Vietnam faced the whole Communist world. It was a modest honor and a great misfortune to the South Vietnamese Nationalists.

The political war in Vietnam has to be clarified because of the controversy in the 1960s. It seems that we all tend to see the Vietnam War according to our own point of view. But solme evidence and truth could be used as a basis to understand many complicated aspects.

At least, the following aspects must be clarified: nature of the Vietnam war (was it a civil war?) and the principles of political war adopted by the Vietnamese Communists. Of the first aspect, we need to understand the structure and origin of the National Liberation Front, the nationalist elements in that front and the relationship between the NLF and North Vietnam.

According to some scholars and journalists, there was a fairly strong anti-Diem insurgent current of non-communist origin in the NLF even before the 1956 deadline on elections between the two zones had passed.

Bernard Fall wrote: "A modest attempt was made in August 1954, to keep alive a legal struggle overt front organization in the form of the Saigon Committee of Defense of Peace and the Geneva Agreements, headed by Nguyen Huu Tho, a lawyer born in South Vietnam in 1910, who was later to become chairman of the National Liberation Front. The committee began to set up branches in various South Vietnamese provincial capitals, but in November 1954, South Vietnam police cracked down on the organization. It was disbanded and its leaders, including Tho, were jailed . . .".(1)

Thus, what was accurately called "the embryo for the National Liberation Front" was crushed only three months after its birth. Later on, without Hanoi taking direct control of the insurgency movement in South Vietnam, one could be sure that nothing was left from that embryo.

The conclusion that there was a strong anti-Diem insurgent current of non-communist origins even before the 1956 deadline on elections, is hasty. Such conclusions give the impression that the South Vietnamese people did not want the non-communist government existing from early 1954 and that there were no nationalists in South Vietnam after the Geneva Agreements of July 1954.

On June 16, 1954, Ex-Emperor Bao-Dai called upon Diem (Ngo Dinh Diem) to form the new Vietnamese government. Early in 1954, with the defeat of Dien-bien-Phu looming, Bao-Dai asked Ngo Dinh Diem to take the Premiership of Vietnam. Diem refused the offer because it was still hedged with the restrictions that overall military command would remain in French hands while hostilities were under way.

Invited by Bao-Dai once more, Diem demanded full and complete civilian and military powers. After three days of hesitation, Bao-Dai granted Diem absolute dictatorial powers on June 19, 1954. Diem arrived in Saigon on June 26. On July 7, 1954, Ngo Dinh Diem completed his first cabinet.

At first, few people really believed that a non-communist South Vietnam could survive for any length of time. It appeared that this belief was also shared by North Vietnam because from 1954 to 1958, it concentrated on internal development. North Vietnam apparently hoped to achieve reunification, either through the elections provided for in the Geneva settlement or through the natural collapse of the weak Diem regime.

Diem's finest hours came in the spring of 1955 when his chances of staying in office seemed very remote. He had to face many adversaries simultaneously. His first enemy was General Nguyen van Hinh, a French trained officer and also, the South Vietnamese Chief of Staff who retained French nationality (his real name is Jean-Marie Louis Nguyen Van Hinh and his wife is a French woman).

One could easily see the inevitable frictions between the Americans and the about-to-be evicted French. The Diem Government was caught in unpleasant

13

situation and the relationship between Diem's Government and the French Government was not encouraging. During the various Vietnamese/French negotiations, Ngo Dinh Diem remained peremptory: Diem would not allow the French to maintain any military base in South Vietnam, although the French had hoped to retain at least an aero-naval base near Cap St. Jacques (in Vietnamese, province of Phuoc Tuy). Diem informed the French that: "The presence of foreign troops, no matter how friendly they may be, was incompatible with Vietnam's concept of full independence." It was no surprise when General Hinh defied Diem and tried to organize a coup against him. After Bao-Dai personally intervened in Diem's favor (by sending messages from France) and after the United States threatened to cut off all but humanitarian aid to South Vietnam, Diem defeated General Hinh's plot.

The armed politico-religious sects were another kind of enemy which was even more difficult to oust. In some areas, they had a certain degree of popular support partly because the local population was still uneducated. In the case of the Binh Xuyen sect, they controlled the police forces of the Saigon-cholon area, and they were willing to fight to retain their privileges. At times, the Binh Xuyen sect was called the Binh Xuyen pirates. It would be hard for an impartial observer to deny that besides his qualities of personal courage and stubborness, Diem displayed an admirable ability to divide his enemies by many intricate maneuvers. Of course, at that time, there were generous amounts of American money to help Diem bribe key sect leaders.

So, slowly very slowly, the idea of non-communist South Vietnam viability began to grow. An illusion became a reality. Among articles written about South Vietnam, could be read: "The Tough Miracle Man of Vietnam"—Life Magazine; "The Bright Spot in Asia"—The Saturday Evening Post. Also, there was a lobby for Diem. There were many speeches in Diem's honor. Among them, these modest words from Walter Robertson, Dulles' Assistant Secretary of State for Far Eastern Affairs in 1956, ". . . Among the factors that explain the remarkable rise of Free Vietnam from the shambles created by eight years of murderous civil and international war, the division of the country at Geneva, and the continuing menace of predatory Communism, there is in the place the dedication, courage and resourcefulness of President Diem himself."

According to official figures after the Geneva Conference in 1954, the Communists had withdrawn about 90,000 men from the South, leaving from 6,000 to 10,000 armed men as a skeletal apparatus. This "army" had the main task of preparing for the scheduled 1956 reunification elections. The cadre members of this apparatus were ordered to carry out only a "political struggle" (meaning that there will be largely propaganda activity and infiltration of the Saigon Government). A document captured early in 1955 from a Communist field organizer revealed that the Communists in Vietnam apparently believed that they would get control of South Vietnam either through the elections of 1956 or by the collapse of the Diem regime through its own weakness.

How effective was the Diem Government from July 1954 to the end of 1959?

In 1967, a captured Communist who was in charge of propaganda in the Saigon area testified, "The period from the Armistice of 1954 until 1958 was the darkest time for the Viet Cong in South Vietnam. The political agitation policy proposed by the Communist Party could not be carried out due to the arrest of a

14

number of party members.''(2)

Another cadre member reported, ''. . . The cadres who had remained behind in the South had almost all been arrested. Only one or two cadres were left in every three to five villages.''(3)

But most important was a document captured in 1966 by the United States First Infantry Division during a major operation near Saigon, in the area called Iron Triangle. This document stated, ''The Diem's Government harsh security policies had truly and efficiently destroyed our party . . . The majority of party members and cadres felt that it was necessary to immediately launch an armed struggle in order to preserve the movement and protect the forces.''

Why had most of all the Communist cadres who had remained behind in the South been arrested by the Diem Administration? These cadres were the infrastructure of the Communists in South Vietnam. Only people living in rural areas and in shantytowns could know who the Communist cadres were. If these people believed in Diem's Government, if they thought they would be protected properly, and more important, if they thought that Diem's Government was worth effort and sacrifice, then they would volunteer to help the Government and denounce these Communist cadres. They did.

Other evidence: from July 1954 to 1957, Ngo Dinh Diem made many tours of all South Vietnamese provinces to obtain his own view of his Government's efficiency and of popular support. At that time, almost every village had some Communist cadres. On these trips, Diem rode in a military jeep at low speed because many provincial roads were in very bad condition. It would be false to think that the Communist Command in South Vietnam did not want to kill Ngo Dinh Diem. They did. But the Communist cadres were unable to organize an assassination. They were too weak and sensed correctly that the majority of South Vietnamese people did not hate Ngo Dinh Diem. The South Vietnamese people wished to give Diem his chance to build a strong and non-communist country in South Vietnam, an answer to the challenge of a communist country in North Vietnam.

Thus, the effectiveness of the Diem Government played an important role in building and maintaining a non-communist South Vietnam from July 1954 to December 1959. By the end of 1959, North Vietnam had to take complete control of all insurgency activities in South Vietnam. Of course, the United States' economic and military aid to South Vietnam during that time must be seriously considered, but could a non-communist South Vietnam have been preserved if there had not been a consensus of support from the South Vietnamese people?

Another question to be clarified about the structure and the origin of the National Liberation Front: were there nationalist elements in the National Liberation Front and how many? A great deal can be learned about the nature of the National Liberation Front and the nature of the Vietnam War, if one can fine adequate answers to these questions.

As mentioned earlier, during the period of 1954 to 1959, the Diem Administration was successful. Even the Communist had to recognize the effectiveness of his Government. Unfortunately, there were no real political changes in South Vietnam. It was still a feudal society. The political base of the Diem Government became over the years narrower and narrower. Faced by so many great political problems and lacking necessary political resources, he turned inward. Born suspicious, he alienated his few allies in the government and turned more and more to his family, to his police forces and to the American aid.

The disappointment of South Vietnamese people began to grow.

According to some scholars and writers, when the Diem Government began to deteriorate, many dissenters joined the National Liberation Front. That line of reasoning was somewhat oversimplified. As mentioned earlier, the life of the embryo of the National Liberation Front composed only of a handful of men was shortened by the effectiveness of the Diem Administration. Without the direct participation of North Vietnamese cadres and regular armed forces, the National Liberation Front would hardly have become something more than an armed rebellion, certainly unable to overthrow the non-communist government in South Vietnam. Had the majority of the South Vietnamese dissenters joined the National Liberation Front, a non-communist South Vietnam would never have lasted from July 1954 to April 30, 1975 (nearly 21 years).

As a direct consequence of the deterioration of the Diem Administration, the number of the dissidents among the South Vietnamese population multiplied. But how did these dissidents think and react? At first, there were some people among those born in South Vietnam who thought that the essence of the National Liberation Front was nationalist. There was no surprise in that line of thinking because in South Vietnam before 1954, people really did not have the opportunity to enjoy political independence. Japanese conquest was succeeded by French domination. After the surrender of Japan in August 1945, the French came back, with overt support of the British and with the tacit assent of the Americans. Then , there came the Geneva Agreement of July 1954 dividing Vietnam. To some persons born in South Vietnam, the Vietnamese Communists were heroes because they did not let foreigners "touch down" on the soil of Vietnam. Thus after 1954, of the two Vietnams, the side which knew how to conceal the military aid from foreign countries was praised. Candid people tended to blame the other side which, by the nature of its regime, did not want to conceal the aid it received from friendly foreign countries.

But to praise the Communists and to admire Ho Chi Minh was one matter. To become a communist was another. Among the South Vietnamese dissidents after 1959, there were those indeed who did think that the National Liberation Front was not a communist organization. It seemed clear that they were only a minority and of this minority, few belonged to the intellectual (the habitual highly esteemed in the traditional Vietnamese society) class.

The majority of the South Vietnamese dissidents had detected very soon the communist nature of the National Liberation Front. Though they may have wanted Diem to effect radical political reforms in South Vietnam, or wished to see Diem replaced, they did not want to join the National Liberation Front. Had this majority joined the National Liberation Front, the collapse of the non-communist South Vietnam might have occurred in 1961.

This does not mean that that majority remained inactive during the time the Diem Regime was disintegrating. Many tried to convince Diem to bring radical reforms which would improve South Vietnam's image abroad and gain strong support from the population. But all efforts of that nature did not bring any result because of Diem's innate shrewdness, and also because of the shrewdness of Diem's close advisers, including his family. That the South Vietnamese dissidents and the silent majority did not try to use violence after so many vain efforts in convincing Diem, was quite understandable. Among the characteristics of Vietnamese Nationalists, there were two which related directly to the South Vietnamese political situation after 1959. First, Vietnamese Nationalists are always apalled at bloodshed. Secondly, Vietnamese Nationalists have always preferred a strategy of non-violent opposition to all dictatorships. The positive aspect of such strategy is that it helps avoid bloody uprisings, bloody purges. In brief, it was quite a humanitarian approach to solve political problems. But against a man like Ngo Dinh Diem, such a non-violent strategy proved useless.

On March 15, 1958, in a pathetic letter entitled, "Letter to My Deputy," Mr. Nghiem Xuan Thien, publisher of the South Vietnamese daily paper, Thoi Luan, wrote what many South Vietnamese no doubt were thinking:

"What about your democratic election? During the city council and village council elections under the medieval and colonialist Nguyen Van Tam Administration (under Bao Dai in 1953), constituents were threatened and compelled to vote. But they were still better than your elections, because nobody brought soldiers into Saigon by the truckload to help with the voting. What about your Presidential regime? You are proud of having created for Vietnam a regime that you think is similar to that of the United States. If those regimes are similar, then they are as related as skyscraper is to a tin roofed shack, in that, they both are houses to live in . . . In the U.S.A., Congress is a true parliament, and Congressmen are legislators, i.e. free and disinterested men who are not afraid of the government, and who know their duties and dare to carry them out. Here, the deputies are political functionaries who make laws like an announcer in a radio station, by reading out loud texts that have been prepared (for them) beforehand . . .".

The publisher of the Thoi Luan paper was sentenced ten months in jail and confiscatory fines. The paper was closed.

On April 26, 1960, eighteen highly respected citizens including several former Cabinet ministers, sent an open letter to Ngo Dinh Diem, warning him of the disaffection of the people, ". . . The people do not know a better life or more freedom under the republican regime which you have created. A Constitution has been established in form only, a National Assembly exists whose deliberations always fall into line with the Government antidemocratic elections; all those are methods and comedies copied from the dictatorial Communist regimes . . . Continuous arrests fill the jail and prisons to the rafters . . . public opinion and the press are reduced to silence. The same applies to the popular will as translated in certain open elections, in which, it is insulted and trampled as was the case, for example, during the recent elections for the Second Legislature . . .".

But, it can not be claimed that the Vietnamese Nationalists never used violence in their efforts to save a non-communist South Vietnam. The paratroop putsch of November 11, 1960 was the first indication, although the putsch was conducted in a gentlemanly and somewhat, amateurish fashion. It was more an attempt to reform the regime (keep Diem but compel him to get rid of his entourage) than to overthrow it.

After surviving the putsch, the Diem regime for the first time, announced on November 17, 1960, a large "reform program." But at the same time, it began a terrible purge of known opposition. The total number of people arbitrarily put in jail and in concentration camps remains unknown.

Faced with such blindness by Diem, the Vietnamese Nationalists finally resorted to genuine armed insurrection: a military revolt, strongly supported by the population on November 1, 1963. Both Ngo Dinh Diem and Ngo Dinh Nhu (his brother) were killed inside an armored personnel carrier after having been

17

captured in a Catholic church.

From the Diem Administration to the Nguyen van Thieu Administration, the political image of a non-communist South Vietnam became darker and darker. But in spite of this deterioration, in spite of the increasing military political efforts of the National Liberation Front directly commanded by North Vietnam, non-communist South Vietnam still held on.

What was the influence of the National Liberation Front vis-a-vis the South Vietnamese people? Whatever the Communists might say about the extremely strong support from the population of South Vietnam for the National Liberation Front, world opinion had acquired this evidence: whenever there was battle between government forces and Viet Colng forces, one only saw people seeking safety in the government controlled areas.

Of course, the pro-communist press always exploited the high degree of desertion among South Vietnamese Armed Forces to provide the illusion that South Vietnamese soldiers did not want to fight against the Communists. But the Communist side never dared tell the truth, the simple truth about the desertion of South Vietnam Armed Forces. There indeed was a monthly average rate of desertion of 20,000 soldiers. Where did these soldiers go? They never went to the Communist side, although they might be terribly disappointed about their non-communist government. They deserted, but only to do a simple thing: to help their families because their relatives were short of everything after so many years of war. That was a practical gesture but it was also a clear political attitude: they did not accept Communism, but since they had seen that successive non-communist administrations did not want to effect radical and vital political changes, they simply said farewell to the battles. This political apathy was an inevitable result of so many disillusioned years.

Further, and perhaps unknown to most Americans, among those deserters, there were those who quit their units to volunteer for service in other units of their choice. And, unfortunately, there were also those who quit their units because they were commanded by unqualified and dishonest officers.

It was true that this deserter's attitude was negative. But since they did not flee to the Communist side, they continued to bring a modicum of political stability to all government controlled areas. Their contribution to political stability coupled with the "voting by foot" of so many South Vietnamese civilians and the consensus of the silent majority to accept a non-communist regime instead of a communist one prevented the take over of South Vietnam for many years.

To repeat, the classic objective of all wars is to break the enemy's will to resist. To attain this primary objective North Vietnam had resorted to many tactics, from political persuasion and subversion to outright invasion. These tactics destroyed houses, bridges, factories, killed South Vietnamese civilians and soldiers, including old persons, women and children, but they were unable to break the will to resist Communism of South Vietnamese people. Those observers who missed this point and those who did not follow closely the struggle of the Vietnamese nationalists will now be able to understand why South Vietnam could survive for nearly twenty-one years in spite of successive corrupt non-communist administrations.

Only a terrible and precipitous accumulation of many disastrous factors would break their will to resist and force the collapse of South Vietnam. Among this accumulation were: international politics upset by an oil blackmail; turmoil in the U.S. politics because of Watergate; new isolationist trend in the U.S.

spawned by the frustration of American people over U.S. policy in Indochina; increase in both economic and military aid of Russia and Red China to North Vietnam; and in South Vietnam, Nguyen Van Thieu's Administration more and more corrupt and more and more remote from South Vietnamese people, etc.

Even such terrible accumulation had not completely destroyed the will to resist of Vietnamese nationalists, 'though the government has fallen. From Bangkok (Thailand) on June 16, 1975, the Associated Press reported: "Viet Cong soldiers have wiped out a pocket of anti-communist resistance in the Mekong Delta, Liberation Radio reported yesterday. The action took place between May 29 and June 8 in the Dinh Tuong Province, 45 miles southwest of Saigon, the broadcast. It said that in the Cho Gao District, a group of unreported military men were encircled and completely crushed, and that many other reactionary elements who had failed to register with the new regime and were working against the peaceful life of the people were brought to light. There were no further details." On June 16, 1975, U.S. News and World Report wrote: "South Vietnam: Headache for Communist Victors . . . The Communists are discovering that South Vietnam is a hard nut to crack. North Vietnamese and Viet Cong officials have moved fast since their conquest of late April. But problems are so vast that it's evident that the Communists will need many months—if not years—to subjugate the South fully . . . Some diehard South Vietnamese troops, in fact, still are holding out, mainly in the Mekong Delta. And many of the 1.1 million men in the defeated armed forces and the 2 million in civilian militia units are believed to have hidden their weapons for possible use later against the victors . . .". And on July 3, 1975, The San Diego Union daily newspaper reported: "Diehard Vietnam troops still fight—From Vientane (Laos) A.P. Diplomats arriving yesterday from South Vietnam reported clashes between the new Communist rulers and diehard troops holding out in the Saigon area and around the country. A former resident of Saigon reported nightly bursts of weapons fire in the capital and what sounded like occasional changes of fire. Saigon's Liberation Radio reported continued efforts to hunt down holdouts in both Saigon metropolitan area and in the countryside. The diplomats who arrived in Laos on a United Nations airlift for foreigners said the Saigon Government was also concerned with recovering hidden weapons and weeding out civil servants and army officers who have ignored orders or register with the government."

And a year after their three-pronged takeover of Spring 1975, Indochina's communist rulers continue to encounter outbursts of armed resistance. The shoot-out at a Catholic church in North Saigon on February 12, 1976 was neither the first nor the most violent such incident in Vietnam.

Predictably, the communist authorities blamed the CIA for the rebellion by the self-styled "anti-communist popular front." But an important feature of what resistance there has been in Vietnam, Cambodia and Laos is the complete lack of American help.

The rules applied to communist soldiers in Saigon—they are forbidden to walk the streets of the capital alone at night—are another sign that opposition is still alive. Combined forces of soldiers and policemen carried out many massive sweeps in Saigon.

It is more difficult to assess the strength and nature of resistance in the countryside but serious incidents have been reported by Saigon radio in Khanh Hoa province and in other provinces: Soc Trang, TuyEn Duc and Lam Dong.

In most areas, resistance appears to take form of guerilla groups acting independently. Still, they are an irritant to the new regime and they may become more troublesome in the long run.

And there could be trouble from another quarter, too. The Cao Dai and the Hoa Hao religious sects who were staunch supporters of the previous regime, and the montagnards of the Central Highlands who have long resisted being governed by anybody in Saigon are likely to be more serious rebels, Guerillas hiding in the highlands could hold out for years.

There is a potentially more serious resistance movement in Laos. Some parts of the southernmost provinces of that country are said to be in open revolt. Travellers in northeast Thailand recently saw battles taking place across the Mekong river, the border between the two countries, around the Laotian town of Savannakhet. These battles erupted when people attending a re-education camp revolted, disarming their Pathet Lao guards.

We come now to the relationship between North Vietnam and the National Liberation Front.

Based on data of 1964 and 1965, Douglas Pike wrote in *Viet Cong: The Organization and Techniques of the National Liberation Party of South Vietnam,* (Cambridge, Mass., MIT Press, 1966): "The National Liberation Front was not simply an indigenous organization in which the Communists played a part. Neither was it simply a robot like instrument of the Democratic Republic of Vietnam (North Vietnam)." Pro-communist scholars, pro-communist writers and anti-American people tended to praise only the National Liberation Front, to exaggerate any performance of the National Liberation Front and of course, to ignore the bloody self-defense struggle of the Vietnamese Nationalists. They repeatedly said that the National Liberation Front was really a political entity and that it was an independent entity. Once again, an important aspect of the Vietnam War was oversimplified.

Since 1954, there have been many changes in the Vietnam War. If reasoning is based on outdated information and political factors, it is difficult to avoid erroneous conclusions.

As mentioned earlier, there might be a modest attempt to keep alive an overt legal struggle of a front organization headed by Nguyen Huu Tho under the Saigon Committee of Defense and Peace and the Geneva Agreements. Bernard Fall stated in his book, *The Two Vietnams,* that it was "the embryo for the National Liberation Front" (based upon a conversation between Nguyen Huu Tho and the Australian leftist journalist Wilfred Burchett in 1974) and that "There apparently was no doubt in Tho's mind as to the organic relationship between the Saigon Committee of 1954 and the more recently created National Liberation Front."

Let's clarify this point. First, the political attitude of North Vietnam about the division of Vietnam. Some writers, including Professor P.J. Honey, maintained that Hanoi had accepted the existence of a non-communist South Vietnam at Geneva in 1954. Once Hanoi accepted that fact, it began to create de facto conditions to make that fact tolerable. North Vietnam leaders were realistic enough to acknowledge that North Vietnam would always need South Vietnam rice and that they needed to sell coal and cement to South Vietnam. The first interzonal agreement, The Postal Agreement, was signed by authorities of both North and South Vietnam at Haiphong on April 12, 1955. Haiphong is the most important port of North Vietnam. Had Ngo Dinh Diem accepted the conditions for a "de facto coexistence," could the Postal Agreement have been the first step, opening the way to other agreements such as economic and cultural exchanges, etc.? The chance was about fifty percent.

What were the reasons behind the shift in North Vietnam strategy? There might be many. The successful first years of the Diem Administration, the aborted elections of 1956. 1956 was really a bad year to the international Communist movement: the uprising of the Hungarian people; the revolt of North Vietnamese peasants against the Communist harsh land reform program. This peasant revolt was bloodiest at Nghe An, Ho Chi Minh's native province. Nearly two crack North Vietnamese divisions were sent to Nghe An Province to crush the peasant revolt. There were many dead and wounded Vietnamese.

Then, there were the letters sent from North Vietnam Prime Minister Pham Van Dong to Diem on July 20, 1957, on March 7, 1958 and on December 22, 1958. The last one was very important, because it included the four point program for the normalization of relations between the two Vietnams: military deescalation in both zones and withdrawal of all foreign military personnel, commercial exchanges between North and South Vietnam, deescalation of the propaganda war followed by exchanges of cultural, scientific, economic and sport groups.

Ngo Dinh Diem did not reply to these letters. Diem's intransigence and the increasing desintegration of his regime were among many other motives North Vietnam had to commit aggression.

From 1956 to 1958, North Vietnamese leaders in Hanoi engaged in a serious reconsideration of their policy. Sometime in 1957, after two years in South Vietnam, Le Duan returned to Hanoi. Duan was a southerner who had participated in the fight against the French during the French Indochina War. Duan carried news that the struggle in South Vietnam was going very poorly. Le Duan is said to have urged military pressures from North Vietnam to replace the political struggle. That same year, 1957, Le Duan was named member of North Vietnam Politburo. Later, in September 1960, he became First Secretary of North Vietnamese Communist Party.

By December 1958, Hanoi apparently decided that the time had come to intensify North Vietnamese efforts. A directive was sent from Hanoi to the Central Highlands Headquarters that month. This directive stated that the Lao Dong Party (the Workers Party, a camouflage of the Vietnamese Communist Party) Central Committee had decided to "open a new stage of the struggle." In January 1959, Le Duan made a secret visit in South Vietnam. And there was an order issued from Hanoi to establish two guerilla operation bases—The first in Tay Ninh Province, near the Cambodian frontier and the other in Western Central Highlands.

The fifteenth meeting of the Central Committee of the Vietnam Lao Dong Party convened in May 1959, was vitally important to future events of the Vietnam War. In that session, the decision previously made by the North Vietnamese Politburo was ratified by the Central Committee. This was considered "the point of departure for the armed struggle of North Vietnam." In May 1959, Ho Chi Miknh made an important speech in which he openly promoted liberation of the country by all means.

The intelligence reports of the United States showed that infiltration from North Vietnam began early in 1955, but only in 1959 did the CIA obtain evidence of North Vietnamese large scale infiltration. After the resolution of the 15th plenum of the Central Committee was issued, there was a rapid build-up of

21

Hanoi's potential for infiltration in order to take a decisive role in the insurgency in the South.

A group of montagnards (tribesmen) from Quang Tri and Thua Thien Province received a special training in North Vietnam in 1958 and in 1959 to operate the infiltration trails. Also, at the beginning of 1959, the 559th Transportation Group received the order to report directly to the Party's Central Committee. This group served as a headquarters for infiltration activities. Special border crossing teams were formed in 1959. These teams were composed of southerners who went to North Vietnam after the Geneva Agreement of 1954. Early in 1960, two big training centers for infiltrators were established at Xuan Mai and at Son Tay Province near Hanoi.

From interrogations of captured infiltrators, United States Intelligence officers learned that until 1964, almost all the infiltrators were native southerners who had gone to North Vietnam after the Geneva Agreements of 1954. At least, two thirds of the infiltrators were members of the Lao Dong Party. They had received very intensive training in North Vietnam before being sent south. Most of them were officers, non-commissioned officers or party cadres.

Later, evidence showed that Hanoi's decision to switch from political struggle to armed struggle was responsible for the rising wave of terrorist attacks in South Vietnam during the second half of 1959. A special report from the U.S. Embassy in Saigon issued in January 1960 noted that while there were 193 assassinations in all of 1958, there were 119 assassinations in the last quarter of 1959 alone.

The full impact of that dangerous situation was reflected in the first attacks of the Viet Cong on South Vietnamese units of division level strength and on United States servicemen. In January 1960, the U.S. Embassy in Saigon passed to Washington two significant comments made by North Vietnamese Premier Pham Van Dong. "You must remember we will be in Saigon tomorrow, we will be in Saigon tomorrow." (Words of Pham Van Dong in a conversation with the French Consul, Georges Picot on September 12, 1959). "We will drive the Americans to the sea." (Pham Van Dong's conversation in November 1959 with the Canadian Commissioner Erichsen Brown who was stationed in Hanoi and who was the Canadian representative in the International Control Commission).

All strategic preparations completed, North Vietnam was ready to introduce the political arm to carry out its aggression. The timing for this introduction was important to the success of the strategy. The National Liberation Front for South Vietnam was born on December 20, 1960 and became that political arm.

It was a good timing. And it was also a good tactics for the North Vietnamese.

North Vietnam learned the lesson from the Korean War of 1950. A good formula for the invasion of South Vietnam would be the one that prevented the outside world, including the United States, from intervening. In 1960, there were a lot of favorable factors to help North Vietnam carry out their strategy. North Vietnam needed a political organization to conceal the invasion, a strategic supply line from the North to the South to sustain the armed struggle and a political atmosphere disadvantageous to the non-communist government in South Vietnam.

Although the prestige of the Diem Administration began to decrease from the end of 1959, world opinion was still very friendly to the Vietnamese Nationalists. An open, armed invasion from the North would almost surely bring

22

more support, more aid from the Free World to the South Vietnamese Administration. The creation of the National Liberation Front was in a large part the answer to that touchy problem. Besides, North Vietnamese leaders did not forget that in the south, there was almost permanently a certain tendency to separate the south from the north. Even among the Vietnamese Nationalists, there was also the same tendency of which the champions were General Duong Van Minh (Big Minh); the South Vietnamese politician Tran Van Van (assassinated by some secret political organizations in Saigon many years ago); and a group of young South Vietnamese intellectuals (The Inter-Schools Group of South Vietnam). When he was Commander of the Capital Military Region of Saigon, General Big Minh bluntly and openly said that he "did not want to have any North Vietnamese or any Centre Vietnamese officer in his staff" (Vietnam was composed of three parts: North Vietnam, Centre Vietnam and South Vietnam). The French colonialists had divided Vietnam in three parts and encouraged suspicion and hatred among each region. After World War II, this separatist feeling among the majority of the Vietnamese had almost been dissipated, although it was still strong among certain classes.

North Vietnam gave the world the illusion that the National Liberation Front was composed exclusively of Southerners; that the National Liberation Front was struggling to liberate South Vietnam from foreign domination (the American aid to South Vietnam); and more important, that the war in South Vietnam was only an internal war among South Vietnamese.

To carry out the North Vietnamese policy in the South, the NLF needed a strategic supply line. Before the Geneva Agreements of 1954, North Vietnamese Communists had built the Ho Chi Minh trail, running from North Vietnam territory deep to the south through the Laotian and Cambodian border. It was safe. War planes and bombs had repeatedly attacked this trail, but those attacks could only lessen or postpone the flow of men and arms that Hanoi daily and regularly sent to the south. Dense vegetation and the annual rainy season allowed the Communists to build many caches for arms and for ammunitions without fear of attack by Nationalist forces.

Through the highly efficient techniques of Communist propaganda, the Ho Chi Minh trail has become a respectful myth. It should be noted that Laos and Cambodia protested to North Vietnam against the building of the Ho Chi Minh trail. But since these two countries had many miles of common border with North Vietnam, and since their armed forces were too weak, the protests were silenced very quickly. After the Paris Accords of January 27, 1973, North Vietnam concentrated many efforts to modernize the Ho Chi Minh Trail. At the end of 1974, it had become a two way and all weather highway running to the gate provinces surrounding the Capital of Saigon.

The political arm, the National Liberation Front, and the strategic supply line must be coupled with a favorable political atmosphere in the south. The end of 1960 and the beginning of 1961 was considered a good time. The Diem Administration had begun to create more and more resentment among the South Vietnamese population. The military putsch of November 11, 1960 did not succeed. But it had paved the way for the Vietnamese Nationalist to think about means other than non-violent opposition to force Diem down. The National Liberation Front was born on December 20, 1960, 40 days after the putsch. This was no coincidence. This North Vietnamese tactical timing succeeded in making a lot of naive people accept the illusion that the Vietnamese nationalists and the

South Vietnamese dissidents had chosen the National Liberation Front to oust Diem.

This timing was also aimed to create trouble for the new American Administration. President John F. Kennedy had just taken office. One of the first problems he had to face was the war in Vietnam. In political warfare in underdeveloped nations, the Western world had usually been behind the Communists in taking the initiative. So was this American Administration. Kennedy had to face a situation in Vietnam in which the Communists had gained the advantage of being the first to move. Hanoi launched the National Liberation Front as a new factor in the Vietnam War at the dawn of the Kennedy era. It hoped that the new American Administration would be overloaded with the new aspects of the Vietnam War, as well as many other serious problems throughout the world.

With these necessary strategic pawns in place, North Vietnam was ready to direct the armed struggle in the South.

At first, there might have been some non-communist elements in the National Liberation Front. But given the hard line conduct of the Communists throughout the world, it was impossible to imagine that these non-communist elements could do anything to reverse policy, strategy and tactics imposed by the North Vietnamese leaders. The presence of some non-communists was no more than symbolic to help North Vietnam argue that the National Liberation Front was really a political organization of the Southerners. Other Southerners in the National Liberation Front were members of the Lao Dong Party, or at least, they were members of the People's Revolutionary Party (the overt Communist Party of the National Liberation Front). They blindly followed the orders and the directives of North Vietnam's Lao Dong Party. Another North Vietnamese tactics and it worked well: some prominent members of the National Liberation Front were allowed to cry loudly that they were non-communists. Of course, these self-proclaimed persons could not change the nature of the National Liberation Front since it was a creation of North Vietnam. And it is quite easy to prove that all real key functions in the National Liberation Front were assigned to Communist members.

During recent years, American intelligence has succeeded in establishing a solid dossier on the structural relationship between Hanoi and the National Liberation Front. This dossier was compiled through the interception of radio traffic, documents and interrogation of the prisoners.(4)

Overall direction of the Viet Cong movement is the responsibility of the Central Committee of the Lao Dong Party. In charge of the policy determination was the Reunification Department under General Nguyen Van Vinh, Politburo member Le Duc Tho and Vice Premier Pham Hung. Pham Hung was formerly a southern guerilla leader for the Viet Minh. The Reunification Department supervised the highest administrative unit in the south, the Central Office for South Vietnam (COSVN or COSVIN). For policy execution, there was the Council of Ministers and that Council supervised the Reunification Commission. This Reunification Commission supervised the National Liberation Front.

To sell the image of an independent National Liberation Front abroad, North Vietnam relied upon three persons: Two men and a woman. The men were Huynh Tan Phat and Nguyen Huu Tho. The woman was Nguyen Thi Binh. Phat is 65 years old. He was a pretty well-known architect in Saigon and has been considered chief theoretician of the National Liberation Front. A former lawyer, Nguyen Huu Tho is 65 years of age and was the loudest voice of those self-proclaimed non-communists. From Ben Tre Province South Vietnam, Madame Nguyen Thi Binh is 47 years old and had been foreign minister of the National Liberation Front many years ago. She was the head of the Viet Cong delegation to negotiate the Paris 1973 Accords on Vietnam. Nguyen Huu Tho and Nguyen Thi Binh travelled extensively abroad, attempting to convince the world that the National Liberation Front was a non-communist organization and that the National Liberation Front was truly the representative of South Vietnamese people.

Two other persons, less well-known than the three previously mentioned, were more important in their function and in their influence within the National Liberation Front. These were Vo Chi Cong and Tran Nam Trung. Both were overt communists and were vice-chairmen of the National Liberation Front. Vo Chi Cong was once described as the Viet Cong's Anastase Mikoyan.

Despite all efforts made by North Vietnam and by the National Liberation Front to deny direct control by North Vietnam of the war in South Vietnam, there was much evidence to the contrary. One June 2, 1962, the International Control Commission in Vietnam issued its formal report to the co-chairmen of the Geneva Conference of 1954 (Russia and Great Britain). The Commission formally and officially recognized that the Government of Hanoi was responsible for the war in Vietnam and had violated the Geneva Accords 1962 on Laos.

There were many additional factors to the Vietnam War after the creation of the National Liberation Front. The most important of these were the openly great offensives of 15 North Vietnamese regular divisions in the south in 1972 and of nearly 20 North Vietnamese divisions in March 1975. The offensive of 1975 accelerated the collapse of the non-communist South Vietnam on April 30, 1975. Without these North Vietnamese regular divisions, the National Liberation Front forces would have had to continue the struggle many more years with no assurance that they would win.

Nevertheless, there still are those people who continue to talk about an independent National Liberation Front Government in South Vietnam after the collapse of the South Vietnamese non-communist government. A French official declared a few days after the defeat of South Vietnamese non-communist Armed Forces that "The Provisional Revolutionary Government has ceased to exist. Now, it's the Government of South Vietnam, and there is nothing provisional about it."

The last pages of this chapter outline the technical aspects of political war in Vietnam, involving principles adapted by the Vietnamese Communists and various factors exploited by them.

For Ho Chi Minh and for the Vietnamese Communists, the departure point was the day they vowed to place Indochina under the control of the Vietnamese Communist Party. Therefore, the political war from 1954 to 1975 in South Vietnam was only a temporary objective of long range planning: all Indochina under the control of Hanoi.

In the new international communist strategy, Vietnam was considered a sacred war. The outcome of that war would have serious consequences to the Third World. It was not surprising to see the Communist World devoting full support in terms of arms, finance, manpower and propaganda. As we have mentioned earlier, in the Vietnam War of 1954 to 1975, the Vietnamese Nationalists had to face not only the Vietnamese Communists, but the whole Communist World.

Of course, there were many reasons for the collapse of non-communist

25

South Vietnam. Among them, we must include the divisiveness of the non-communist world after World War II. Had this divisiveness existed in World War II, the world map might have been quite different from the world map of today. The war against Nazi Germany, Fascist Italy and imperialist-militarist Japan was conducted as a sacred war. All nations knew that their freedom was at stake. Should they fail to defend and to preserve that freedom, they might have been enslaved indefinitely.

It is with the post World War II era that the existence of nuclear weapons has at least given the leaders of superpowers the necessary wisdom not to destroy each other in an atomic war. But to the national interest of some powers, war was sometimes considered necessary. In this thermo-nuclear age, instead of directly participating, the major powers fought their battles by proxy.

In such proxy wars, the international communist movement carefully chose their strategic objectives. Once these objectives have been selected, the international communists would provide support to their pawn country. The line of thinking was clear: the success of the pawn country would be the success of the whole Communist world. This unified command, this unified objective and that ideological solidarity were and are terrible weapons and constitute the most dangerous threat to mankind.

To face that threat, the Free World has been stymied by national selfishness and divisiveness. In each Free World country, individualism is worshipped. That way of life has been scientifically explored by international Communism. To date, there are already worrisome advances of Communism in Western stronghold bastions such as Portugal, Spain and Italy.

In his book entitled, *The Politics of Surrender,* author M. Stanton Evans wrote: ". . . The 'new prospects for advance' of the Communist Empire were spelled out by Khrushchev in his speech to the 20th Congress, and are everywhere visible in the world around us. They include new and unconventional methods of waging aggression under assumed conditions of coexistence and strategic stalemate: proxy wars, guerilla uprisings, coups d'etat, terrorism, espionage, all under the rubric of 'wars of national liberation.' As pointed out by Khrushchev, these types of warfare are definitely not ruled out by 'peaceful coexistence.' In fact, they are part and parcel of the definition of that concept. "The Communists," Khrushchev said, "fully support such just wars and march in the front rank with the peoples waging liberation struggles . . .

"Wars of this type in Algeria, Vietnam, the Congo, Laos, Angola are permissible under 'peaceful coexistence,' and even more important from the Communist point of view, they are aided by 'peaceful coexistence'." Since the doctrine means, in essence, that both sides renounce direct strategic confrontation, the Communists employ the threat of such confrontation to prevent Western resistance to their advances. At any point where the United States might feel impelled to intervene in one of these struggles, the threat is conveyed that such intervention would lead to "nuclear holocaust." "There are only two ways," Khrushchev said in his 1956 speech, "either peaceful coexistence or the most destructive war in history.

"The communists know that, when Cuba falls to Fidel Castro through internal revolution, war is being waged and that world Communism is winning. The west, defining 'war' in the conventional sense of armies marching across borders, seeks its solace in the absence of nuclear exchange. It clings to the notion that, despite the Communist advances, 'peace prevails.'

26

"One of the chief objects of 'coexistence policy' is to encourage the development and persistence of precisely these thought patterns in the West. So long as we conceive of war in a narrow sense, and congratulate ourselves on the presence of 'peace,' when in fact, the new style of war is everywhere being waged against us, the West is going to lose . . ."

In terms of the political war in Vietnam, it was necessary to explain why 1954 was a point of departure for the Vietnam War. Among the scholars and writers who have been long-time Indochina watchers, there were those who have repeatedly said "After three decades of guerilla warfare . . ." That remark is not false, nor a mistake. The problem has been simply oversimplified.

There is a difference between the French/Indochina War (1946-1954) and the Vietnam War (1954-1975). The war in Vietnam really became ideological after July 1954 with the Geneva Agreements. Before July 1954, it would be unfair to say that it was the war of the Vietnamese Communists against the French colonialists. During the French/Indochina War, evidence showed that, much like the situation in mainland China before 1948, nationalists and communists had temporarily forgotten their ideological differences to fight the common enemy. Only after July 1954 did the Vietnamese nationalists have to make up with their minds. The Geneva Agreements decided to place North Vietnam under the control of the Vietnamese Communist administration. The coalition experience with the communists in Vietnam before 1954 was too bitter and too bloody to forget. Each time the Vietnamese Communists arranged a coalition, Vietnamese nationalists lost many excellent cadres. They were massacred by the Communists. Vietnamese nationalists had only one option left, to the South, if they did not want to live under the Communist regime in the North. These Vietnamese nationalists accepted the challenge to rebuild a truncated land (South Vietnam) into a viable non-communist Vietnamese state.

So, the war in Vietnam became the ideological war after 1954, and that name did fit with the political aspects of the war. The outcome of that war was to be very important to the new nations in the world. If the Communists could not win, it would mean that the new nations would be able to build a new valid philosophy, a new strategy for an effective balance to Marxism.

As the international Communist Movement developed a new global strategy, North Vietnam changed its strategy accordingly. It developed a new kind of aggression. North Vietnam could not invade South Vietnam openly, as North Korea did in the Korean War of 1950s. A political war, emphasizing guerilla aspects, mounted from external bases with rights of sanctuary, would be a terrible burden for any South Vietnamese non-communist government to carry in a society making its way toward moderniztion. It would be difficult for the United Nations to intervene in that new form of aggression because there was not the appearance of an invasion. Nor would it be easy for the United States to try to help the Vietnamese nationalists. Military and economic aid from Russia and from Red China were well concealed, and North Vietnam never confessed that it received quantities of military equipment from the two communist giants. Meanwhile, any aid from the U.S. to South Vietnam was challenged by Hanoi and by other communist countries as "aggression."

To control all Indochina, North Vietnam must have intermediate objectives. For Laos and Cambodia, a neutralist status would be necessary so that North Vietnam could use these two countries as external bases with rights of sanctuary. North Vietnam would be the big rear area to the long range planning conquest of

Indochina. To South Vietnamese people, North Vietnam offered an alternative Vietnamese solution. North Vietnam promised further existence of a separate bourgeois but neutralist southern state. It was offered in order to split away from the Saigon regime those middle class elements which may still cling to this as an alternative to a social revolution. Later, the world would discover the tool for that alternative Vietnamese solution was the National Liberation Front.

North Vietnam had its own problems. If it did control Indochina too quickly, Hanoi might be overextended. Intermediate objectives would begin to accomplish Ho Chi Minh's dream: the ultimate control of the whole Indochina under the Communist regime of Hanoi. These intermediate objectives would help Hanoi buy time to acquire favorable conditions from South Vietnam—sociological, political and ethnic factors which proved to be so crucial in winning the battle of the Vietnam political war.

Before starting the war in South Vietnam, the physical environment of the fighting had been carefully studied by North Vietnam's leaders. They did have a high degree of flexibility in the application of revolutionary principles and in making the most of different factors.

First, the principle of popular representation. To a large body of international opinion, Ho Chi Minh is a legendary hero. Nobody could deny his influence in Indochina or even within the International Communist movement. At the time the Sino-Soviet dispute was most intense, it was Ho Chi Minh who wrote an important letter which brought about a reconciliation and temporarily preserved the unity of the International Communist movement. To compete with Ho's popularity, the non-communist South Vietnamese would be hard pressed to find a leader. And if South Vietnam could develop a leader of international prestige, it would still have to face this dilemma: the leader of non-communist South Vietnam might be popular, but his government might not be "strong" enough to resolve the vital problems of building a non-communist South Vietnam. In a non-communist developing country, it is almost impossible to find a popular leader and a strong and effective government simultaneously. If the leader wants to resolve vital problems of a country in a relatively short time, he may have to undertake unpopular measures which will label him a dictator. Faced with a revolutionary war promoted by the Communists, the future leader of a non-communist South Vietnam might have to sacrifice his popularity to national survival. In either case, North Vietnam was in an advantageous position to profit. If the South Vietnamese population did enjoy many individual rights and freedoms, the Communists would take advantage of the opportunity to infiltrate and to overthrow the legal government. If, on the contrary, South Vietnamese people were ruled by unpopular leaders, the Communists would use the slogan "Down with dictatorship" coupled with their usual infiltration and sabotage.

Secondly, there was the problem of foreign aid. As discussed in the first chapter, without the direct help of the United States, there might not have been a non-communist South Vietnam after July 1954 for the Vietnamese nationalists. Therefore, one of the primary objectives of North Vietnam was to deny American aid to South Vietnam. Foreign aid and common borders were two factors so vitally important as to affect radically all other elements in the equation of the political war in Vietnam. A review of the French Indochinese War (1945 to 1954) would demonstrate the importance of the common border factor. Experts on Asian affairs remember that after the surrender of the

Japanese in August 1945, the mountainous area in the northern part of North Vietnam was the Viet Minh stronghold (originally, it was the name of the Vietnamese communist organization). The northernest provinces of North Vietnam had many miles of common border with mainland China. Vietnamese Nationalists and Vietnamese Communists used to cross that common border when pursued by the French.

A big change came when the Chinese Communists took over mainland China in 1949. The Viet Minh began to receive arms and ammunitions from Red China. After consolidating their power in mainland China, however, the Chinese Communists could not increase their aid to the Viet Minh because of the Korean War. Red China entered the Korean War in November 1950 to prevent the collapse of Communist North Korea. Red China also shared many miles of common border with North Korea. Should Communist North Korea fall (meaning the South Koreans could take over North Korea), Chinese national security might be endangered. And the Korean War went on without victory for either side. Finally, in July 1953, an agreement to stop fighting was signed. Korea was once again divided at the 38th parallel. From then on, Red China was able to rush economic and military aid to the Viet Minh. The French Indochinese War dragged on from 1946 to 1953 (7 years) but it needed only one year after the end of the Korean War to accelerate the defeat of the French Expeditionary Corps.

In the Vietnam War (1954 to 1975), common border once again played its vital role. From July 1954 to April 30, 1975, Hanoi never had to complain about foreign aid to North Vietnam (aid from Russia, Red China and from some other communist countries like Cuba, Czechoslovakia, East Germany). Russia and Red China may be short of wheat, corn and rice. But they are never short of arms and ammunitions to provide to North Vietnam for the sacred war of the International Communist movement. Of course, North Vietnam high officials travelled many times to friendly communist capitals to negotiate the renewal and/or the increase of foreign aid. The Vietnamese Communist soldiers were never in short supply of weapons to kill the Vietnamese nationalists. After the 1972 great winter/spring offensive of North Vietnam across the D.M.Z. (Demilitarized Zone) separating the two Vietnams (only theoretically), one Western journalist reported that in a casual conversation with some North Vietnamese peasants helping North Vietnamese soldiers in moving many brand new Russian made 130 millimetres guns across paddy fields, one said that: "Never, we have had so many modern weapons as we have now." And it was not only 130 MM guns. There were plenty of other kinds of weapons as well, all of them heavily sophisticated and of course, deadly: SAM Missiles, anti-aircraft guns, tanks, trucks.

North Vietnam had three ways to get supplies and weapons from abroad: the railroad through mainland China, the seaway through the Haiphong Port and finally, the airway. Practically, there was no means for the Free World to know and to check the quantity of foreign aid to North Vietnam. No international organization, including the United Nations, no country in the world, including the United States, could prevent North Vietnam from receiving foreign aid. Even blockades of the U.S. Navy for many days could not stop the ceaseless flow of arms and ammunitions to North Vietnam.

Another remarkable aspect of the Vietnam War (1954 to 1975) was that there was practically no limit to foreign aid to North Vietnam. For Moscow and Peking, the victory of the Vietnamese Communists was to be the victory for the

International Communist movement. Therefore, arms and military equipment were to be given to North Vietnam according to the needs of the war to conquer South Vietnam, Laos and Cambodia. The procedure to aid North Vietnam was simple and fast: Moscow and Peking never had to report to their people about motivation, quantity and purpose of any kind of aid to any country.

At the height of the Chinese-Russian dispute, there were those optimistic people who thought that North Vietnamese war efforts in South Vietnam would be jeopardized; that this might bring some hope for an eventual cease fire in the Vietnam War. It was sublimely naive: the Chinese-Russian dispute never hurt the delivery of foreign aid to Hanoi. There was a tacit division of responsibility between Peking and Moscow. Peking provided light weapons and light equipment to Hanoi, and heavy equipment came from Moscow. Peking and Moscow might not have agreed with each other about revisionism, but they had never denied Communism. They might disagree about North Vietnamese tactics but they never asked Hanoi to stop fighting the Vietnam War. They gave Hanoi different advice, but Chinese advice as well as Russian advice were centered around the same strategic long range objective: a unified Vietnam under the Vietnamese Communist regime. Thus, in spite of the Chinese-Russian dispute, aid from two giant communist countries complemented each other. Of course, it might also be the result of a North Vietnamese clever and flexible attitude in the dispute between Moscow and Peking.

The world very well knew about the flow of arms and supplies from outside to North Vietnam but nothing could be done. To demonstrate that world opinion would never have any effect on Communist strategy and tactics, Russia and Red China doubled their aid to North Vietnam after 1970—a time when the world was elated by the detente between the United States and the two Communist giants. The result was two North Vietnamese great offensives in South Vietnam, one in spring 1972 and the other in spring 1975. During the last months of the Vietnam War, North Vietnamese armed forces were equipped with weapons which were even more sophisticated than the weapons of most American units in Europe.

The aid formula from Russia and from China was rewarding and tactful. They exported their weapons and their ideology, but they avoided sending their troops, excepting some civilian and military advisors. Thus, Russia and China could loudly say they never interferred in the Vietnam War. North Vietnam was their sales representative to sell Communism in Indochina and the North Vietnamese had the monopoly to kill the Vietnamese in the North as well as in the South of Vietnam. For that killing, North Vietnam was never short of manpower. Some American reports said that North Vietnamese manpower has been drained by so many years of war. North Vietnam infiltrated thousands of men in the south since 1954 and of course, thousands were killed in action. But it was far from drained. Reliable documents from experts showed that North Vietnam could afford to lose 300,000 men each year. And one could not forget that North Vietnam was known as having the hardest Stalinist Communism: everybody had to do as ordered by Communist rulers. In North Vietnam as well as in any other Communist country, individual human life has never been considered. Therefore, North Vietnam was ready to wage the Vietnam War for many, many years until ultimate victory.

Third, there were two principles underlying the political war in South Vietnam after 1954: the principle of legitimacy and the principle of violence.

Theoretically, the principle of legitimacy means that North Vietnam had the sacred mission to liberate South Vietnam from foreign domination. Since non-communist South Vietnam had to rely upon foreign aid (mostly upon American) to survive, it was easy for North Vietnam to choose the United States as target for their propaganda purpose. Any kind of American aid to non-communist South Vietnam was seen as an act of aggression against the Vietnamese and was loudly accused by the whole International Communist movement.

Practically, the principle of legitimacy would try to win the Vietnamese peasants to two causes. The major cause was liberation: North Vietnam would liberate the peasants from foreign domination and would give land to the peasants. The minor cause would aim to better everything directly related to the daily life of the peasants.

Vietnam is primarily an agricultural country with nearly 90% of its population involved in farming. In the Vietnam war, the winning side would be the one which did not lose its grass root contacts with its own people. In Vietnam, by the word people, one must understand that people means the majority, particularly those peasants who live and who die in the countryside. The Vietnamese Communists are masters in the art of winning hearts and minds of common people no matter by what means. The principle of legitimacy did emphasize that majority, more specifically, the peasants. Being an agricultural country, South Vietnam offered an agrarian theater of hostilities because the non-communist South Vietnam government did not know how to communicate with the majority of the peasants. The peasants are water and the communists are fish. According to revolutionary doctrine, fish will die if there is no water. At first, this principle seemed to be an elementary one but soon, it became one of the fundamental principles of political warfare throughout the world. During the French-Indochinese war and the Vietnam war, the Communists never underestimated that principle. Of course, the wise observance of that principle was to contribute a great part to the success of their political war.

But of course, the Vietnamese Communists did not win the people's hearts and minds by smiles and roses alone. They won by the observance of the principle of violence as well. There were at least two ways to win hearts and minds: by friendly persuasion or by terrorism. The Communists used both, with emphasis on the tactics of violence. Whether you liked communism or not, you would surely die if you did not support the communists. And violence always brought results faster than friendly persuasion.

In the countryside, there were not many armed communist members at the village or at hamlet level. The Communists needed only a team (the minimum was three men) in each village or hamlet to completely control the villagers. The team lived day and night together with the villagers and became their rulers.

To counter that tactics, the government side must develop effective counters. The experience of the French-Indochinese war showed that the classical tactics of search and destroy did not succeed: if government forces were strong, the communists simply evaded (which explains why many major operations using large forces and modern weapons failed).

On the contrary, if government forces were weak, the communists would destroy them by building a temporary concentration of strength. If the government side could not develop suitable counterbalance to the communist strategy and tactics, the war would either drag on indefinitely or would end in the defeat of the government forces.

At higher level, the principle of violence was much more appalling. After the delivery (from Russia and mainland China) of rockets to North Vietnam, those weapons become the deadliest Communist tools to win hearts and minds. Under normal circumstances and according to current international conventions, any army at war must avoid harming the civilian population. But in the Vietnam war, the civilian population become the target of the principle of violence. To the Communists, raining rockets and mortars on civilians was a most rewarding tactic: the Communists did not need to select the objectives. Any civilian could be destroyed, any civilians could be killed if they continued to support the government cause. In the offensive of spring 1968, the Communists deliberately sent rockets and mortar shells on any group of civilians trying to flee to government controlled areas. In the offensive of 1972 and in the offensive of 1975 as well, the most sophisticated Russian weapons were used to kill any civilian who fled to government controlled areas.

Another principle fully observed by the Vietnamese Communists was their maximum propaganda effort to sell their image abroad. These efforts paid off. The fall of Dien Bien Phu in May 1954 was seen by a great part of the world as a famous Communist victory. North Vietnam produced a film about the fall of Diem Bien Phu. Later, that film was shown in many foreign countries. Of course, those who saw that film were deeply impressed by the Communist performance. And, of course, it detracted from the prestige of the western world. Such film shows combined with many other propaganda tactics helped North Vietnam to acquire the admiration of many countries. Communist propaganda tactics were so sophisticated that few people thought of the negative aspect of the battle of Dien Bien Phu. An average observer could easily find out that the Dien Bien Phu victory was not difficult. A glimpse at the map of Dien Bien Phu and of its surrounding area would do: how could Colonel De Castries' French garrison or any other garrison survive when Dien Bien Phu was established in a valley and when all the surrounding heights were occupied by many well-equipped North Vietnamese units? The Dien Bien Phu garrison got supplies only by air. And only a few days after the beginning of the battle, North Vietnamese artillery destroyed the only runway. One could see that Dien Bien Phu was lost in advance. But Communist propaganda techniques turned it into a famous legend.

Another example: in 1969, a few months after the opening of the Paris Conference on Vietnam, the French weekly *Paris Match* prepared a story to introduce French readers to the life of the Viet Cong and of the South Vietnamese delegations in Paris. Of course, the South Vietnamese delegation and the Viet Cong delegation both tried to give the *Paris Match* their most advantageous documents and photos. When the readers received that *Paris Match* issue, they had simultaneously two patterns of propaganda. The readers could easily reach an appropriate conclusion. The photo of the Viet Cong delegation showed Mme. Nguyen Thi Binh, Foreign Minister of the National Liberation Front playing ping pong with another Vietnamese woman (possibly member of the Viet Cong delegation) in the courtyard, while the other Vietnamese were watching chickens in a poultry cart. All of them had a peasant bearing.

In the other photo, the reader saw Mr. Pham Dang Lam, chief of South Vietnamese delegation sitting in the living room of his villa near his wife and his little daughter, all dressed at their neatest. The villa looked very nice. They were the image of a perfect bourgeois family. Nobody really knew in fact how the Viet

Cong delegation members behaved in their daily routine life but the two opposite pictures did provide a grim contrast. Although this was only one article, a few photos in a foreign magazine, it reflected quite well a concept about the political aspect of the Vietnam war. Mr. Pham Dang Lam might be sincere when he gave the *Paris Match* magazine the photo in which, he was having a good time with his family. But unfortunately, to the world (watching closely the activity of every delegation attending the Paris Conference on Vietnam), that photo only emphasized the individualistic aspect of the South Vietnamese non-communist society. That perception was bad for the South Vietnamese cause. Why didn't Mr. Lam take a photo in which, he and his assistants were together, talking or even participating in a friendly game?

In selling a better image abroad, the Vietnamese Communists chose a daring formula: each Communist diplomat must be a propaganda specialist, a fighter. Normally, a western diplomat handles his embassy affairs in a classical way; routine working hours every day at office, attending parties, courtesy visits, sending periodical reports. To the Communists, more specifically, to the Vietnamese Communists, these routine activities were only of secondary importance. In the Vietnam War, the diplomatic front was as important as the military or the economic front. Propaganda service diplomacy was the daring formula of the Vietnamese Communists. Diplomatic activities were seen by the Communists as a crucial weapon in political warfare to win hearts and minds.

The primary objective of any Vietnamese Communist diplomat abroad was to try to make the world believe that the Communists are the true and honorable representatives of the Vietnamese people. To carry out that crucial objective, the Vietnamese Communists invested considerable sums of money. That investment paid off: more countries paid attention to the fighting of the Vietnamese Communists. From attention to sympathy was a short step.

One key to their diplomatic success was their tactful and wise use of public funds. If they thought that in the future, such and such areas would be needed to reinforce their political front abroad, they gave full support to that area: money, manpower, resources, etc. Years before, the Vietnamese Nationalists had not paid attention to the many new African countries. Yet, the National Liberation Front had already sent Mme. Nguyen Thi Binh as special Envoy on many good will visits in Africa. In Northern Europe, there was also a strong diplomatic offensive by the Vietnamese Communists.

The diplomatic battle to win the support of the Vietnamese living abroad was equally important to the Vietnamese Communists. Where there were Vietnamese (businessmen, students, refugees, politicians), there was at least a man who acted on behalf of the Vietnamese Communists. At various capitals where there were many Vietnamese, the Communist diplomatic offensive became active, particularly in France, West Germany, Australia, Canada and in the United States. In these countries, there was a desperate fight to win hearts and minds between the Vietnamese Nationalists and the Vietnamese Communists. According to most reports and many eye witnesses, it was again an unequal combat. Bureaucratic, remote and selfish was the attitude of South Vietnamese diplomats. When a Vietnamese student required assistance, he was rarely received by a South Vietnamese representative. The Vietnamese Communists were always ready to help any needy Vietnamese. In France, as soon as a new Vietnamese student landed at Orly airport, he met covert or overt Communist members. If the student did not know what hotel to select, what places to go, he would surely be "guided" by the Communist agents or by Communist

33

sympathizers. And if that student agreed to live together with some other Vietnamese (introduced by those who had helped him at the airport), he could not escape the Communist influence.

Even in the United States, the Vietnamese Communists were very active. Aided by American leftists and by so-called liberal elements, the International Communists organized a keen and subtle long-range propaganda campaign. The United States is a democratic country. The human and civil rights observed there served the interest of the International Communists well. Even as more than 500,000 American soldiers were fighting in South Vietnam to help preserve a non-communist South Vietnam, there was a stream of Communist books funnelled into the United States via Canada. The propaganda offensive was so strong that in many U.S. schools and universities, professors and students knew much more of North Vietnam and the Viet Cong than they knew of the non-Communist South Vietnam. It was no surprise to see that the Communist propaganda efforts played a considerable part in building a strong anti-war movement in the United States.

Finally, came the factor of destruction and construction in the Vietnam War. The Vietnamese nationalists had to request foreign aid to build highways, hospitals, schools, markets, bridges while fighting against the Vietnamese Communists. But these construction efforts were not to last. While the nationalists needed many months, even years to build a bridge, hospital, a highway, the Communists needed only a few minutes to blow it up. It was purely International Communist's vandalism.

But because of many complicated reasons, only a few countries wanted to criticize these acts of vandalism.

Should the Free World be less divisive and should it be more cooperative, there might have been a chance that South Vietnam could be saved.

Having seen the disastrous divisiveness among Free World countries, the International Communists increased their destructive efforts in South Vietnam. They were sure that passivity and divisiveness in the Free World were two blessings which gave the Vietnamese Communists the most terrible power the world has ever had: the monopoly to kill Vietnamese without fear of punishment.

There are different opinions about the American aid to non-communist South Vietnam. At least, the American aid to non-communist societies has been able to help millions of people maintain the way of life they have chosen. Had American aid to South Vietnam been used reasonably and adequately and should the Vietnamese Nationalists been less inactive and less conservative, there might not have been the collapse of South Vietnam on April 30, 1975.

Let's summarize. To prepare the aggression in South Vietnam, North Vietnam Communist leaders tried to sell to the world the image of a national hero (Ho Chi Minh) who gave to himself the sacred mission of reunifying the two Vietnams, the emergency of the Vietnamese Communist-led Nationalism, the Vietnamese alternative (the National Liberation Front) to the Vietnamese Nationalists and many patriotic slogans.

Behind these slogans was an immense rear area which included mainland China and Russia with ceaseless flow of arms and ammunitions to North Vietnam.

There will never be peace in the world as long as the international community accepts the outcome of a political war mounted from outside a nation as tantamount to a free election.

Chapter Three
U.S. POLICY ON VIETNAM
UNDER FIVE U.S. PRESIDENTS

The Eisenhower Administration

A few weeks after the signature of the Geneva Agreement of July 1954, President Eisenhower, in response to a request from Prime Minister Ngo Dinh Diem of South Vietnam for "economic assistance," pledged American support "to assist the Government of Vietnam in developing and maintaining a strong, viable state, capable of resisting attempted subversion or aggression through military means."

The Eisenhower letter to Diem contemplated only economic and political support for the Saigon Government. It was not a warrant for military intervention. At the end of Eisenhower's Administration, there were really in South Vietnam fewer than 800 American military personnel. But Eisenhower's letter did draw a line in Southeast Asia. In politics, it committed the U.S. to hold that line. Of course, that line could have been drawn elsewhere, but it was drawn in South Vietnam.

As Eisenhower had written Diem, the object of American policy in South Vietnam was to "discourage any who might wish to impose a foreign ideology on your free people." That mood was essentially moralistic. The commitment to South Vietnam followed directly from the Dulles conception of the world as irrevocably split into two unified and hostile blocs.

The Eisenhower administration had assumed that economic and political support alone would be sufficient to assure the survival of South Vietnam as an independent state. In 1954, this was a reasonable judgment. For a time, it seemed to be working: a rise in production; a token land reform program; an army with the help of American advisers.

Beneath the surface, things were far less rosy; too little of the American

35

economic assistance went to the Vietnamese peasants (about 90% of South Vietnam's total population). Diem's concept was to remake a Vietnamese society according to a model which required the concentration of total power in the hands of a small trusted group. In the first year in office, Diem moved to consolidate his control by crushing all sources of opposition.

Among the first U.S. officials who saw the danger to South Vietnam in the policy of Ngo Dinh Diem was General Lawton Collins, the U.S. special representative. He urged the removal and replacement of Ngo Dinh Diem as the leader, or the "reevaluation of our plans" for aid to South Vietnam. But Dulles replied that he had "no other choice but to continue our aid to Vietnam and support of Diem."(1)

As his later writings make clear, President Eisenhower recognized not only Ho Chi Minh's popularity but the high cost of any effort to crush Ho's movement. He resisted ambitious schemes for building up Diem's regime as a western style alternative to the Viet Minh. The proposition of General Collins reflected Eisenhower's point of view. But the Eisenhower Administration was vulnerable to political pressures, and therefore, during the unsettled period after the signature of the Geneva Agreement of July 1954, the pre-Geneva lobbying for Diem began to bear fruit.

The strongest voice publicly raised on behalf of a hard line of full support for Diem was that of Cardinal Spellman. On August 31, 1954, in a speech before the American Legion Convention, he said "If Geneva and what was agreed upon there means anything at all, it means . . . Taps for the buried hopes of freedom in Southeast Asia: Taps for the newly betrayed millions of Indochinese who must now learn the awful facts of slavery from their eager communist masters!Now, the devilish techniques of brainwashing, forced confessions, and rigged trials have a new locale for their exercise."

Cardinal Spellman emphasized the essential thesis of the cold war containment policy. He said that the danger lay in the illusion of peace with the communists. Others of Diem's early supporters followed: Wesley Fishel, the Michigan State University professor who had originally induced Diem to come to the U.S., Wolf Ladejinsky who found the Research Institute of America and was also President of the International Rescue Committee (an organization aimed at helping refugees from Communism). After so many moves of Cardinal Spellman and from the spring of 1955 on, the U.S. commitment to Diem was complete. There was even the celebration of the "Miracle of Vietnam."

During the first five years of Diem's regime, it was generally accepted in the United States that American aid to South Vietnam had produced a great success: according to the "miracle thesis" formulated by the lobby (and that thesis was accepted by most of the mass media), the Diem Administration had turned back the threat of communism by "initiating vast programs of economic and political reforms." Life of the people has been greatly improved. These lobbyists said that the American aid and advice had helped to develop a nationalist alternative to the Viet Minh and that the country was making "rapid strides toward political stability and economic independence."

In considering the politics of the Diem Administration, it must be kept in mind that in Vietnam as in most Asian countries, there was no tradition of formal representative government. The Vietnamese nationalist political parties formed during the French domination were secret parties, accustomed to operate clandestinely and often warring with each other. This tradition continues today. Diem really accomplished one thing tantamount to a miracle when he put together a relatively stable government and attracted support from many key factions of the elite in South Vietnam.

But unfortunately, Diem had taken other actions which made the renewal of revolutionary warfare both inevitable and successful. Haunted by a strange desire to bring back into being the society of former days, when there were no sects and no communists, the Diem Administration accentuated its authoritarian and repressive character. The de facto integration of South Vietnam within the American military defense structure implied that South Vietnam ought to be secure and ought to be purged of anything which might be considered by Diem as "bringing profit to the Red cause."

In 1956, there were uprisings in North Vietnam and in Hungary. That was really a bad year for the International Communist movement. Profiting from the emotion aroused by these uprisings, the Diem Administration launched a series of man hunts in 1957. In theory, this repression was aimed at the communists but in fact, it affected all those who were bold enough to express their disagreement with the policy adopted by the ruling oligarchy. Even those who attempted to criticize Diem through the regular channel of parliament and press were suppressed by this secret police. To the common people in South Vietnam from 1957 onwards, U.S. aid was greatly responsible for that terrible man hunt because Americans had trained and financed the police apparatus. It soon became evident to many observers that this policy was playing into the hands of the communists.

The Diem Administration also drew almost exclusively from the Catholics and from the Catholic refugees of North Vietnam, causing friction with the largely Buddhist population of the South. That friction was the strongest motivation to the coup of November 1, 1963 resulted in the death of Diem and of his brother Nhu.

No less important was the appointment of village chiefs in South Vietnam. Throughout history, Vietnam's thousands of villages were traditionally governed by village chiefs or headmen. These men had their family roots deep in the local soil, ancestors having lived in the same village for centuries. Diem chose to replace many of these village headmen with appointees of his own from Saigon, causing deep resentment among the villages so governed.

In addition to Diem's incomparable stubborness, South Vietnam had an official political philosophy: Personalism. That philosophy was developed in the post depression of 1930s, first in France by a group of young Catholics led by Emmanuel Mounier. Ngo Dinh Nhu (Diem's brother) convinced Diem that personalism was capable of counterbalancing the primitive Marxism of the Viet Minh.

To compete with the Viet Minh, Diem and his brother Nhu imitated the totalitarian methods of the communists. After 1957, there was virtually only one legal political party in South Vietnam and it was Ngo Dinh Nhu's Can Lao Nhan Vi Cach Mang Dang (Revolutionary Personalist Worker's Party). This party had its secret membership and five-men cells whose members could swiftly and quietly do away with any oppositionist. That party did, within its own system, exactly what a communist party would do: acted as a state within a state in its own government's machinery.

All this was far from enough to be estimated as an available alternative to the South Vietnamese. The Eisenhower Administration has been criticized for not pushing Diem harder on political reforms. To talk of superimposing western democratic institutions overnight on the Vietnamese culture is pointless. There exists no truly democratic nation from Burma to the gates of Red China in all of Southeast Asia. Therefore, President Eisenhower only stuck to his basic position that if there was a solution in South Vietnam, it would be political and not military, insofar as the U.S. was concerned. That fundamental precept was not to be altered until 1961 when the new administration of J.F. Kennedy took office.

Pushing Diem on political reforms? Once again, the problem has been oversimplified. By western standards, the first five years of the Diem Administration were successful. There were both political stability and economic independence plus—according to western standards—a sort of alternative to South Vietnamese. In fact, South Vietnam needed much more than that to counterbalance the primitive North Vietnamese Marxism.

In Vietnam and in Asia, after World War II, the exaggerated expectations of the champions of freedom and modernization were usually doomed to serious disappointment. The life of the average citizen was lived in the context of a world of spirits. There was virtue in excessive industry looking toward the accumulation of wealth. But, many lacked training in the ordered discipline of the modernist tempo. Spirit or ancestral shrines were still maintained in most homes. Social security in Asia continued to be rooted principally in the family system.

The modernizing elite leaders of Southeast Asian countries had to start virtually from scratch. Lacking the traditional credentials of ruling status and substantial economic power, they assumed authority arbitrarily, but tried at the same time to enlist popular backing of their programs. These leaders fully exploited their patriotic reputations to justify their exercise of arbitrary power.

A sharp contrast was presented in the character of the successor governments in French Vietnam. After the abdication of Emperor Bao Dai in August 1945, communism became solidly entrenched in North Vietnam, operating through the agency of a one party dictatorship. French alignments were gradually replaced by close connections with Moscow and Peking. The contrasting regime in South Vietnam in 1954 was politically weaker than the communist regime in the north, partly because Ngo Dinh Diem was Catholic (moreover, he only used relatives and close friends in key positions in the government) and partly because he incurred the hostility of France by his acceptance of aid from the United States.

Whether democratic government could take root and survive in Vietnam was a controversial question. From the colonial period, there was the idea that progress toward self government and independence was to be measured in terms of increased popular representation in election. But once in control, nationalism was more likely to express itself in traditional than in alien patterns of government. Constitutions and elections provided no more than an empty facade. The resulting attitude of political apathy and passivity of the population generally provided facile reason for dictatorship and authoritarian direction.

After World War II, while new nations adopted a wait and see attitude, Marxism commended itself to many people in Asia as a modern shortcut to industrialization. By comparison, the centuries old liberal system of the westerners seemed old fashioned. To the developing nations, the more rapid communist techniques of economic and of political regimentation might presumably avoid the compromises in the slower processes of democratic adjustment.

In the Vietnam War, North Vietnamese were confident that they could gain ascendancy in the south, either through elections or through subversion and guerilla warfare. They were a modern force and the one opposing them in the south was feudal. At the Geneva Agreement of July 1954, they were the heroes who had driven out the French and stirred the powerful feelings of nationalism in the country. In the south, the old feudal order still existed, soon to be preserved by the conservative force of American aid. The force which divided the various political groups from one another was more powerful than that which bound them together. The tradition of the old Vietnam had been loyalty to family alone. Symbolically, the Ngo Dinh Diem government was a family government (and so was the government of Nguyen Van Thieu later). And until the time of his downfall, Diem trusted only his family. From the very starting point, one Vietnam lived in the past and the other in the present.

By comparison with North Vietnamese leadership after 1954, the legitimacy of Ngo Dinh Diem was weaker than that of Ho Chi Minh. Diem was a Catholic in a Buddhist country. He was a Vietnamese from centre Vietnam in the south. But most important of all, he was really a mandarin, a strong supporter of the feudal aristocracy in a country swept by revolution.

Facing such unfavorable factors, would political reforms be enough to counterbalance the alternative offered by North Vietnam to the South Vietnamese? The answer was clearly no. To compete with the communists, Ngo Dinh Diem would have to carry out essential political changes which would be indispensable to win the political war in Vietnam, something no less than a real social revolution in South Vietnam. But given the education of Diem (mandarin), given his self defeating policy, no one could expect any reform from him.

Many western observers had few illusions about the recovery of the non-communist Vietnamese. The disproportion between the monolithic power of the north and the weakness of the Vietnamese Nationalists was such that in July 1954, few people thought that the two years delay provided by the Geneva Agreement could be anything more than a respite to salvage the wreck. But Hanoi had realized quickly that the political situation was evolving in a disturbing way to North Vietnam. Not being a signatory, South Vietnam was already declaring that it was not bound by the Geneva Agreements and the consolidation of South Vietnam was taking shape rapidly with massive aid from the United States. That aid reminded South Vietnam that it was not alone in the ideological war. To Washington, after the Geneva Agreements, it was necessary to save South Vietnam and to transform it into a bastion of the Free World in Southeast Asia. With strong aid from the U.S., South Vietnam had enough time to recover.

The second unfavorable factor to North Vietnam was an important political regroupment in the south. Having decided to hold on to the 17th parallel at all costs, the conclusion of the Americans was that South Vietnam could only be held and preserved with the help of anti-communist nationalism. For the Vietnamese nationalists, the only hope to fight against a take over of communism was to rely heavily on the American alliance coupled with radical political reforms.

Furthermore, the exodus of thousands of people southward from the victorious North Vietnamese communists showed that many Vietnamese (like the East Germans) pereferred to risk their lives than to live under communist rule.

Thus, North Vietnam underestimated the importance of the non-communists in South Vietnam. For the first time since the French Indochinese War,

North Vietnam was not confronted by people linked in one way or another to ignominious colonial authorities, but by a man whose partriotism and integrity had been tested and whose uncompromising anti-communism did stem from deep religious convictions, not from calculated self interest. South Vietnam was emerging from chaos.

On February 4, 1955, North Vietnam proposed the restoration of normal relations between the two Vietnams. It was the first round in a diplomatic offensive which lasted seven years over two crucial questions to North Vietnam: the normalization between the two zones and the implementation of the Geneva Agreements concerning preelectoral consultations and general elections. The proposal of February 4, 1955 was repeated many times, particularly on March 7, 1958 and on October 4, 1960.

Ngo Dinh Diem bluntly rejected the proposition of North Vietnam on the ground that the normalization proposed by North Vietnam had no other aim than the infiltration of agents, arms and propaganda war into the south. Some western writers tended to accuse Diem of being extremely intransigent and they wondered whether the anti-communist's lowering of this iron curtain (revealing a singular inferiority complex on their part) had not ultimately caused much injury to the Vietnamese nation, and had not made the ordeal of the whole people more difficult.

But was it possible for Diem to seek some accommodation policy with North Vietnam when south depended so vitally on American aid? In the generation following World War II, the Presidents of the United States concluded that they could not lose another inch of territory to communism anywhere. The Republicans challenged the Democrats by saying they had been weak or treacherous about China and had accepted less than total victory in Korea. The Democrats countered the Republicans by saying that they had lost Cuba and dissipated American prestige and missile strength.

Later on, there was evidence that all elaborately staged offers of negotiation and compromise with the communists were privately acknowledged in the American administration as demands for its virtual surrender. And there was evidence scattered over the years that the often proclaimed goal of achieving self-determination for the South Vietnamese was in fact acceptable to the United States as long as no South Vietnamese leader chose neutralism or any other form of non-alignment. In a cablegram to his ambassador in Saigon in early 1964, President L.B. Johnson said "Your mission is precisely for the purpose of knocking down the idea of neutralization wherever it rears its ugly head."(2)

When proposing normalization to South Vietnam, Hanoi might have put its reconstruction policy and its economic development upon a Pan-Vietnamese basis: if the two Vietnams could reach an agreement of normalization, South Vietnam would be able to make good the North Vietnamese food deficits, and therefore, North Vietnam will not have to intensify its agricultural production at a costly price and in difficult conditions. The intransigence of South Vietnam might have contributed in pushing the north into the arms of Red China. And had not South Vietnam by its refusal, condemned itself to an ever increasing state of dependence on the United States?

Have the American Administrations had any serious study on the aspirations of the Vietnamese people, on the physical environment of the battle areas of the Vietnam War and on the nature of the political war in Vietnam? The planners of American Administration wrote different scenarios of U.S. policy on

Vietnam in the cold but confident spirit of efficiency experts. Assistant Secretary of Defense, John T. McNaughton had professed ignorance of the Vietnamese people. His sincerity best typified this style of thought and planning at high levels of the U.S. government.

Had Ngo Dinh Diem been less closely tied to the U.S. policy of containment, had Diem been less near-sighted after 1957, an effective nationalist alternative might have been reached for the Vietnamese and so many atrocities, so much suffering might have been avoided. Unfortunately, Ngo Dinh Diem had not only rejected the repeated proposition of normalization from Hanoi, but more tragically, it seemed that he wanted to exterminate the communists. Thus, by his intransigence vis-a-vis the communists and by his home policy, the Diem Administration finally destroyed the confidence of the South Vietnamese which Diem had won during his early years. He practically drove them into revolt and despair.

From the end of 1959, many civilian and military elements in the nationalist camp realized clearly that things were moving from bad to worse and that if nothing were done to end Diem's dictatorship then the communists would finally end by gaining victory, even by the political passivity of the population. From 1959 onward, one could hardly see how Diem could restore his authority among South Vietnamese. And finally, even the Americans were themselves aware of that desperate situation. In May 1961, Secretary of State Dean Rusk emphasized that it was no longer possible to oppose the Viet Minh by pure military means. Later, the Taylor/Rostow mission has confirmed that point of view.

The methods and the nature of the Diem regime reflect a sad history. The people of Vietnam have always been caught between communism and a form of anti-communism which they could not accept. Under the French domination, the Vietnamese had to choose between communism and an unpopular colonial regime. Then, the Americans gave them a choice between communism and a dictatorship which was simultaneously fascist and backward. To make sure that the Saigon Government was capable of inspiring confidence, it would be necessary to get out of the terrible formula "either Diem or the communists." It would require another pole of political influence: a popular and democratic nationalist regime, an advanced economic and social policy and a positive attitude regarding relations with the north. Such a government in Saigon would likely be able to destroy many debating points of North Vietnamese propaganda. And finally, why should a popular and democratic government in the South fear any contact with the North? After all, the Geneva Agreements did not mean that all the Vietnamese wanted to live as foreigners and enemies to each other.

Of course, the Americans could have provided South Vietnam with another alternative to the old formula "either Diem or the Viet Minh" after 1959. But unfortunately, nothing like that was done, although an American intelligence estimate of May 1959 already described the situation in South Vietnam as follows: "President Diem continues to be the undisputed ruler of South Vietnam. All important and minor decisions are referred to him. Although he professes to believe in representative government and democracy, Diem is convinced that the Vietnamese are not ready for such a political system and that he must rule with a firm hand, at least so long as national security is threatened. He also believes that the country can not afford a political opposition which could obstruct or dilute the government's efforts to establish a strong rule. He remains a somewhat austere and remote figure to most Vietnamese and has not generated widespread popular enthusiasm. Diem's regime reflects his ideas. A facade of representative government is maintained but the government is in fact essentially authoritarian. No organized opposition, loyal or otherwise, is tolerated and critics of the regime are often repressed." And in January 1960, the U.S. Embassy in Saigon concluded in a special report on the internal security situation in Vietnam: "The situation may be summed up in the fact that the government tended to treat the population with suspicion or to coerce it and has been rewarded with an attitude of apathy and resentment. The basic factor which has been lacking is a feeling of rapport between the government and the population. The people have not identified themselves with the government." Finally, the report pointed to this "growth of apathy and considerable dissatisfaction among the rural populace" as a major cause of the insurgency.

The U.S. intransigent policy of containment, the Diem nearsightedness, the increasing disintegration of the Diem Administration under political pressures from both sides (from North Vietnam and from the Vietnamese nationalists) coupled with the consolidation of the Communist power in North Vietnam provided a great part of a rationale to Hanoi for starting the aggression.

The Eisenhower Administration was the first American one to become involved directly in the political situation in Vietnam. Therefore, its view, its attitude and its decisions vis-a-vis Vietnam continued to be the guidelines to successive American administrations.

In terms of the U.S. policy of containment in Southeast Asia, under Eisenhower, were the Vietnamese ends or were they simply means to the U.S. objectives? There was some evidence that South Vietnam was simply a means to the U.S. own objectives. The Ngo Dinh Diem Administration had only brought to South Vietnam few successful years after 1954 and adopted a self-defeating policy after 1957. However, the lobbying for Diem made the Diem miracle thesis accepted by the American people during the first five years of his regime. These lobbyists propagandized to the world the American concept of a friendly anti-communist regime in Southeast Asia: that regime might be unpopular, remote to local population, but if that regime showed its strong anti-communism it would receive full American support.

In maintaining its hard-line anti-communism, did the Eisenhower Administration realize that should the proposition of normalization of North Vietnam fail, Hanoi would likely seek reunification by any means, including armed aggression? In this light, did that administration consider the big and safe rear area (Red China and Russia) and the safe infiltration route through Laos and Cabodia of the North Vietnamese?

To provide adequate assistance to South Vietnam, the Eisenhower Administration needed the approval of the American people. How much did that administration explain to the American people the precise national interest in Vietnam?

These questions have never received clear and adequate answers.

The Kennedy Administration

In early 1961, when he took office, President Kennedy had most of the same options Eisenhower had in 1953. He could choose to continue economic and military aid with the same emphasis on a political solution. He could increase aid.

42

He could cut aid. He could phase aid out. He chose to believe that everything could be resolved if the proper American was sent to fix it.

Successive Democratic Administrations have assumed since 1961 that the revival of the war in South Vietnam was undertaken solely at Hanoi's initiative. According to Secretary of State, Dean Rusk, the war in the south "could end literally in 24 hours" if Hanoi so decided. There was in fact some evidence to reinforce the Democratic assumptions. On January 29, 1961, forty days after the birth of the National Liberation Front, Hanoi Radio recognized the National Liberation Front, praised it and almost immediately thereafter North Vietnam stepped up the infiltration of men and weapons in the south. Assassinations, terrorist acts and attacks on South Vietnamese armed forces rose sharply in number and in ferocity.

In his news conference of May 5, 1961, President Kennedy told newsmen that the use of American forces in Vietnam was under consideration. It meant clearly that Kennedy saw the answer to Viet Cong insurgency in counter-insurgency. He understood well that guerilla warfare was essentially political warfare. The Viet Cong could never be defeated unless the Saigon regime could enlist the support of Vietnamese peasants. Magsaysay's campaign to destroy the Huks insurgents in Philippines might be served as model: tough military action against the enemy, generous provisions for amnesty, real and sweeping social reforms.

So, the first efforts of the Kennedy years was to persuade Ngo Dinh Diem to move along the Magsaysay's model. In the meantime, President Kennedy reverted to old fashioned gunboat diplomacy: he sent an aircraft carrier to demonstrate off Haiphong (biggest seaport of North Vietnam). U.S. troops were sent into Thailand and then were withdrawn to show the U.S. strength and readiness. From the vantage point of 1975, these maneuvers may appear as merely thrust and feint of shadow boxing but they were military actions. They made more fateful military actions which were to follow easier.

And in 1961, too, President Kennedy used the parade tactics. Many political, diplomatic and military figures were sent to Saigon. On May 11, 1961, Vice-president Lyndon Johnson was dispatched to Southeast Asia. After a two day session in Saigon, a session which was described as very warm and cordial, Johnson compared Ngo Dinh Diem to George Washington, Andrew Jackson, Woodrow Wilson, Franklin Roosevelt and Winston Churchill.

On May 13, 1961, in a joint statement in Saigon, Ngo Dinh Diem and Johnson said "The United States recognizes that the President of Vietnam, Ngo Dinh Diem, who was recently reelected to office by an overwhelming majority of his countrymen despite bitter communist opposition, is in the vanguard of those leaders who stand for freedom on the periphery of the communist empire in Asia."

On returning from Southeast Asia, Vice-president Lyndon B. Johnson wrote a memorandum to President Kennedy dated May 23, 1961 in which he suggested that "The fundamental decision required of the United States and time is of the greatest importance is whether we are to attempt to meet the challenge of communist expansion now in Southeast Asia by a major effort in support of the forces of freedom in the area or throw in the towel."

After the Lyndon B. Johnson trip, the U.S. needed a basis to form a new program of American aid. Professor Eugene Staley visited Saigon close upon LBJ's heels to direct an all embracing study.

Professor Staley proposed a new prescription for South Vietnam: large increases in the South Vietnamese Armed Forces, civil Guard and village militia, together with large increases of arms and radio communications, creation of the Strategic Hamlet (scattered villagers would be brought together in compounds better to protect them from marauding Viet Cong). It was based on the successful British tactics in Malaya. President Kennedy approved Staley's program and on September 17, 1961, Mr. Robert Thompson, former permanent Defense Secretary in Malaya, was brought to Vietnam to put the Staley Program in action. Along with that move there was the Taylor-Rostow Mission in Saigon for a fact finding tour.

Staley's Program was a good one, except that it brought to the U.S. and to South Vietnam a self-delusion. The program was based on the British situation in Malaya a decade earlier, without paying attention to some basic differences between the situation of the two countries. First, with the close and sincere cooperation of the Thailand Government, the British were able to seal the border and therefore deny the communists in Malaya any overland supply routes. Second, it was easy to identify the Malaysian communists because they were merely Chinese aliens, squatters. Finally, Malaysian people were willing to cooperate because of the hostility with which they regarded these Chinese aliens. At the peak of the insurgency in Malaya, hard core communists numbered only about 8000 and the total Chinese population was something over 400000. During the French Indochinese War, the French had tried that formula but it failed.

In Vietnam, it was practically impossible to seal off the Laotian and the Cambodian borders. The communists closely controlled these borders because they were vitally important to the supply of the communists in the southern part of Indochina. These borders were, therefore, the best route of infiltration. It was impossible to distinguish a Viet Cong, a North Vietnamese cadre from a South Vietnamese villager: they were all indigenous. In Vietnam, peeasants used to live on the same land for generations and they vehemently rejected any move from their villages into what could often be described as concentration camps.

The Taylor-Rostow mission in Saigon on October 11, 1961 was to find out "whether Vietnamese Nationalism had turned irrevocably against communism." At that time, General Maxwell Taylor was President Kennedy's military adviser and economist Walt W. Rostow was President's deputy assistant for National Security Affairs.

It was reported that the Taylor report contained not simply recommendations to beef up and improve military operations but it made a strong case for sweeping political reforms in the Diem Administration. Unfortunately, Taylor's report was peevishly denounced by the government-controlled Saigon press for what it termed an attempt to infringe on South Vietnamese sovereignty. Diem refused to be swayed by broad diplomatic hints that the U.S. might recall the U.S. ambassador if reforms were not effected. The result was a joint American Vietnamese eleven point declaration of Janary 1962, which was clearly a compromise in favor of Ngo Dinh Diem. Political reforms were watered down but military and economic support were increased.

It was a deep mystery among observers throughout Southeast Asia when the senior American diplomatic and military officials in Saigon decided that Diem was "the key to stability" and that the only policy was to win Diem's confidence by assuring him of Washington's unconditional support. In the view of Ambassador Frederic Nolting and General Harkins, attempts to being pressure on Diem would be self defeating. American newspapermen in Saigon called the support to Diem the policy of "Sink or swim with Ngo Dinh Diem."

How great was the influence of the reports sent to Washington by the U.S. Embassy in Saigon? After the Taylor-Rostow mission, the Vietnam problem passed from the Department of State to the Department of Defense. And although there was the Kennedy early insight into the political character of the Vietnam War, the projected American solution in 1961 and 1963 was increasingly framed in military terms. How was this permitted to happen? One reason was that Vietnam was still a low level crisis (less urgent than Cuba or Berlin) in these years. Another reason was that the senior American officials in Saigon assured the President that the Diem regime was increasingly deteriorated, but Ambassador Nolting and General Harkins listened uncritically to Ngo Dinh Nhu's claims (Nhu was Diem's brother) and passed them back to Washington as facts where they were read with elation.

After many hasty visits in Saigon, Washington officials confirmed the picture. Having other matters on his mind, President Kennedy accepted the optimistic report from men in whom he had great confidence. This optimism continued well into 1963. In March, the Secretary of State said that the war in Vietnam "was turning an important corner . . . Government forces clearly have the initiative in most areas of the country." A month later, he concluded that the South Vietnamese "are on their way to success." Ambassador Nolting: "South Vietnam is on its way to victory over communist guerillas." General Harkins: "The war would be won within a year."

It is necessary to note that by the end of 1961, it became apparent the Kennedy Administration had decided on military intervention. The decision to commit 15,000 U.S. servicemen in Vietnam was a critical step towards international tragedy and a domestic crisis of politics and morality.

Searching for a motive in President Kennedy's decision to opt for a military solution in Vietnam, the two principal historians of the Kennedy Administration (Theodore Sorensen and Arthur Schlesinger) plead that past American policy gave Mr. Kennedy virtually no alternative. Schlesinger stated that President Kennedy "had no choice now but to work within the situation he had inherited" and Dulles' "policy in South Vietnam had left us in 1961 no alternative but to continue the effort of 1954." Sorensen agreed. But if one accepts this thesis at face value, one will have to accept its consequence: the thesis pictured President Kennedy as a mere robot with no responsibility for whatever actions he took in Vietnam.

Meanwhile, there were two separate accounts of Kennedy's decision. The first account was that of James Reston (New York Times Editor): "A few minutes after this meeting (with Khrushchev in Vienna in June 1961), President Kennedy told me that apparently Khrushchev had decided that 'anybody stupid enough to get involved in that situation (Bay of Pigs) was immature, and anybody who didn't see it thru was timid and therefore, could be bullied.' " Mr. Reston said President Kennedy then put 12,000 American soldiers in Vietnam as an offset to Khrushchev's estimate of him, although he was amply warned that he was creating an unlimited commitment and was violating all his pronouncements about not allowing the U.S. to get into an Asian land war. (Washington Daily News, June 2, 1966.)

The second account was found in the book *Facing the Brink* by Edward Weintal and Charles Bartlett. They wrote, "Had he not suffered reverses in the

45

Bay of Pigs and Laos, it may well be that President Kennedy would have thought twice before expanding the Vietnam commitment early in 1962 from 700 to 11,000 advisers. Had he followed a long range policy plan rather than an understandable concern for his image as a result of the Bay of Pigs fiasco, he might have reduced rather than increased the Vietnam commitment."

There was another view of the situation in South Vietnam, the view of American newspapers and magazines. American newsmen saw Diem as an oriental despot, "hypnotized by his own edless monologues and contemptuous of democracy and the west." Their visits to dismal stockades were peasants had been hearded, sometimes at bayonet point, to engage in forced labor confirmed their worst misgivings. They stopped believing Diem's communiques and, when General Harkins and Ambassador Nolting defended Diem, they stopped believing Harkins and Nolting.

International historians may someday discover the motivation of American high senior officials in sending to Washington cheerful reports even when the Communists multiplied their victories in the south. On January 2, 1963, a force of 200 communists attacked and defeated a force of 2000 South Vietnamese regulars in the Mekong Delta. Five helicopters were shot down. Three Americans were killed. Yet, on March 8, 1963, Secretary Rusk said that the struggle against the Viet Cong was "turning an important corner" and concluded that "Diem's forces clearly have the initiative in most areas of the country." Never, the U.S. senior officials in Saigon wanted to tell the truth about the demoralization of South Vietnamese armed forces under the authoritarian rule of Ngo Dinh Diem. Commanders in South Vietnamese armed forces were more political appointees than military qualified commanders. In the defeat of January 2, 1963, (as in other defeats) South Vietnamese units were badly guided. The Commander of the 7th Infantry Division had never participated in any important battle. The commanding officer of the armored unit in the battle of January 2, 1963 was so confused by the Communist tactics that he virtually did not know how to use his armored vehicles. And the whole operation against 200 communists completely lacked cooperation between units of different branches (Battle of Ap Bac, province of My Tho in the Delta).

On May 8, 1963, in the ancient city of Hue (Centre Vietnam), government troops fired into a great many Vietnamese who were protesting Diem's strictures against flying the Buddhist flag during a festival to celebrate Buddha's birthday—equivalent to Christmas of Christians. Then, demonstrations spread to Saigon. On June 11, a monk committed suicide by setting fire to himself, to be followed a few weeks after by six other self immolations. On August 21, 1963, Buddhist pagodas in Saigon, Hue and other cities were attacked by Diem's special forces. Many buddhists were arrested. Diem's Minister of Foreign Affairs Vu Van Mau resigned in protest. Even Madame Nhu's father (Ambassador of Saigon in Washington) also resigned along with most of his staff. Thousands of students joined the Buddhist demonstrations. About 4,000 were arrested. Discontent in key segments of South Vietnam's rickety power structure was transformed into rebellion.

But on July 11, 1963, Ambassador Nolting returned to Saigon from Washington with assurances of continued U.S. support to Ngo Dinh Diem's government.

Meanwhile, in response to news reports, American officials even gave the astonishing impression that there would be no trouble in Vietnam if only the journalists would follow the line. David Halberstam of the New York Times, wrote: "The U.S. Embassy turned into the adjunct of a dictatorship. In trying to protect Diem from criticism, the Ambassador became Diem's agent!"

By the end of summer 1963, the Kennedy Administration could no longer maintain the confidence. On September 2, 1963, in a CBS interview, Kennedy admitted that Diem's regime had "gotten out of touch with the people" and that he believed it could regain support only if there were "changes in policy and perhaps with personnel."

On September 21, 1963, Secretary McNamara and General Taylor once again flew to Saigon. While they were there, elections were held for the National Assembly. All candidates were approved in advance by Ngo Dinh Diem. Obviously, there was no change in policy or personnel.

The Diem Administration did not want to recognize the Buddhist trouble beginning on Buddha's 2587th birthday was as much social as religious. It was an uprising of the new generation of Vietnamese Nationalists, drawn largely from the middle class and the lower class in revolt against traditional Vietnamese society. This uprising was wholly unforeseen by American diplomats.

Finally, the South Vietnamese Army brought off its coup. It killed Diem and Nhu, and the war in Vietnam entered a new phase on November 1, 1963. Political chaos was immediate in South Vietnam. However, on November 15, a U.S. military spokesman promised 1,000 U.S. military men would be withdrawn from Vietnam beginning on December 3, 1963.

On November 22, 1963, President Kennedy was assassinated and his vice-president, Lyndon Johnson took office.

U.S. involvement dating from the Kennedy era used only limited means to achieve excessive ends. Although he resisted pressures for putting U.S. combat units into South Vietnam, Kennedy's tactics deepened the American involvement in Vietnam piecemeal, with each step minimizing public recognition that the American role was growing.

During his term of office, President Kennedy faced three main questions in Vietnam: whether to make an irrevocable commitment to prevent a communist victory; whether to commit U.S. combat units to achieve the ends of the United States; whether to give top priority to the military aspect to the battle against Viet Cong or to the political reforms for winning popular support for the Saigon government. While President Kennedy and his senior advisors were described as considering defeat unthinkable, Kennedy had to conduct the U.S. policy on Vietnam in the context of a global power competion with the Soviet Union. He was confronted by other crises: Berlin, Cuba, Laos while he had to make his harshest decisions on Vietnam with restraint.

The Kennedy strategy on Vietnam was flawed from the outset for political as much as for military reasons. It depended on successfully prodding President Diem to undertake political, economic and social reforms to win the hearts and minds of the people. If Diem could not reform, the U.S. plan to end the war was foredoomed from its inception, for it depended on Vietnamese initiative to solve a Vietnamese problem.

And, in the end, the Kennedy Administration concluded that President Diem could not reform sufficiently. Then in 1963, that administration abandoned Diem. One has to remember that as early as September 1960, the U.S. Ambassador in Saigon, Elbridge Durbrow, had suggested abandoning Diem. That proposition was repeated shortly before Kennedy took office in December

1960. One of Durbrow's themes on September 24, 1960 suggested that if President Diem was unable to regain support through political and social reforms, "it may become necessary for U.S. Government to begin consideration alternative courses of action and leaders."

However, there was no serious demand for pressing Diem to make the kind of reforms that secretary Dean Rusk felt necessary. Was it because of an unfounded optimism in the spring and summer of 1962? The development of the strategic hamlet program at first was the special object of praise and of American offical confidence. By September 30, 1962, Diem's government stated that more than one third of the total rural population was living in completed hamlets.

To assess popular allegiance was difficult work in South Vietnam. Therefore, American officials in Saigon turned more and more to physical aspects for statistical evaluation of progress. The result was that Vietnamese reports were exaggerated and that situation was only uncovered after Diem had been overthrown in 1963. Later, a Pentagon study said that "principal responsibility for the unfounded optimism of U.S. policy in 1962 and early 1963 was on inadequate and relatively uninformed American intelligence and reporting systems."

The American involvement grew to 16,732 men in October 1963 while the phase-out continued, but the analyst of the Pentagon commented that this planning took on an "absurd quality" based on "the most Micawberesque predictions" of progress. And during the final five months of the Kennedy Administration, the situation in South Vietnam had so deteriorated that the entire phase-out had to be dropped in early 1964.

The decision to build up the combat support and advisory missions was made almost by default because the Kennedy Administration paid so much attention to the question of sending combat troops to Vietnam in the fall of 1961.

It was difficult for anyone to find a conclusive answer to the most controversial question about Kennedy's Vietnam policy: if Kennedy had lived until 1965, would he have been compelled to undertake full scale land war in South Vietnam and air war in the North?

The legacy left by President Kennedy was a legacy of crisis, of political instability and of military deterioration. It was a deterioration at least as difficult to the American policy makers as the situation Kennedy had inherited from Eisenhower.

Because President Kennedy had his senior advisers described as considering defeat unthinkable, the Kennedy Administration bluntly rejected two opportunities to seek a political solution to the Vietnam War.

The first opportunity was the request of Peking on February 24, 1962. Red China requested that the co-chairmen of the 1954 Geneva Conference, and other countries concerned to consult regarding Vietnam. On March 1, 1962, Secretary Dean Rusk commented on the Chinese request and said, "The United States is always prepared to talk about situations which represent a threat to the peace, but what must be talked about is the root of the trouble. In this case, it is the communist aggression against Vietnam in disregard of the Geneva Accords." Of course, no talks were held.

The second opportunity was the offer of French President Charles De Gaulle on August 29, 1963. The French Chief of State proposed to help work for an independent but neutral South Vietnam. The proposition was rejected by the Kennedy Administration.

The Johnson Administration

When Lyndon B. Johnson took office on November 22, 1963, once again, a new American President had an opportunity to reassess the American position in Vietnam. He could deal with a new government in Saigon. At that time there were still fewer than 20,000 U.S. troops committed in Vietnam. The opportunity existed to make the American involvement worthwhile by insisting on a sound civilian government in Saigon capable of leading and attracting the people.

And there were also opportunities for a political settlement. President Johnson still had before him the De Gaulle offer on August 29, 1963 to help work for an independent but neutral South Vietnam. And in December 1963, Cambodian Prince Norodom Sihanouk invited South Vietnam to join his country in a neutral confederation. But the new American Administration simply ignored these propositions.

On November 4, 1963, the U.S. Ambassador in Saigon, Henry Cabot Lodge, cabled Washington to predict that the change of regime in South Vietnam (after the death of Ngo Dinh Diem and of his brother Ngo Dinh Nhu) would shorten the war against the communists because of "the improved morale" in the South Vietnamese Armed Forces. But immediately after the fall of Ngo Dinh Diem, Viet Cong activity jumped dramatically and only at that time did the observers realize the tragic failure of the strategic hamlet program.

Three months later, General Nguyen Khanh, ex-commander of the 1st Infantry Division in Hue (Centre Vietnam) seized power for himself. In doing that, he stated a round of intramural power struggle that plagued the United States for the next two years, drawing the U.S. deeper and deeper into the Vietnam War.

President Johnson had made his choice: he allowed the military junta to continue its total dominance of the civilian government. Meanwhile, the Johnson Administration shipped in more money, more guns and more American troops. In the 18 months that followed, ten governments passed in rapid succession, but each more disorganized than the last. For each of these ten governments, the Johnson Administration expressed high hope.

At first, some observers thought that there might be a mystery about such hope placed in each of these ten governments. But later, a memorandum from Mr. McNamara clarified this mystery. In the cablegram to Saigon on January 11, 1965, Secretary Dean Rusk instructed Ambassador Taylor "to avoid actions that would further commit the United States to any particular form of political solution" to the turmoil there. If another military regime emerged from the squabbling, "we might well have to swallow our pride and work with it." Another memorandum to Mr. McNamara from Mr. McNaughton on January 27, along with Mr. McNamara's penciled comments on it, added perspective to that viewpoint. Mr. McNaughton stated and Mr. McNamara agreed that the United States objective in South Vietnam was "not to help friend" but "to contain China."

As a result of the U.S. objective mentioned above, General Khanh, who replaced General Minh in January 1964, was described my McNamara as an "able and energetic leader" who demonstrated his grasp of the basic elements— political, economic and psychological as well as military required to defeat Viet Cong, etc. Khanh "bounced" in and out of the premiership for a year after Mr. McNamara's speech. Finally, on February 25, Khanh went into permanent exile as an Ambassador-at-Large.

From all accounts, President Johnson was concerned with maintaining the appearance of continuity in both domestic and foreign policy. He really made his choice in December 1963 in his New Year's message to General Minh of South Vietnam, "The United States will continue to furnish you and your people with the fullest measure of support in this bitter fight. We shall maintain in Vietnam American personnel and material as needed to assist you in achieving victory . . . The U.S. Government shares the view of your government that netralization of South Vietnam is unacceptable . . . Peace will return to your country just as soon as the authorities in Hanoi cease and desist from their terrorist aggression . . ."

After a While House strategy meeting on February 20, 1964, President Johnson ordered that "Contingency planning for pressures against North Vietnam should be speeded up." The order continued, "Particular attention should be given to shaping such pressures so as to produce the maximum credible deterrent effect on Hanoi." The impelling force behind that order was the recognition of the steady deterioration in the positions of the pro-American governments in Laos and in South Vietnam, and the corresponding weakening influence of the United States on both countries. Accordingly, attention focused more and more on North Vietnam as the root of the problem.

The concept of the dominant intellectual of the Administration, Mr. Walt W. Rostow, was that a revolution could be dried up by cutting off external sources of support and supply. Mr. Rostow tought that a credible threat to bomb the industry of Hanoi would be enough to frighten North Vietnam's leaders into ordering the Viet Cong to halt their activities in the south because "Ho Chi Minh has an industrial complex to protect; he is no longer a guerilla fighter with nothing to lose."

These theories provided the theoretical framework for the Johnson Administration strategy on Vietnam. Mr. McNamara had advocated trying a number of measures to improve the Saigon government performance first, before resorting to overt escalation. He believed that the government of General Khanh was incapable to compete politically with the communists. Therefore, any attempt to negotiate between the Vietnamese themselves would result in a communist take-over and the destruction of the American position in South Vietnam.

Ambassador Cabot Lodge proposed an "essentially diplomatic carrot and stick approach" backed by covert military means. It involved sending a secret non-American envoy to Hanoi with an offer of economic aid, in return for calling off the Viet Cong. If North Vietnam did not respond favorably, the stick would be applied until they did.

One remembers that when Vice President Johnson took office after the assassination of President Kennedy, Vietnam was still not a top problem to the United States. In his first State of the Union message, President Johnson hardly mentioned Vietnam. Later, things became so desperate in early 1965 that he felt he had no alternative but to begin to supply American boys to do the job that he had thought of months before "Asian boys should do."

Yet, President Johnson had made his ultimate objective clear: he was only seeking a negotiated settlement. His judgement was that the way to achieve a political solution is by intensifying military pressure until Hanoi agreed to negotiate. By continually increasing pressures, the "quotient of pain" could force Hanoi at each new stage of widening the war to reconsider whether the war is worth the price.

In other words, widening the war will shorten it. How did this war become

50

Americanized? President Kennedy once remarked that the war in Vietnam could be won so long as it was "their war." If it were ever converted into a white man's war, the U.S. would lose as the French had lost a decade earlier. As the record has shown, a qualitative shift in the American commitment in 1961 from arms, money, advisors to armed combat troops set the stage for increased U.S. involvement.

In retrospect, Vietnam was a pattern of the politics of inadvertence. The U.S. became entangled not after due and deliberate consideration, but through a series of small decisions. Each step led only to the next until the U.S. found itself entrapped in a land war, a war which no President desired.

On February 7, 1965, eight Americans were killed and sixty-two wounded in an attack by the Viet Cong. President Johnson promptly ordered the U.S. Air Force to retaliate on targets in North Vietnam. Soviet Premier Kosygin was in Hanoi at the time of the first bombing attack. There were many speculations about the trip of Soviet Premier. One of these was that because Red China had not given Hanoi enough material support as promised, Kosygin was in Hanoi to promise more arms and supplies. On February 9, Kosygin made his first public announcement of stepped-up Soviet support for the Hanoi regime.

During that period, the military situation in South Vietnam was deteriorating badly. Succeeding military governments did little to remedy this situation. They were incapable of providing the type of political leadership that would attract the loyalty of the peasants and make the struggle against the Viet Cong seem worth the risk. At the top, leaders in Saigon were preoccupied with keeping their grasp on power. At just about every level below the top was a government of local thieves, run by entrenched military sycophants or petty underpaid civil service officials. District or province chiefs bought their jobs and imposed their "own form of taxes." The peasants were caught between the Viet Cong and these corrupt sychophants.

It was not a surprise to any observer when Vietnamese units were defeated frequently, district capitals were falling weekly, village strong-points overrun nightly. On March 26, 1964, Secretary McNamara admitted, ". . . Indeed, there can be no such thing as a purely military solution to the war in South Vietnam."

Within this framework, President Johnson stepped up the bombing of North Vietnam, no longer as retaliatory raids but as an effort to break the supply route to the south which North Vietnam was using to supply the Viet Cong. The escalation continued.

Meanwhile, after two visits of Mr. Seaborn, Canadian emissary to Hanoi, the U.S. received the report that during the second meeting as in the first meeting with Mr. Seaborn in June and in August, "Pham Van Dong (North Vietnam Premier) showed himself utterly unintimidated and calmly resolved to pursue the course upon which North Vietnam was embarked to what he confidently expected would be its successful conclusion."

In the summer of 1966, a secret seminar of 67 U.S. leading scientists representing the cream of the scholarly community in U.S. technical fields under U.S. government sponsorship was studying the overall results of the bombing in North Vietnam. The scientists pointed out that they felt North Vietnam could not be hurt by bombing: it was primarily a subsistence agricultural country with little industry and a primitive but flexible transport system, and most of its weapons and supplies came from abroad. So, as an alternative to bombing North Vietnam, the scientists suggested that an elaborate electronic barrier, using

51

recently developed devices be built across the demilitarized zone.

The conclusion of these scientists had a dramatic impact on Mr. McNamara and further, contributed to his disenchantment. In October 1966, he sought to persuade President Johnson to cut back the bombing of North Vietnam to seek a political settlement. In May 1967, Mr. McNamara went a step further: he advocated that the Johnson Administration stop trying to guarantee a non-communist South Vietnam and be willing to accept a coalition government in Saigon that included elements of the Viet Cong.

McNamara showed his report to President Johnson on May 19, 1967. President Johnson did not endorse the McNamara recommendations as he had in the past. On the contrary, in a series of decisions on the air war in July and August, President Johnson adopted a course that differed markedly from the strategy of deescalation, that McNamara had urged. (The Pentagon papers identified this as a secret effort to test Hanoi on what became known as the San Antonio formula.)

That formula was made public by President Johnson in a speech at San Antonio, Texas on September 29, 1967. He offered to halt the bombing, provided that action would lead to prompt and productive negotiations, providing that North Vietnam would not take advantage of the halt militarily.

Secret diplomatic probing went on fruitlessly for months while the air war widened slowly. Only in March 1968, a few days after McNamara left the government, did his proposal reemerge and open the way toward negotiations in May 1968 in Paris.

Finally, amid the shock and turmoil of the Vietnamese Lunar New Year of February 1968 caused by the great offensive of the communists, there was the pressure by the joint chiefs of staff and General Westmoreland, Commander of U.S. forces in Vietnam, to force President Johnson a long way toward "national mobilization in an effort to win victory in Vietnam." This pressure came to President Johnson at a time of great domestic dissent, dissatisfaction and disillusionment about both the purposes and the conduct of the war.

On January 27, 1968, four days before the great offensive of the communists, there was a very optimistic year-end assessment by General Westmoreland. And on February 12, 1968, with the communist great offensive at its height, there was a far different assessment by the same man.

The communist great offensive of spring 1968 finally led him to accept the view of the civilian advisors and of the intelligence community.

On April 3, 1968, President Johnson announced that North Vietnam had declared readiness for its representatives to meet those of the United States.

The Nixon Administration

In March 1968, President Johnson announced he would not run for reelection. Another presidential candidate for the Democratic Party would compete with Richard Nixon. It was easier for Nixon to campaign than for his opponent regarding the Vietnam War for the very simple reason that it was under a Democratic Administration that the U.S. was entrapped in the nightmare of the Vietnam War. Once elected, Mr. Richard Nixon would have time to reassess the situation and the American position in Vietnam. He would also find the opportunity to help South Vietnam obtain an effective anti-communist government in Saigon.

It was time for the U.S. to create a new situation and to take advantage of new opportunities.

Unfortunately, this hopeful feeling of the South Vietnamese soon became hopeless in 1968 when they realized that the new American administration seemed willing to maintain the military regime in South Vietnam.

Thus, after November 1968, what the American people once believed to be a crusade against communism degenerated into a war to preserve a dictatorship in power.

Almost daily, one heard from Nixon's administration sources that the president was "winding down the war." People were told that Nixon inherited this war from President Johnson. In a certain respect, it was true. But it was no less true that in his campaign of 1968, Richard Nixon repeatedly said that he supported the Johnson war policies. And it was true, too, that in 1954, at the time the French were pulling out of Indochina, Richard Nixon was the first important official (vice-president) to advocate sending American combat units to a land war in Asia.

During the campaign of 1968, one of the principal themes of candidate Nixon was that he had a "secret plan to end the war." American people and world opinion believed him serious, partly perhaps because Eisenhower had made a similar promise in 1952 in his campaign.

The secret plan of President Nixon was the Vietnamization of the war in Vietnam. This plan revealed a special psychohistorical character of Richard Nixon: he was ambivalent, especially on the issues of peace and war and paradoxical in his foreign policy.

Of course one has to believe that President Richard Milhous Nixon really wanted the "winding down" of the war in Vietnam, but on his own terms. The essential element in the Vietnamization was the preservation of a center of American influence and strength in South Vietnam. Whatever his terms, Nixon would wind down the Vietnam war in one aspect and only one: the withdrawal of American soldiers. And money appropriated for foreign aid under Nixon's Administration was going to finance the Nixon doctrine wars in Southeast Asia . . . wars financed by American money but fought by local people. This has been found to be true in Vietnam, Laos and Cambodia.

In June 1969, Nixon met Nguyen Van Thieu on Midway Island. Nobody knew what secret agreements were signed between them at the close of that meeting. A communique announced that 25,000 American troops would be withdrawn in first scale-down of U.S. involvement.

After the death of Ho Chi Minh in September 1969, there was another withdrawal of 35,000 American troops. In November 1969, Nixon announced the Vietnamization program under which fighting would be turned over to South Vietnamese.

In January 1970, President Nixon declared end to the Vietnam war as a major goal of his administration. The world would have the opportunity to see Nixon end the war in Indochina.

On March 18, 1970, while he was traveling abroad for an official tour, Prince Norodom Sihanouk was ousted as Chief of State of Cambodia by Marshal Lon Nol. The Republic of Kmer was proclaimed but it was essentially like the military regime of South Vietnam from 1967 onward.

In April 1970, Nixon ordered an invasion of Cambodia by American and

53

Soluth Vietnamese troops. When he ordered the invasion, Mr. Nixon did not know the bitter hostility that has existed through hundreds of years between Cambodians and Vietnamese. He said the objectives of the invasion were to discover and destroy enemy headquarters inside Cambodian territory and to drive North Vietnamese forces out of their sanctuaries along the South Vietnamese border. As promised, Nixon ordered the withdrawl of U.S. troops out of Cambodia by the appointed date (June), but he imposed no limitation on activities of South Vietnamese troops in Cambodia, although the government of Cambodia has many times demanded that South Vietnamese troops leave. The reason for the plea of Cambodian Government was that some units of South Vietnamese troops were guilty of atrocities against the civilian population of Cambodia.

1971 was the election year of South Vietnam. South Vietnamese people voted a new house of representatives and a new president. The Vietnamese did not deceive themselves: in the North as in the South, consitutions and elections provided little more than empty facade. From the first election organized under President Ngo Dinh Diem, South Vietnamese people became accustomed to political apathy and passivity.

They could predict who would be elected.

The power conflict between Nguyen Van Thieu and Nguyen Cao Ky had reached the point of no return. A large part of the American aid was spent to prevent the candidacy of vice-president Nguyen Cao Ky. All government services received orders from Nguyen Van Thieu to create as many difficulties as possible to other presidential candidates. Thieu avoided appearances before the Saigonese together with vice president Ky. When they had to appear together, Thieu could not camouflage his aversion. This time, there would be no more advice from other generals or from politicians because Thieu's secret police has silenced all kinds of opposition.

To buy time and to prevent the annual offensive of the communists on Vietnamese Lunar New Year Day, in the beginning of February 1971, a major invasion of the southern part of Laos was ordered by Nixon. The official purpose of that big operation was to cut the vital Ho Chi Minh Trail once and for all (the main supply line of North Vietnam to the North Vietnamese troops in South Vietnam). The operation was carefully planned by American advisors and was supported by a massive American logistic and transportation effort. The invasion was called off before the end of March after South Vietnamese troops moved about 50 miles inside Laotian territory.

The invasion was nearly a disaster. South Vietnamese units were caught in bloody traps of the North Vietnamese. They fled after suffering heavy losses and after abandoning large amounts of weapons including tanks, artillery, ammunition and equipment. Washington did not want to reveal the main reason of that disaster: the poor leadership of South Vietnamese Army. The commander of the operation was a two star general. He was also the commander of the 1st Infantry Division. He was reinforced by the South Vietnamese Marine Division, whose commander was a three star general. President Thieu knew that rivalry, but since he trusted the two star more than he trusted the three star general, he gave full power to the two star. General Phu commanded the operation and General Khang commanded the South Vietnam Marine Division. Phu dared not give battle orders to Khang. And it was Phu's 1st Division which participated in the operation from the beginning to the end and which was in charge of all frontal attack efforts. The Marine Division was considered a reserve unit during the whole operation. Vietnamese and foreign reporters who told the truth about that operation were accused of "aiding the enemy by distortion of the truth."

The burden of the war became heavier and heavier to the South Vietnamese as Nixon announced successive withdrawals. Living conditions for South Vietnamese troops were harder and harder. Had it not been for the nationalist spirit in these troops along with American air support, South Vietnam might have collapsed right in mid-summer of 1971. But President Thieu did not mind that gloomy military situation. He gave top priority to the election of October 1971, "his election," according to the ironic language of South Vietnamese people.

To American politicians who sought an excuse for U.S. involvement in Vietnam, there was a time when it appeared worth an effort by the United States to assure the South Vietnamese an opportunity to chose a democratic government freely. In the election of October 1971, that excuse became ridiculous.

Taking no notice of any elementary law of a civilized society, Nguyen Van Thieu prevented other presidential candidates from running against him. The South Vietnamese Supreme Court became the most obedient institution to serve Nguyen Van Thieu's personal power. All Supreme Judges, except only one (Honorable Tran Minh Tiet) invented devices to stop the other candidates. To make his application, a candidate other than Nguyen Van Thieu would meet insurmountable obstacles even at the gate of the Supreme Court. Finally, there remained only the ticket of Nguyen Cao Ky/Truong Vinh Le to run against Nguyen Van Thieu. To make his application, Ky was riding a military jeep, heavily armed and escorted by a motorized platoon of his faithful soldiers. The Supreme Court accepted Ky's application only after the Supreme Judges saw Ky among his platoon of bodyguards. In the history of non-communist South Vietnam, this was the low point. But later, the same Supreme Court of Nguyen Van Thieu rejected the application of the Nguyen Cao Ky ticket on the ground that the application was not "legally suitable."

Before the election of October 3, 1971, a new house of representatives was elected in April 1971. Nearly three-fourths of the new house were Thieu's men. To be elected, each future representative had to sign a blank document in which Thieu would add necessary confession of guilt should the signatory betray Thieu. It was not a surprise to any observer that the new house did not make any protest against the one-man contest organized by Thieu.

On January 25, 1972, (the election year in the United States), President Nixon revealed that for many months, his Secretary of State Henry Kissinger had been carrying on secret negotiations with North Vietnam and that efforts had been going on in secret to try to get an agreement from North Vietnam. It was remarkable that Mr. Nixon revealed such secret negotiations only hours after his controversial budget message had been delivered. And withdrawal of U.S. combat units was scheduled by Nixon to be virtually completed by election day.

In March 1972, North Vietnam launched 15 full strength divisions, reinforced by many armored units, across the demilitarized zone in the biggest offensive since February, 1968. They captured the provincial capital of Quang Tri under strange military conditions: South Vietnamese still had more than enough weapons and ammunitions stored at Ai Tu base, three miles north of that provincial town, but their commander, the one star general Vu Van Giai, ordered them to withdraw south of Quang Tri. General Giai was put in jail immediately after the fall of the city. (He was still in jail when Saigon collapsed on April 30, 1975.) War raged in many other provinces of South Vietnam.

Richard Nixon's reply was the ordering of the bombing of Hanoi and Haiphong and the ordering of naval vessels to the coasts of Vietnam. In a television statement, he said that troop withdrawal would continue but at a slower rate. Ten days after the bombing of Hanoi and Haiphong, Nixon announced that the U.S. would resume Paris talks. The peace talks resumed for a few days, then broke off again.

In May, North Vietnamese troops captured the province of Quang Tri. Mr. Nixon ordered the mining of Haiphong and six other North Vietnames ports.

In June 1972, he announced that the U.S. ground combat role ended. Four months before election day, this announcement surely had a positive impact on the American voters.

In July, the peace talks resumed in Paris. Kissinger and Le Duc Tho (North Vietnam) resumed their secret talks. And in September 1972, South Vietnamese troops recaptured a large part of the Quang Tri Province. Finally in October Kissinger declared "peace is at hand." This was announced on the very eve of the election. In fact, it was not at hand until after Nixon had been safely reelected. In any case, the Kissinger announcement was worth millions of votes for the reelection of Richard Nixon.

After the reelection, in December 1972, the Paris peace talks intensified. Meanwhile, Mr. Nixon ordered a round-the-clock bombing above the 20th parallel of North Vietnam. The heaviest air raids of the entire air war in North Vietnam halted after 12 days.

The case fire agreement was signed in Paris on January 27, 1973.

The last American soldier left South Vietnam on March 29, 1973, officially ending the direct U.S. military role in South Vietnam. U.S. combat death toll was 46,079.

In April, heavy fighting flared. The situation proved to be so desperate that in July, Canada withdrew from International Control Commission and charged that the commission was ineffectual.

The Canadians were quite right: Nixon and Henry Kissinger might be satisfied with the Paris Cease-fire Agreement of January 27, 1973, because it helped them to carry out the total withdrawal of American soldiers from South Vietnam without humiliation. But the killing in Vietnam continued.

Any international agreement becomes useless if there is not an effective control body. The International Control Commission of the Geneva Agreement of July 1954 was paralyzed from its inception. The Agreement of 1954 could not help maintain peace in Vietnam. It was the same with the cease-fire agreement of 1973. The composition of the International Control Commission of 1973 yields an idea about the future of South Vietnam. The commission was represented by four countries: Poland; Hungary; Canada; and Indonesia. Poland and Hungary defended faithfully the interests of the communists. It is their ideological duty. Of course, they would do anything to prevent the agreement from being observed. Instead of administering the agreement, they simply became conspirators of the invaders. Canada is a liberal country, perhaps too liberal, regarding the ideological war in Vietnam. The Canadian liberal policy was exploited by the communist side. Indonesia had repeatedly proclaimed its non-engagement foreign policy. But Indonesia needs American aid. Therefore,

Indonesia would do anything which would please the United States and what was good for the American interests was not necessarily good for the interests of the Vietnamese. In brief, the ICC of the 1973 Agreement was no more than second-rate ornament. The next great offensive of North Vietnam would be carried out without any objection from that International Control Commission. The fate of South Vietnam was sealed.

While outlining the withdrawal of American troops, the Agreement of 1973 did not contain any provision for the withdrawal of North Vietnamese combat troops—although North Vietnam had indirectly confessed the presence of its troops in South Vietnam. This, coupled with the departure of the Americans, would be tantamount to the abolition of the demilitarized zone between the two Vietnams. One of the consequences of that abolition was that North Vietnamese troops would be able to move anywhere in South Vietnam at will.

The cease-fire agreement of 1973, stipulated replacement of weapons and equipment to South Vietnamese armed forces be carried out on the basis of one-by-one, while there would be virtually no control of any reinforcement or supply to the communists.

When the cease-fire agreement was signed on January 27, 1973, there were in South Vietnamese territory about 200,000 North Vietnamese troops, not including 60,000 armed Viet Cong. These troops occupied strategic positions along South Vietnam's borders. At some places, North Vietnamese units were only 30 miles distance from Saigon. With the high speed of North Vietnamese Russian-made tanks, North Vietnamese troops would reach Saigon within an hour.

Theoretically, South Vietnam still had 600,000 regular troops, not including nearly 400,000 regional forces. They were spread thinly throughout 44 provinces and four big cities in South Vietnam. Two strategic units, the paratroop division and the marine division had been assigned the mission of defending Quang Tri Province since 1970. But in fact, these two strategic reserve units were sent to Quang Tri because Nguyen Van Thieu was afraid that they may prepare a coup against him. It was hard to think that General Nguyen Van Thieu, Commander-in-Chief of South Vietnamese Armed Forces could give orders to his units to fight against the invaders without any strategic reserve unit. In 1973, as throughout former years of his regime, Thieu only thought of preserving his personal power without regard to the survival of his country.

Since the great offensive of the communists in 1972, it was clear that they were better equipped than South Vietnamese armed forces. South Vietnam was outgunned and its military leadership was poor. Every important function, civilian or military, could be bought.

Moreover, the Watergate affair had been carefully studied by the communists. They knew that from now on, Richard Nixon would no longer be able to enjoy his presidential war power. The conflict between the executive and the legislative in the U.S. was at its peak and there must be a losing side. Using the power of the purse, the U.S. Congress had tied Nixon's hands. South Vietnam would not have any chance for more aid from the U.S. And that Congress went further by forbidding the support of the U.S. Air Force to South Vietnamese forces. The next North Vietnamese great offensive (and, surely the last one) would be launched according to the decision of the U.S. Congress concerning aid and support to the Thieu regime.

Facing this situation, the people of South Vietnam knew in advance that the collapse of their country was imminent.

After the withdrawal of Canada from the International Control Commission, the United States tried to convince the communist side to accept Iran as replacement. Iran is a pro-American country but it was accepted by the communists because North Vietnam and the Viet Cong knew that Iran may follow the same policy as Indonesia. Each time the communists launched an attack at some government outposts or at some district capital, the Saigon government imitated the communist tactics by organizing an anti-communist demonstration in front of the International Control Commission Office. But the Saigon Government tactics converted a serious and solid-based claim into a ridiculous joke.

Fighting in South Vietnam continued with more and more victims every day. The Nixon Administration repeatedly requested more aid to South Vietnam and to Cambodia, but it was clear the opportunity for more aid was remote. There was evidence that in Cambodia and in South Vietnam, combat unit commanders had sold weapons, ammunition, artillery, tanks, gasoline and rice to the communists. Later, the communists used these weapons to kill the nationalists and to kill the civilians in Cambodia and in South Vietnam. But the American Embassies in Pnom Penh (Cambodia) and in Saigon (South Vietnam) continued to strongly support the corrupt governments in these two countries. In that political battle, the U.S. Congress won. The Communists won, too. The Thieu administration won in terms of tons of gold for Thieu and for his prime minister Tran Thien Khiem. Of course, there were the losers—the South Vietnamese people. And of course, Richard Nixon had won—re-elected by a landslide vote.

In July 1974, the heaviest fighting since the 1973 cease-fire agreement broke out around Da Nang, second largest port of South Vietnam. The Communists seized several outposts of the Saigon Government.

On August 8, 1975, President Nixon resigned. Thieu and his closest aides stayed awake that whole night in Saigon.

The Ford Administration

When Mr. Gerald Ford took office on August 8, 1975, there was some speculation in South Vietnam about his future policy on the Vietnam War. The South Vietnamese people realized quickly that Ford could do nothing more than yield to the will of the U.S. Congress. Gerald Ford became the fifth American President to call on his countrymen to save a floundering Southeast Asia land. But this time, the nation and especially the Congress balked. It seemed certain that Cambodia and South Vietnam would fall into communist hands. And they would be the first two friendly countries to fall since Fidel Castro took over Cuba sixteen years ago.

There was no talk of sending American troops to fight another war in Asia. Gerald Ford only asked for money. But, with 150 billion spent in Vietnam in the past and with economic problems stemming from the Arab oil embargo, most U.S. legislators were deaf to the administration's argument.

The first test to President Ford in South Vietnam in August 1974 was the anti-corruption movement headed by Catholic Father Tran Huu Thanh. Later the name of the movement was changed to the Popular Anti-Corruption Movement. Its origin was a secret meeting of 302 Catholic priests at the Church

58

of Tan Sa Chau, in the suburbs of Saigon. The main theme of this movement was that corruption has damaged South Vietnam so much that it was urgently necessary to crush corruption. In fact, the anti-corruption theme was not new in the political life of South Vietnam. But this time, it seemed that the movement had new impetus: it was headed and backed by Catholic priests. From 1954, South Vietnamese people had been used to Catholics permanently supporting any non-communist regime in Saigon. The military coup in November 1963 which killed President Ngo Dinh Diem was largely motivated by the militant Buddhists in South Vietnam. The fall of Diem meant a great defeat for Vietnamese Catholics. And these Catholics would never forget that defeat.

According to the view of many people in Saigon, the Popular Anti-Corruption Movement of Father Tran Huu Thanh was an opportunity for the Vietnamese Catholics to "clean their face" by claiming that the Catholics were leading a big anti-corruption movement (meaning revenge for the victory of the Buddhists in 1963). But when people looked more deeply into the slogans and the actions of the movement, it seemed nothing more than an amateurish revolution of a Vietnamese Catholic group. From the very beginning, Father Thanh did not promote a revolution. He did not want to see Thieu replaced. And to the South Vietnamese, such a movement would surely fail.

At first, the South Vietnamese hoped that Washington would give some blessing to the anti-corruption movement. But as time ran out, they realized that the caretaker administration of President Ford could not afford a coup after the shock of the resignation of President Nixon. Once again, the American administration needed political stability on the surface of South Vietnam. In other words, Thieu continued to rule South Vietnam.

From the moment the Ford administration failed to approve a big change in the political life of South Vietnam, the Anti-Corruption Movement of Father Thanh lost considerable support from the people of South Vietnam. There were rumors that the U.S. Embassy in Saigon did not give a green light to Father Thanh. Meanwhile, Thieu gave orders to his police forces to use any means to crush the anti-corruption movement. South Vietnamese people once again had the opportunity to see Thieu's mercenaries in action. Rarely, could one see such savage ferocity from Saigon police against a nationalist opposition.

Also, in August 1974, the Vietnamese press corps in Saigon decided once-in-for-all to fight openly against Thieu. Money, corruption, terrorism and many other weapons were used by Thieu's agents to squash the news rebellion. The most fervent nationalist newsmen were accused by Thieu's police as Viet Cong sympathizers, jailed without any charge. These newsmen and many other oppositionists were in jail until the collapse of Thieu's regime.

For the last time, South Vietnamese people were disappointed by the American administration: South Vietnam would never get a pro-peasant leadership to compete with the communist leadership.

From August 8, 1974, the date of Nixon's resignation, there was an important question: when did North Vietnam decide to take over South Vietnam by force? Much evidence showed that after the fall of Richard Nixon, North Vietnamese leaders decided to launch their final offensive in the south. North Vietnam knew that Nixon was quite unpredictable. Past experience showed Nixon was ready to order new bombing in North Vietnam, although American soldiers were going home.

In one respect, the U.S. withdrawal from Vietnam was a success for the

American people because they constitutionally forced an end to the Vietnam War. The American people forced Congress to cut off funds. It was the only way Congress could deflect the American foreign policy.

But in some other respects, the denial of funds by Congress had a very positive effect on the communist strategy: North Vietnam intepreted the attitude on Capitol Hill as a tacit blessing to North Vietnam to take over South Vietnam.

President Ford, faced with the possible collapse of all South Vietnam, was attempting to convince a stubborn Congress to help Saigon withstand further communist advances. But the struggle over the administration's request for military aid to South Vietnam went far beyond the fate of that distant Southeast Asian country. At stake were two historic issues: who controls U.S. foreign policy and what is America's proper role in the world? The Nixon Doctrine had already limited American influence in the post-Vietnam era. This doctrine promised that even if American troops were not available to fight local wars, Washington could always be counted to provide money and material to help friendly nations to help themselves. Now, Congress seemed bent on restricting the perimeter of U.S. influence even further. That tendency, in turn, raised an even more troubling moral question, as one Kissinger aid said: "The issue is what do we do to and for people who relied on us, who believed our commitments? These people fought, they believed and now, they may be let down."

The momentum and the violence in the North Vietnamese military efforts in the South changed according to the reaction of the Capitol Hill. From August to December 1974, there were light attacks at battalion unit level to sound the fighting capacity of South Vietnamese troops and to sound the American reaction. But in Da Nang, second largest part of South Vietnam, from August to December 1974, heavy fightings resulted in government loss of several military bases and district towns.

In January, before the Vietnamese Lunar New Year, Phuoc Binh fell. It was the first province capital to be captured by the Communists since Quang Tri fall in the 1972 offensive. While President Ford asked Congress to approve 300 million, in additional aid for South Vietnam, the fall of Phuoc Binh was the model of the fall of many other provinces, in March and in April 1975: no strategic reserve to reinforce the garrison, no supply (mostly of gasoline and ammunition) and the reluctance of South Vietnamese soldiers to sacrifice for a corrupt regime. The passivity of Congress and the absence of the American air support were important factors to accelerate the fall of many provinces. But the most important factor was panic among the civilians, including the families of South Vietnamese soldiers.

After the Lunar New Year, South Vietnamese adopted a wait and see attitude. Waiting for what? Too many years depending almost completely on Washington's decisions has made a great part of South Vietnamese people passive: they still hoped that the Ford Administration would succeed to convince the U.S. stubborn Congress to support the fight of South Vietnam. Those people believed that the U.S. dollars could reverse the situation in South Vietnam by some miracle.

On March 10, 1975, North Vietnamese troops opened an attack of big unit level (division) in Ban Me Thuot province, about 180 hundred miles northwest of Saigon. South Vietnamese troops were caught by surprise and the province fall quickly. A few days later, Nguyen Van Thieu became the first commander-in-chief to give an extraordinary order to his army: to abandon many strategic military bases without preparation and without having the minimum of time to prepare. But his most horrible order was to abandon the civilian population to the communists. This abandon, coupled with the retreat (soon a rout), created a panic which spread rapidly throughout South Vietnam. From March 10 to March 31, 14 provinces and cities fell. The panic of civilian population was so disastrous that the U.S. emergency refugee air and sealift broke down in confusion.

In the midst of the battle, a six member delegation of U.S. legislators flew to South Vietnam and Cambodia for a first-hand look. They were appalled at the carnage and ironically for the first time since 1954, a delegation of American legislators was able to be in direct contact with the local population without interference of the U.S. Embassy. Their lucidity came too late.

From March 15 to 25, 1975, Nguyen Van Thieu arrested many journalists and oppositionists. Most of them were liberated only after the resignation of Thieu and only one or two days before the collapse of Saigon.

On April 5, President Ford ordered all available Navy ships to stand by near South Vietnam to assist refugees, if necessary. On the same day, Nguyen Van Thieu gave another proof of his dementia: he asked Mr. Nguyen Ba Can, a man that nobody knew, to form a new government. Thieu said that "it would be a united fighting cabinet and there would be no surrender to the communists." This new act of Thieu's madness so disappointed the Saigonese that many predicted the end "is not too far."

While many provinces fell and in some cases, the fall happened without the presence of any communist combat unit, Operation Babylift was launched on President Ford's orders. Then, the communists shelled Saigon for the first time in 15 months. On April 8, 1975, a F-5 jet of South Vietnamese Air Force bombed Saigon's Presidential Palace. Thieu was safe. At least, seven people, including the top aide of former vice president Nguyen Cao Ky were arrested in Saigon for "plotting a military coup d'etat" against Mr. Thieu, government officials said.

On April 9, 1975, in Paris, informed sources said that the French Government had contacted all elements that might be able to contribute to a political settlement in South Vietnam as part of its new peace initiative. The sources said that talks had been held with South Vietnamese neutralists, but gave no indications of names or organizations. Unfortunately, the French new peace initiative was launched too late: North Vietnamese Communists were already near the suburbs of Saigon.

When the communists attacked Xuan Loc, an important strategic province northeast of Saigon, President Ford asked Congress for almost 1 billion in military and humanitarian aid for South Vietnam. From April 9 to April 19, many other provinces were abandoned.

On April 21, Thieu resigned, named vice-president Tran Van Huong as replacement. Government troops abandoned Xuan Loc after 12 days battle. The evacuation of Americans and Vietnamese from Saigon moved into high gear.

On April 22, the Communists launched artillery and ground attacks against Bien Hoa Air Base. On April 23, communist troops concentrated outside Saigon but held off their attacks. In Washington, President Ford declared the Indochina war is over "as far as America is concerned" and he said, "It's over. Let's put it behind us."

On April 25, President Huong told National Assembly that he would step down and turn over power to General Duong Van Minh (Big Minh, 59 years of age). On April 26, Thieu fled to Taiwan. On that day, the Nationalist Chinese

61

Government in Taiwan closed the airport of Taipeh to disembark 10 tons of properties including Thieu's 4½ tons of gold.

On April 27, General Minh was sworn in as President of South Vietnam. He offered to open peace talks with the communists on April 28. Four jets captured by communists bombed Tan Son Nhat Air Base.

On April 29, communist troops attacked Cho Lon and Tan Son Nhat Air Base. Two U.S. Marines were killed, first U.S. military deaths in Vietnam since December 1973. The U.S. began the evacuation of the last Americans, ending two decades of involvement in Vietnam.

On April 30, 1975, South Vietnam surrendered unconditionally to the Communists.

The American press commended on various administration's responsibilities for the collapse of South Vietnam on April 30, 1975.

In the Newsweek Magazine on April 14, 1975, David Halberstam (who won a Pulitzer Prize for his Vietnam reporting) wrote: "To justify the struggle in terms that might seem palatable to Americans, we employed vast numbers of skilled, sophisticated propagandists who proved again and again to their own satisfaction, and to that of their employers, how evil and sinful the other side was, but who could never understand why the other side kept winning. Public relations was a booming industry in Vietnam in the 1960s. It was as if by saying these things often enough to ourselves, perhaps they could come true, illusion would become reality . . . The Pentagon seems surprised this week by the collapse, surprised by the failure of Saigon's command and initiative. And no wonder. A generation of American officers built their own career endorsing ARVN fitness (ARVN for Army of the Republic of Vietnam) because there was no other way an American officer could be promoted . . . All of this is unfair to the ARVN, which deserves better of everyone. They bore their burden honorably and with no small amount of dignity. All the historical failures and political cowardice and mendacity of so many western leaders were placed on their backs. Their job was to live up to the lies of powerful westerners. How unfair it was, how injust to expect an army to be better and more modern and less corrupt than the society that produced it . . . The shame for all this is ours, not the ARVN's . . . The scenes this week from Vietnam were the legacy of peace with honor, which in truth brought neither peace, nor honor, but which was in essence Caucasian face saving, camouglaged defeat . . . The secretary of state remains. A man filled with contempt for Thieu and Saigon who demands that we believe in Thieu and Saigon . . . The truth is we give them not too little but too much. If anything we made them more dependent upon up and our technology than upon their own population. And more important, we gave them the wrong things, not what they wanted but what we wanted for them. . . ."

Other interesting remarks on the fall of South Vietnam came from some well-known journalists, those who had witnessed the tragedy in Vietnam throughout many years. Columnist Worsthorne wrote for the London Sunday Telegraph: "There is general concern at the appalling scale of human suffering involved. But what is surprising and worrisome is the lack of any accompanying sense of indignation or moral outrage aimed at those who are causing it, the power-hungry rulers of North Vietnam who restlessly bent on conquest and domination over the whole of Indochina."

On June 20, 1975, professor Anthony T. Bouscaren wrote: "The tens of thousands aboard the huge evacuation armada sailing away from Vietnam have told endless stories of heroism, loyalty and love in the last hours. But for millions of Vietnamese and not a few Americans, the dominant memory will be sorrow and betrayal and guilt.

"There was scarcely an American in the final weeks who was not forced to share personally in that intense feeling of guilt. It was only the Americans who could do almost anything: cash checks, cut through maddening bureaucratic impediments that had been erected both by Saigon and Washington, and, most of all, get a few Vietnamese to safety.

"Nonetheless, countless Vietnamese, knowing they would remain despite all, worked for their American friends to the last. Some who knew they could not leave, however much they wanted to, tried to send out last precious parts of themselves—photographs, the ashes of ancestors, keepsakes, and children.

"A few minutes before one of the last groups of distraught Americans rushed from their ravaged offices and hotel rooms to look for a bus to the airport, a Vietnamese friend arrived to say farewell. Some of the Americans were in tears, and the Vietnamese, seeking to comfort them, patted their shoulders and tried hard to reassure them: 'You may hear after you leave that some here have died, perhaps even at their own hand. You must not spend the rest of your lives with the guilt. It is just a part of Vietnam black fate, in which you, all of you, became ensnared for a time. Fate is changeless and guiltless.'

"South Vietnam was just getting on its feet by the end of 1974. The people were recovering from war and the rice crop was good. There was a prospect of a shot to the economy by the discovery of offshore oil. There was real hope for the future. But the Communist world did not want South Vietnam to live and the American Congress did not care. It was still debating an aid bill on April 29 when the 'Option 4' evacuation was ordered by President Ford. The events took a Congress which had refused to move for four months. Right after the debacle, 72 congressmen refused to vote for a resolution condemning Hanoi's invasion."

On the Wall Street Journal on May 2, 1975, Pulitzer Prize-winning correspondent Peter Kahn wrote an *Obituary for South Vietnam*. He noted that South Vietnam "did manage to resist" for 25 years and "not always with a great deal of American help." Few societies "that I can think of would have struggled so long."

Kahn's remarks on South Vietnamese Armed Forces: "It was an army that stood and fought with great courage and competence on a few occasions you remember, like the siege of An Loc. It stood and fought well at a score of places whose names we have forgotten. And it stood and fought well in a thousand little engagements and in a thousand little mud-walled outposts whose names no Americans ever knew . . . It was an army that for years watched the Americans try to combat Communists with every wonder of modern weaponry and which then, all too suddenly, was left to face the Communists with American-style tactics but without American-style resources . . . It was an army that for years was ordered to defend every inch of Vietnamese territory and which tried, with greater or lesser success, to do just that. . . . Several hundred thousand of these soldiers died. More than half a million were wounded. And, in the final weeks of the war, when every American in Saigon knew the war was lost, some of these soldiers continued to fight at places like Xuan Loc and thereby bought a bit of time for the Americans and their chosen Vietnamese to escape with their lives. It was a much better army than it appeared to be at the end."

And Kahn concluded in his article: "The stronger side is not necessarily the better side. Better becomes a question of values and much as I may respect Communist strength and stamina I cannot accept that the Spartan Communist society of North Vietnam is better than the very imperfect South Vietnamese society that I knew."

Finally, regarding the U.S. Congress, professor Bouscaren wrote: "We forced South Vietnam to sign the very imperfect agreement of January 1973, promising to help as in 1972 should the Communists again invade. The Communists did invade again, convinced that Congress would block effective defensive action. The Communists knew more about our Congress than the President of the United States."

PART II
Chapter One
THOSE WHO GOVERNED SOUTH VIETNAM

The First Republic: Diem's Administration

Although this book is not intended to be a history of Vietnam, some background on the growth of Vietnamese Nationalism is necessary in this chapter to understand the problems of the First Republic in Vietnam.

The roots of Vietnamese nationalism extend back to the period of Chinese domination. The struggle of the Vietnamese for independence has an equally long historical tradition. Armed opposition to foreign rule continued until 1916, led by high ranking mandarins and by members of the royal family. Beginning in the decade which preceded World War I, the objectives and the leadership of the Vietnamese resistance changed. Under the influence of French economic, cultural and educational penetration, there emerged a group of western-oriented intellectuals who were convinced of the need to modernize their country. They recognized the need to broaden the primarily political anti-foreign struggle to include economic and other goals.

During the 1920s, Vietnamese scholars and nationalists made attempts to achieve moderate reforms by means of cooperation with the colonial regime. When their programs were rejected, they returned to their armed struggle. Among the many underground nationalist societies which existed in the twenties, there were two remarkable organizations: the dominant nationalist organization bearing the name of Vietnamese Quoc Dan Dang (Vietnamese Nationalist Party), and the Vietnamese Communist Party. The former, referred to as the VNQDD, aimed at the revolutionary overthrow of French rule to establish a republican government along the lines of the Chinese Kuomintang.

The line of thinking of the Vietnamese Communist Party was the same as the International Communist movement.

To foment a general revolution, on the night of February 9, 1930, the

VNQDD led an uprising. The Vietnamese garrison at Yen Bay (a province in the highlands of North Vietnam) rose to revolt. The rebellion was easily crushed by the French because they were alerted by some betrayers. Thirteen leaders of the VNQDD were beheaded. The political activity of the VNQDD was reduced to token action for nearly fifteen years. They did not reappear until World War II, under the auspices of the Nationalist Chinese.

The disappearance of the VNQDD for nearly fifteen years from the political scene facilitated the rise of a new Vietnamese Communist Party. In 1930, the Comintern representative in Southeast Asia, Nguyen Ai Quoc (pseudonym of Nguyen Tat Thanh, better known to the world as Ho Chi Minh) arranged the fusion of three competing communist groups into a united Indochinese communist party (ICP). Soon after that fusion, the ICP sought to rival the VNQDD uprising by organizing mass peasant demonstrations. It was an attempt to dramatize the agrarian misery as a result of many crop failures. The demonstrations were followed by strikes in plantations and in factories. The strikes culminated in peasant revolts in the two provinces of Ha Tinh and Nghe An, where there was the creation of "soviets" (a communist organization). These soviets distributed communal land to peasants and took over local administration. The French quelled these revolts quickly and brutally. It was estimated that by 1932, 10,000 political prisoners languished in 81 prisons, not including labor reform camps. Many communist leaders were executed. With the arrest of Nguyen Ai Quoc in Hong Kong in 1931, the organization of the ICP was disrupted.

The eve of World War II found the leadership of the VNQDD and of the ICP forced to reorganize in exile in southern China. Later, the ICP tried to gain preeminence in the revolutionary movement in Vietnam. Meanwhile, another nationalist party of the Vietnamese in exile in Southern China also tried to emerge to rival the ICP revolution. It was the VN Cach Mang Dong Minh Hoi (The Vietnamese Allied Revolutionary Party) led by the old politician Nguyen Hai Than.

In Vietnam, a new situation developed in August 1945 when the Japanese surrendered after atomic bombs decimated Hiroshima and Nagasaki. The ICP accelerated its activities in Vietnam. All of its armed forces were unified into the Vietnamese Liberation Forces and the Vietnamese territory was divided into many "strongholds." ICP agents promoted violence among the population against the then pro-Japanese government of Tran Trong Kim (also a long time nationalist fighter in Vietnam and one who clung to obsolete ideas about popular revolution). The VNQDD and the VNCMDMH also increased their activities to exploit the new political situation in Vietnam.

On August 7, 1945, Ho Chi Minh formed the Committee for Liberation of the People of VN, comprising fourteen commissioners (eleven of whom were communist). Realizing that the mood of the people was favorable to a revolution, Ho Chi Minh gave orders for a "general uprising" on August 13, 1945 although his forces were not ready.

In Hanoi on the afternoon of August 17, 1945, the Vietnamese nationalists organized a demonstration of 20,000 people to protest the French attempt to land forces in Saigon. The organizers of this demonstration belonged to the committee of civil servants of Hanoi. Communist cadres infiltrated among the demonstrators and raised red flags. The VNQDD and the VNCMDMH recognized their mistake too late: throughout many years of struggling against the French, the

66

VNQDD and the VNCMDMH were always too honest and too naive to promote revolution. And exactly because of that honesty many Vietnamese historians consider them as amateurish and bourgeois revolutionaries. They thought that the demonstration had been organized by many pressure groups and they dared not raise their flags. They paid the price for their honesty: they were bypassed by the Vietnamese communists. They were so passive that nobody in their party thought of protesting. The people of Hanoi did not understand the delicate difference between these two opposite political parties. They only thought of applauding those who organized that demonstration. And because of the political passivity ingrained since French colonialism, they were ready to accept the idea that the communists were really the organizers of the patriotic demonstration when the communists whispered that idea.

That passivity opened the way to the communists and two days later, on August 19, 1945, they were able to organize without any difficulty a marching demonstration in the streets of Hanoi.

In the meantime, the High Command of the Japanese Armed Forces in North Vietnam gave plenty of arms and ammunition to the communists after only a few hours of negotiation. In other provinces in North Vietnam, it was because of the immature organization of the Vietnamese Nationalists that the communists were able to take over local administration so easily. The audacious maneuvers of the communists worked so well that even the communist leaders might have been astonished.

But in South Vietnam, the communists' maneuver did not work because of the lack of adequate armed forces. So, the communists tried to convince other nationalist forces to participate in a unified front called Viet Minh. Later, westerners used to say Viet Minh when they wrote about the North Vietnamese communists. On August 25, 1945, there was a massive demonstration in downtown Saigon. The Viet Minh Front established the Provisional Administration Committee of Nam Bo ("Nam Bo" was the name given by the communists to South Vietnam). There were nine commissioners among them, seven communists.

After taking power in North Vietnam, the communists ran into difficulty because they did not have enough cadres and agents to assume responsibilities at all levels. Moreover, there was a greater threat: the Chinese Nationalists began to march into North Vietnam to disarm the Japanese in accordance with a treaty among the winning powers of World War II. The communists knew that the Chinese nationalists strongly supported the VNQDD.

To cope with that new danger, Ho Chi Minh hastily gave orders to his lieutenants to eliminate any trace of communism in organizations related to the Viet Minh. The Indochinese Communist Party was disbanded in November. It was converted into the "Association of studies of Marxism." A new front including the Communist Party and its satellite parties was formed and it was named Mat Tran Lien Viet (The Pan Viet Front).

A special week was set aside to organize the collection of gold from the people in North VN. It was named the "Gold Week." Communist cadres explained to the population that the government needed that gold "to buy arms and ammunition" for the defense of the Fatherland. Coupled with persuasion was terror: secret communist agents gave severe warning to those who refused to "volunteer" to give gold to the Government. Tons of gold were collected to become gifts from Uncle Ho Chi Minh to the Chinese Nationalist Army

Commander-in-Chief in North VN (Lu Han). At that time, the conflict between Viet Nationalists and Viet Communists became particularly bloody. Finally, the Chinese generals were bought by Ho Chi Minh and they adopted a neutralist attitude in the brotherly carnage in North VN. Ho Chi Minh needed only this attitude. And then, communist soldiers and secret agents received Ho Chi Minh's instructions to exterminate all members of the VNQDD and the VNCMDMH.

On November 19, 1945, through the intermediary of the Chinese general Tieu Van, there was another agreement between the VNQDD and the Communist Party. A first agreement had been reached on October 23, but it was rejected by the VNQDD because the Communists failed to observe it. This time, the new agreement included a common policy, the unification of armed forces and the formation of the National Union government.

But on December 3, 1945, Ho Chi Minh said that there was no need to form a new government because general elections would be held. Recognizing that once again, they had been cheated by Ho Chi Minh, all Nationalist forces prepared to boycott the election.

Realizing his weak position, Ho Chi Minh once again returned to his treacherous delaying tactics. He signed a third agreement and promised that Nguyen Hai Than, leader of the VNCMDMH would be vice-president, the VNQDD would have 50 seats in the Parliament, the VNCMDMH 20 seats, the ministries of Economy and of Health to the two Nationalist parties, the ministries of National Defense and the Interior would be to neutral people and finally, the general election would be postponed until January 6, 1946.

A coalition was formed. The Communists faced new difficulties: the People of VN still venerated the VNQDD. On the anniversary of the death of Mr Nguyen Thai Hoc, leader of the VNQDD in 1930 and beheaded by the French after the abortive coup in Yen Bay Province, there were many people attending a memorial ceremony. Resentment rose high among the population after the firing of many civil servants because the government's financial difficulties . . .

The political situation in VN reached a turning point when the French and the Chinese Nationalist concluded at Tchoung Kinh (capital of the Chinese nationalist government) an agreement which resulted in the replacement of the Chinese Nationalist army in North VN by the French.

With this new agreement, Ho Chi Minh faced three dangerous pressures: the VNQDD, financial difficulties and the French.

Here again, Ho Chi Minh used delaying tactics. He began to negotiate with the French through two French diplomats: Leon Pignon and Jean Sainteny. A temporary agreement was signed on March 6, 1946 accepting the French troops into Vietnam. To avoid being accused of selling out the country, Ho Chi Minh convinced some nationalist leaders to sign that agreement.

To protest the signing of the agreement, vice president Nguyen Hai Than resigned on March 1, 1946 (five days before the signing day). On March 2, 1946, Ho Chi Minh was advised by the communist party to form a new government which was named union government of resistance: six ministries to the communists, two to the VNQDD, two to the VNCMDMH, one to a non-party and there was to be a committee of resistance of which, Vo Nguyen Giap (communist) would be the chairman and Vo Hong Khanh (VNQDD) the vice-chairman.

The new formula did not get the approval of the Vietnamese nationalists: secret strongholds were formed in many provinces. After many bloody battles, the nationalists fled to China.

In the evening of November 11, 1946, a new government was established by the communist parliament.

The coalition had been used by the communists as a successful strategy to take power. The same strategy was used in China and in Czhekoslovakia. In the coalition formula in Vietnam the Vietnamese communist party cooperated twice with the foreigners to destroy the Vietnamese nationalists.

But, it was not the last time that there was to be a coalition between two ideologically opposite sides in Vietnam. On December 19, 1946, when the French Indochinese War erupted, the Vietnamese Nationalists once again forgot the ideological differences with the communists and accepted a new coalition formula to fight against the French invaders.

Being honest and shy by nature, they were cheated and cheated again. Under the treacherous propaganda tactics of the communists, the outside world believed that the victory of the Indochinese War belonged only to the Vietnamese communist party.

The greatest lesson for the Vietnamese Nationalist after the Indochinese war was that to fight the International Communist movement, a classical concept of revolution would never succeed. It would never be easy for the Nationalists to invent an alternative to replace the tricky but attractive marxist philosophy. If they failed to find an effective alternative they would surely be defeated by the communists. So, in South Vietnam after July 1954, the Vietnamese Nationalists finally had an opportunity to think about an alternative philosophy to compete with the primitive marxist philosophy of the Vietnamese communists. If the Nationalists failed this time, the failure would bury them forever.

With many Vietnamese Nationalist leaders to choose from after the years of fighting against the French and the Japanese, it was strange to many observers that the Americans considered Ngo Dinh Diem as the anti-communists' last card in South Vietnam. They played that card at the eleventh hour and played in the worst conditions. Just after the Geneva Accords of July 1954, Diem found himself practically without means of action and isolated in the midst of the remnants of the French Administration (amateurish politicians, sects, army, police, etc. . .). But he managed to survive until November 1963.

Ngo Dinh Diem took power on July 7, 1954. He learned quickly enough that his full powers, civil and military existed mainly on paper. His survival required strong leadership, considerable political flexibility and manipulative skill. During his first four ruling years, his regime was assuredly one of the most stable and honest on the periphery of Asia. One of his earliest supporters wrote of him in 1959 as "the prophet of an indigenous Asian form of democracy." But after Diem and his brother had been assassinated, the same writer made a reevaluation and found that the philosophy of Diem was nothing less than "peasant-based revolutionary fascism."

The strange metamorphosis of that writer (Wesley Fishel, Diem's advisor) suggest interesting questions about the success and the fall of Diem. Did he have the background to be as popularly supported as Ho Chi Minh? What was the nature of the alternative to a communist-dominated Vietnamese Nationalism? Why with so many American friends, did Diem fall?

Born in 1901, Ngo Dinh Diem was one of the sons of a well-educated mandarin. His family had been among Vietnam's earliest Roman Catholic converts during the 17th century and was said to include several members who had suffered martyrdom in defense of their religion. Ngo Dinh Diem was made less of the kindness of the apostles than of the ruthless militancy of the Grand Inquisitor. His view of government was the tyranny of a tradition-bound mandarin. He was a spiritual son of a fiercely aggressive and militant faith rather than of the easygoing and tolerant approach of Gallican Catholicism.

Ample justification in evaluating his political behavior can be found in his paternalistic approach to what he considered to be a proper relationship between those who governed and those who are governed. This irritated many of Diem's supporters. William Henderson who, in an otherwise laudatory article, said that "Diem's conversation reflects an archaic mandarin temperament."

Ngo Dinh Diem wrote: "A sacred respect is due to the person of the sovereign. He is the mediator between the people and heaven as he celebrates the national cult." The concept of executive power subject to popular recall simply went against the grain of the man. In his own eyes, it hurt his stature as a predestined leader. While Diem's South Vietnam was structurally a republic primarily because that system of government is most familiar to the Americans, it was an absolute monarchy without a king, in terms of the relationship between government and the governed. According to Diem's philosophy, only national survival counted. He did not pay attention to popular representation. Thus, during his entire period of leadership, Ngo Dinh Diem was considered by the people of South Vietnam to be a remote leader with a remote philosophy.

Diem's concepts were vitually important to the political future of South Vietnam. They were to provide the base upon which the South Vietnamese built their struggle against the primitive Marxism promoted by North Vietnam. Should Diem's alternative fail, there would be no alternative for South Vietnam except the one proposed by the communists.

The alternative Ngo Dinh Diem offered was "one man democratic rule," supported by a family dictatorship.

In Vietnam as in many other new states after World War II, independence could not have been achieved and could not be maintained without strong leadership. Generally speaking, the people of Southeast Asia are not sufficiently sophisticated to understand what westerners mean by democracy, they do not know how they can exercise and protect their own political rights.

This was not to say that the noble principles of the U.S. Declaration of Independence did not exercise a magnetic attraction for Asian peoples. But the unlettered majority is far more interested in the more immediate and tangible issues of securing independence, developing the country and raising standards of living.

Ngo Dinh Diem was the man who, in four short years led his truncated country from the edge of chaos to peace, stability and a tempo of development. Those who knew Diem were impressed by his determination to keep his country alive.

Unfortunately, Diem was not interested in distrubing the hierarchical structure of the classical Vietnamese society. His shrewdness made him forget that so long as he did not change that structure radically, the communists could and would promote their alternative.

In brief, Ngo Dinh Diem set up the pattern of democracy for South Vietnam in the fight against communism. According to Diem, he had the support of the army, the civil servants and police forces.

Ngo Dinh Diem did not see himself as the type of leader that the Americans would like to have in Vietnam. He saw himself representing God to the People of Vietnam and he believed that it was the duty of the people to honor and to obey him. Moreover, his family tied his hands.

To compete with the communist alternative, Diem deprived himself of the support of the majority of the population. He destroyed political parties other than his own. He did not tolerate any kind of opposition. Three pillars of his regime: the army; the civil service; and the police were used by Diem and by his family as tools.

Up to his fall on November 1, 1963, it was a continuing surprise to foreign observers that South Vietnam had not been controlled by the communists from 1957 onward. Two serious situations prevented the communists from taking over South Vietnam, although Diem's administration became more and more remote from the South Vietnamese. The first situation was that the communists were not politically and militarily strong enough to overthrow Ngo Dinh Diem. The other was that South Vietnamese Nationalists and the silent majority had a strong sense of anti-communism, at least as long as they still had some hope of improving a non-communist government.

It must be noted that the Nationalists, and not the communists, overthrew Ngo Dinh Diem. It was a good opportunity for the Nationalists to find a new formula, a new philosophy to compete with the alternative of communism. Could they succeed in saving South Vietnam after the fall of Diem?

On November 4, 1963, three days after the fall of Diem, Ambassador Lodge cabled Washington predicting that the change in regime would shorten the war against the Viet Cong because that change improved morale in the South Vietnam.

Diem ruled South Vietnam for nearly ten years. It had been a lost decade for the Vietnamese Nationalists. Ngo Dinh Diem did not prepare a successor because he thought his dynasty would last for a long time, and because he was so sure of himself. Diem's legacy was a dangerous precedent: civil servants and military men might be promoted or demoted on political and personal, not military grounds. Key military units had been kept out of the war zones in order to protect Saigon from a coup. A credibility gap was left after the death of Ngo Dinh Diem.

From one man democratic rule, South Vietnam moved to democracy in uniform.

Democracy in Uniform

Between the death of Ngo Dinh Diem and the rise to power of air marshall Nguyen Cao Ky, there was a string of ephemeral juntas and civilian cliques.

First, there was a leadership of General Duong Van Minh and his military revolutionary council. Minh choose Nguyen Ngoc Tho to become his prime minister. Tho was an economist and had been Diem's vice-president. General Minh and Tho were both born in South Vietnam, a clear psychological advantage to win the support of South Vietnamese people.

For many years, the Viet Cong had used as their main drawing card the fact that Diem's administration was a hated mandarin administration backed by the United States. The Viet Cong propaganda line of My Diem (My Diem means "Americans and Diem") collapsed with Diem's death. If South Vietnam were to have a new and effective leadership, the communists might be deprived of their main propaganda theme.

71

But to have such an effective leadership would have required a great deal of hard decisions in Washington. And at that time even Washington was in the midst of a dramatic change of government (after the assassination of President Kennedy). Therefore, the decision to carry out a big change in the political leadership of South Vietnam after Diem's death was left in the hands of the U.S. ambassador in Saigon and of those who overthrew Diem.

General Minh was known as a moderate man and he did not have an extremist view of the Viet Cong. His religion was Buddhism and more important, he was born in South Vietnam. One might think that the Viet Cong would be willing to deal with General Minh's team on a compromise basis.

In the meantime, members of the Vietnam Quoc Dan Dang (VNQDD) had tried to seek the support of the population in order to form a civilian government to cope with the new situation. There were some meetings and some demonstrations organized by the young generation of the VNQDD in Saigon. (After 1954, the VNQDD was divided into three branches: Central, North and South branches. Of course, these branches did not like to cooperate with each other in their struggle to take power. It was the common mistake of almost all non-communist political parties: divided among themselves and never formed a common policy to fight against communism. It was a waste of manpower and a waste of time. It was also the kind of weakness that made them so vulnerable to any communist political offensive.)

Another weakness of the nationalist parties was the lack of support from the population. Since 1930, the VNQDD had never tried to establish a pro-peasant base for its long range policy. Almost all its members came from the intellectual class and they did not realize that a pro-peasant base was vitally important to any revolution in the Vietnamese society.

And finally, their philosophy dated from 1930s. They continued to use that obsolete philosophy to compete with Marxism. It is difficult to understand why Nationalist political parties seemed to be afraid to be identified with the peasants and with low-income people. Therefore, the Vietnamese Nationalists tacitly accepted the fact that the communists had the monopoly of being "friendly" with the peasantry and with low income people. And to developing nations in the cold war, to accept that meant acceptance of defeat. The truth is, however, so simple: being essentially an agricultural society, Vietnam could not be adapted blindly to any western style revolution.

About the revolution of November 1, 1963, it is unfair to say that there was no civilian participation. The resentment of the population and the struggle of the Buddhists were factors crucial to the success of the revolution. The Vietnamese armed forces were necessary tools to carry out the revolution.

The VNQDD is the oldest Nationalist party in Vietnam. But throughout the ten ruling years of Ngo Dinh Diem, it had lost much of its prestige among the population. Common people are forgetful and besides, they had to think about their daily life first. The revolution of November 1, 1963 was a good opportunity for the VNQDD to regain prestige and more important, to prevent South Vietnam from being ruled by military men. But because of its lack of preparation and because of divided policy among many VNQDD branches, the VNQDD failed. The military junta succeeded because it had the armed forces, the most disciplined organization in South Vietnam through the troubled years before the fall of Diem.

The remaining nationalist political parties in South Vietnam were not luckier than the VNQDD in the historical event of November 1, 1963: they, too, had to surrender to the power of guns.

However, there was at first some hope from the population that the junta would know enough to request advice from wise politicians to avoid making political mistakes. But this faint hope vanished very soon when it faced reality.

General Duong Van Minh was among the military heroes of South Vietnam. He was born in South Vietnam and did not get many favors from Ngo Dinh Diem. He was one of those who promoted the slogan "South Vietnam belongs to South Vietnamese" for a long time. (That means those who came from North Vietnam would have to leave South Vietnam to the North and after that, everything would be all right.) His formula might please the Viet Cong. Unfortunately, General Minh was not a qualified politician. After the success of the military coup, instead of doing something to unify South Vietnam in order to get strong support from the population and to seek a solution from a strong position, General Minh gave full political power to his friend, Nguyen Ngoc Tho, Diem's former vice-president. To the South Vietnamese, Tho was neither a good nor a bad man. However, he was identified with the Ngo Dinh Diem administration and he did not have the necessary aureole to win "hearts and minds" of the peasants. The passivity of General Minh and of his friend Nguyen Ngoc Tho made the Americans feel uneasy. They were afraid of a "neutralist South Vietnam."

On January 30, 1964, General Nguyen Khanh overthrew General Minh with the charge that General Minh and his aides had not hesitated "to ally themselves with the French colonialists and have a tendency to advocate neutrality." If General Duong Van Minh was not a qualified politician, he was at least a relatively virtuous military man. Nguyen Khanh was a professional military man and at the same time, he was tricky. He had neither virtue, nor political qualification. However, the U.S. television cameras recorded the enthusiam with which the rise of Khanh was greeted in Washington.

Being one of the most favorite adoptive sons of Ngo Dinh Diem, Khanh followed Diem's example in conducting military affairs. To get support from the armed forces, Khanh promoted many officers to higher rank. Of course, many other officers were fired for political reason. Under Diem's rule, there were many high ranking officers without any function because they were distrusted by Diem. After the military coup, there were more and more high ranking officers without commands. This situation hurt the prestige and the morale of the army. Newly promoted officers began to distinguish themselves from those promoted by the "revolution." In other words, officers promoted to higher rank under normal conditions considered themselves "insulted" if somebody said they got their new rank from the revolution.

The political power of South Vietnam had been weakening since 1960 and so was the military power. Now, Duong Van Minh and Nguyen Khanh made everything go from bad to worse. The last bastion of South Vietnam to fight against communism since 1954 had been the army. As long as that army continued to fight, South Vietnam could not be defeated militarily. Of course, the military aspect was only of secondary importance in the Vietnam War but if that aspect become dark, there would be no hope for the survival of South Vietnam.

Ngo Dinh Diem could not deny the importance of the South Vietnamese armed forces. But because of his formula democratic one man rule, family dictatorship, he tended to see that army was his tool. The political appointment of civilian servants and officers under Diem's administration had already weakened South Vietnamese armed forces.

After the fall of Diem, military rank became a trade, a market. To get support from army officers, Vietnamese generals promoted their subordinates to higher rank according not to political grounds as under Diem's regime but to the degree of friendship. In other words, the so-called revolutionary generals had corrupted South Vietnamese armed forces. The result of this situation was that many combat units were led by unqualified commanders. Another result was more dangerous to the fighting spirit of South Vietnamese armed forces. Soldiers and small unit commanders began to wonder why they gave their lives to such men as Duong Van Minh, Nguyen Khanh and a lot of corrupt generals. And when an army wonders about its *raison d'etre* for fighting, its efficiency is destroyed. This was one of several major reasons which explain the increasingly deteriorated military situation in South Vietnam after Diem's death.

Between August 16 and September 13, 1964, there were at least four distinct coups: August 16, August 29, September 3 and September 13. Foreign observers saw a very strange picture in Saigon: Government combat units moved from the battle front to Saigon. One unit was for this general, some other unit for that general. But while their generals were bargaining, Vietnamese soldiers scornfully commented, "Well, that is their business, it is not ours. We should not shoot at each other. Let the generals kill each other." Blinded by power, money and personal ambition, these generals could not see how their behavior had damaged the morale and the fighting spirit of South Vietnamese armed forces. If communist forces had been strong enough at that time, South Vietnam would have collapsed at the end of 1964.

After so many coups from November, 1963, to November, 1964, there came an interlude. On November 1, 1964, a year after Diem's death, Nguyen Khanh surrendered power to the civilian regime of Phan Khac Suu and Tran Van Huong. Like every junta, they also enacted a constitution. But, like other juntas having not the slightest effect on the harsh realities of South Vietnamese political life. Yet, there was a faint hope for democracy when that civilian regime organized local council elections on May 30, 1965. Over 74% of South Vietnamese allegedly voted. And then, once again, the military uniform took the reins of power. On June 12, 1965, Air Marshall Ky was named Prime Minister and General Nguyen Van Thieu Chief of State by the junta. Nguyen Khanh wandered into exile, having had enough time to send some of his closest aides abroad with many millions of dollars.

When Air Marshal Nguyen Cao Ky took power, political passivity was still in order. But Ky's words created faint hope. Maybe this time, South Vietnam would have a pro-peasant government. Ky repeatedly emphasized improving the the life of "poor people." He once stated that his government was the government of poor people. While Nguyen Van Thieu's role was only symbolic with no real power, Ky had full power.

Born in Hanoi (North Vietnam) in 1930, Ky was called to serve in the Vietnamese Armed Forces in 1951. Graduated from a Vietnamese Military Academy, he moved from the army to the air force after having been trained in France as a cargo pilot. Later he received complete training as a fighter pilot. His military career was brilliant: Ky was among the youngest generals of the South Vietnamese armed forces.

Had he been able to avoid political involvement, Ky might have become a famous and flamboyant hero of the South Vietnamese armed forces. In every combat mission, he showed clear contempt for death. As a commander, he tried to protect and to defend his subordinates. In short, Ky was a good officer with a bright military future. Facing death every day, Ky quickly became careless about everything, including the survival of his country. Western papers and magazines called Ky a playboy. In Saigon, while still an air force officer, he used to drink at some splendid bars on Tu Do Street, the Broadway of Saigon. His familiar dress was a black pilot uniform with an orange neckerchief and two beautiful silver inlaid pistols.

Nobody really knows whether Ky thought that he was a predestined leader, but he eagerly accepted the role of Prime Minister. Ky continued to behave as he had when he was still an ordinary officer. From time to time, he and his wife went to have breakfast at a famous and popular restaurant on Vo Tanh Street, in Saigon. His wife imitated him in dress: she used to wear a pilot black uniform with an orange neckerchief. They had an appearance of a happy couple.

Unfortunately, in June 1965 South Vietnam needed much more than a demagogic air-marshal.

Prime Minister Nguyen Cao Ky succeeded in carrying out three things in his ruling months (nearly sixteen months). The first was his policy to choose his assistants and his contributors. While Ngo Dinh Diem trusted only the Vietnamese born in Central Vietnam, Ky trusted almost only those who were born in North Vietnam. In doing that, and doing that in South Vietnam, Ky stirred resentment. The second thing was his attitude vis-a-vis the so-called Chief of State, Nguyen Van Thieu. Although almost everybody knew that the Thieu's role was symbolic, at least, a chief of state deserved some special respect from his citizens, including his Prime Minister. Nguyen Cao Ky did not show a minimum of respect to Nguyen Van Thieu. There is an idiom in Vietnamese language which says, "As cunning as a dog trying to secretly snap up some food." That described Thieu's attitude each time he appeared together with Ky before the Saigonese population. Thieu would never forgive Ky's arrogance.

The third performance of Prime Minister Ky was the convention of June 19, 1965, seven days after he took power. Ky's 1965 convention exhorted the South Vietnamese people to fight until victory at any price. It well reflected the human nature of Air-Marshal Nguyen Cao Ky: he never once mentioned the rights of every individual citizen.

From Ngo Dinh Diem to Nguyen Cao Ky, the quality of the leaders was tragically downgraded. The democratic one-man rule of Ngo Dinh Diem had at least been carried out by civilian politicians. But democracy in uniform was carried out only by the military men who lacked even minimal political background.

THE SECOND REPUBLIC: Nguyen Van Thieu's administration

Nguyen Van Thieu ruled South Vietnam from 1967 to 1975. He had been Chief-of-State since June 1965 but he really ruled in absolute dictator in South Vietnam only after the election of October 1967. How could a dictatorship arise where the United States spent many billions to help build a democratic non-communist society? And how could that dictatorship last ten years with continued assistance from the United States? Why did the United States continue to support that democratic banditry rule for so many years?

Nguyen Van Thieu was born in 1924 in Phan Rang Province, a Vietnamese coastal area and one of the poorest lands of all Vietnamese territories. He came from a peasant family.

Because his father was financially unable, Thieu was obliged to interrupt his studies. The only exit for him and his family was to volunteer in the French Army. After a few years, Thieu became a sergeant and was sent to the Ecole Militaire Inter-Armes of Dalat (the French Joint Military School of Dalat), a resort city about 250 miles northwest of Saigon. After the departure of the French in 1955, this Military School got its new name: Vietnamese Military Academy of Dalat. Graduated second lieutenant from that school, Thieu became platoon leader in a French-led Vietnamese battalion. At that time, every eight months, there was a graduate class for non-commissioned officer students. That brief training was to satisfy urgent needs of military cadres in French combat units in Indochina. After 1955, the training time was increased to three years. That detail was important in our psychohistorical inquiry about Nguyen Van Thieu. Having received military training of four and one half months, Second Lieutenant Thieu had only elementary knowledge to lead an infantry platoon of 36 soldiers.

As far as Thieu's classmates could remember, Thieu had the reputation of being shameless in any kind of activity. Thieu had the courage to calmly receive insults from some friends and then, continue to keep company with those friends. But at the first opportunity, he would kill those who had insulted him.

Years of service in the French army converted Thieu into a model of a French mercenary: unmannerly language, carelessness about human life, an inferiority complex before any virtuous person, permanently hungry for money.

While he was an inferior officer, Thieu was married to the daughter of a bourgeois Catholic family in My Tho Province. To gain favor from Ngo Dinh Diem, Thieu did not hesitate to drop his traditional family religion (Buddhism) to embrace Catholicism. Thieu became one of Diem's many "adoptive sons." Because of his conversion, Thieu rose quickly in his military career. When the militant Buddhist movement began its open protest, Thieu was the commander of the 5th Vietnamese Infantry Division. This division had the responsibility of protecting Saigon from any attack coming from the North. Thus, prior to the coup of November 1, 1963, Colonel Nguyen Van Thieu was not an ambitious high ranking officer.

Nobody knew what Thieu was planning in November 1963, when he participated in the coup. But the fact was that he was also a member of the military revolutionary council. Later, he managed to be among the so called Young Turk Leaders, too. Thieu began to build his power base since being named (symbolic) chief-of-state on June 12, 1965.

Cunning and vengeful, Thieu would never forgive Nguyen Cao Ky for making him lose face in June 1965, when Thieu was named Chief of State and Ky Prime Minister. Thieu tried to oust Ky and to build his own group. Promising that they would be materially rewarded if he could take power, Thieu got enough support from many Vietnamese generals to oust Ky.

South Vietnam received a new constitution in April 1967 (voted upon by the constituent assembly of September 11, 1966). Like its 1956 predecessor the 1967 constitution was born with the help of an American expert, professor John Roche Brandeis. All powers were still shared by a constellation of military commanders at the top, extending down to lower ranking officers, who were province and even district chiefs.

After Diem's fall, South Vietnamese armed forces and the silent majority realized the nation was weak politically. They also knew that it would be vitally important to maintain the unity of the armed forces, because military men were the last anti-communist bastion for South Vietnam. Thus, South Vietnamese people were anxious when they knew about the Thieu/Ky conflict. The political and military situation in South Vietnam might be more pessimistic should leadership in South Vietnam be split. They tried to advise Thieu and Ky to run on the same ticket to "save national unity" and to bring confidence to South Vietnamese armed forces. With such advice, Thieu had to comply with the popular wish. The Thieu/Ky ticket won easily in September 1967. It provided the faint hope that the new government would reach a settlement to end the war. But later evidence showed that war was the vital ingredient to Nguyen Van Thieu's regime and that Thieu could only stay in power if the war continued.

Now that he had full power, Thieu began to carry out his philosophy of competition with the communist alternative: South Vietnam would have the democratic banditry rule supported by the old Vietnamese proverb, "If you have money, you can buy even angels." Thieu's tactics were quite simple: provide money for their function and they must be faithful to you. Honest and qualified military and civil servants were fired quickly. Within a short time, every administrative position, every important unit of the armed forces was occupied by Thieu's men or by men introduced or guaranteed by Thieu's aides. Those who had been in trouble with the national police easily got a job in Thieu's administration. It was a very ingenious blackmail tactic: their files were kept by Thieu's staff in a black list. At the first sign of betrayal, Thieu used the black file to put them in jail.

Good politicians and qualified generals began to leave Thieu's administration. This time, vice president Nguyen Cao Ky could not but accept that unhappy truth: he did not have enough money and anyway, he was still too honest to help Thieu's democratic banditry rule. Sooner or later Ky would be ousted.

The number one problem for Thieu's regime was finance. It was vitally important to him and to his staff to finance a secret army and a secret police as well as buy any person necessary to the strengthening of his regime. If Thieu and his staff were weak in their war against the communists, they were effective in fund raising for their regime. They divided South Vietnamese society into three markets, all of them to be fed by the war: the trade of power, the trade of blood and the trade of justice.

Thieu imitated communist tactics to promote stability for South Vietnam. In other words, he would rule South Vietnam by blackmail and by terror. He would be the anti-communist champion through oral anti-communism. His anti-communism would be the screen to cover banditry. To carry out his philosophy, Thieu would need mercenaries. To hire these mercenaries, he needed money. His constitutional powers would be his weapons, the war his business.

Except for the presidency and the prime ministership, all government functions could be bought. Buyers could either pay cash or on the installment plan. For instance, the position of chief of province of a prosperous area could be bought by 30 millions VN$. This chief of province could pay cash (1/4 or 1/5) and pay the balance in the coming months; i.e., bribery and corruption would bring him money to pay his account.

Theoretically, a citizen from 18 years of age onward would be called to serve in the army. But there would be permanently somebody to help him be free from military service, providing he paid certain sum of money. If a young man could not avoid the military service, he could still avoid being sent to combat unit. He could pay a sum of money to his commander and be permitted to stay at the safe rear area. This trade of blood flourished under Thieu's ruling years. Prices changed according to the degree of danger of battle areas. The young man need not pay only one time. After the first payment and after a certain time according to the degree of money hunger of his commander, he would have to pay a second time then a third time, etc. Of course, his commander could not enjoy this sum of money alone. The commander had to "pay" his superior and so on . . .

The trade of justice was still more expensive. No matter who was right, the winner would be the one who could pay money to the policeman, to the judge from the county court up to the supreme court. If the guilty person could afford to pay, there would be somebody at the court to "destroy" his file. As was the case of the trade of blood, the county judge had to "pay" to his superior . . .

Thus, by the passivity of the silent majority, by the cowardice of South Vietnamese intellectuals, by the amateurish behavior of various Vietnamese political parties, by the contemptible and slavish line of conduct of many Vietnamese generals and by the tacit complicity of some American diplomats in Saigon, Thieu succeeded in imposing his banditry rule for ten years.

To carry out his rule, Thieu had to have an important staff. Under normal conditions in any country in peacetime, it would be very difficult to get such staff. But in Vietnam, war changed everything. Vietnam had been a poor country since the days of French colonialism. Only a small minority could be considered as rich. "Get rich" therefore became an important objective to many people in Vietnam. It was a long way to come for those who wanted to make money honestly. Of course there were always those who wanted to make money easily, not caring whether their way of making money would damage their country or not.

Thieu knew quite well that he could not rule alone. Those who followed him must have their share. His formula brought a lot a dishonest people to him. He recruited his staff among those Vietnamese who wanted to become rich in a short time. No matter what they might do, they would receive the blessings of Thieu and anything done by Thieu would be explained by Thieu himself as for "national security."

The one chosen by Thieu to be his prime minister was Tran Thien Khiem, ex-commander of the Vietnamese 4th infantry division. After successive coups, Khiem got his four star rank, although he did not win any battle since he served in South Vietnamese armed forces. Khiem had many brothers and it worked well with his planning: each one of his brothers would occupy an important position in the administration as long as he was still prime minister.

The port of Saigon and the Tan Son Nhat airport were two places where one could do colossal business. Prime minister Khiem named one of his brothers director of the Saigon port and one of his men director of the Tan Son Nhat airport. The bribes alone offered every day by the smugglers brought millions to Khiem's family. Khiem's wife had another way to get rich: she cooperated with some Vietnamese generals to sell heroin and other foreign items to the Vietnamese. Originated from a low class people, Khiem's wife looked clumsy but arrogant. She had the reputation of being never satisfied about getting money.

78

Khiem named one of his brothers chief of press and media relations bureau and Khiem gave him the rank of full colonel. The new colonel was only graduated from an elementary school and never had the opportunity to attend a formal party. He had to learn and to practice many days but after few dinner parties, he gave up, because "it was too difficult" to him "to wear a coat and tie," too difficult "to choose assorted colors" to his dress.

Khiem's wife had still another way to get money: selling the position of *chief of province* and chief of various precincts in Saigon capital. There was a secret agreement between Thieu and Khiem. They drew boundaries on the map of South Vietnam and on the map of Saigon. Thieu's men would be named chief of such and such province while Khiem's men would be named chief of other provinces . . . and so on . . . The 5th precinct of Cholon area (vicinity of Saigon) was considered the richest area of Cholon. Therefore, Khiem's wife sold the function of chief of police of that precinct for VN 50 million. It was not a problem with anybody who wanted to do business: Cholon area was inhabited by nearly one million Chinese and among them were many millionaires. These Chinese were always very responsive to any new chief of precinct police. They paid millions but after that, they were free to do any kind of business. As ever, the permanent losers were the Vietnamese common people.

As we have mentioned earlier, Thieu's family had truly hard days when he was only a French mercenary. He could never forget that his father, at times, had taken mango tree leaves for food. His closest aides would be in charge of making money for his family. Nha, his nephew, became his "eminence grise" because Thieu trusted everything reported by Nha. A lot of Vietnamese civil servants and military officers began to flatter Nha to get favors and to get better positions (in term of buying their function). Nha's mother practiced the trade of rice in all provinces of Central Vientnam. From time to time, all the provinces of Central Vietnam were suddenly in short of rice, although there were one or many security rice stock houses of the government. On the surface, there was a rice shortage, but if the buyers paid a higher price (two times or even three times the normal price), they could get rice at any quantity.

In many provinces in South Vietnam, relatives of Thieu's wife used the same tactics to make money. Thieu and his wife became proprietors of thousands of acres of land scattered throughout many provinces and cities. It wasn't until September and October 1974, when South Vietnamese newspapers decided to open their courageous campaign to fight against Thieu's corrupt regime. When a daily newspaper published incontestable documents about Thieu's illegal and dishonest orders to buy land, he dared not put the publisher of that paper in jail. A few days after, a government-financed newspaper published an announcement that Thieu had given up some land property around Dalat City.

Thieu's assistant of National Security Affairs was General Dang Van Quang. One time serving as a French mercenary, Quang was permanently hungry for money. When he was commander of the 4th Military region, he had a secret agreement with the Viet Cong: the Viet Cong would be free to move from such and such areas, providing that they did not prevent Quang's private convoys of rice and coal. Quang's wife came from the same lowest-class people as Prime Minister Khiem's wife. She was active in making money and business with various kinds of smuggling. She was especially active in selling heroin. Since her husband was the assistant of National Security Affairs, nobody dared worry about her deadly and inhuman business.

Another actively capable man in making money for Thieu was General Lam, long time commander of I Corps (he was the warlord of five provinces: Quang Tri, Thua Thien, Quang Nam, Quang Tin and Quang Ngai). Each time he went to some dangerous area by helicopter, he always consulted a fortune-teller first. His main duty was selling heroin and getting money for Thieu. When Lam was replaced, South Vietnamese Air Force had to provide many cargo flights during many days to move Lam's possessions from Da Nang to Saigon.

One Chinese in Cholon area was greatly appreciated by Thieu: Ly Long Than, businessman. Through the intermediary of Nguyen Thi Hai, female pharmacist (she became a representative in 1971), Ly Long Than became one of Thieu's finance supporters. When Thieu or Thieu's wife needed a certain big sum of money, Ly Long Than offered money and later, Thieu gave him opportunities to make money. For instance, Ly Long Than received in advance some warning from Thieu's administration that taxes on certain items was to be increased. He transferred that warning to Chinese businessmen and they stopped selling those items until the government fixed new prices. Of course, with the new prices, they got profit of hundreds of millions.

These were only few among many tactics of Thieu's gang to get money during his ruling years. One important source of finance of Thieu's regime was American aid. A considerable part of this aid has been diverted from public interest to Thieu's private interest. In this light, Thieu had quite a capable servant: Pham Kim Ngoc, long time minister of Economy. Ngoc carried out many unpopular economic measures and he accepted all public critics and all insults on behalf of Thieu's administration. Thieu rewarded him largely in terms of money, favors and economic interests.

Thus, from 1967 to 1971, Thieu succeeded in establishing a solid base for his democratic banditry rule. With the continuous support of the United Embassy in Saigon, Thieu's regime became so deep-rooted that only the collapse of South Vietnam could remove Thieu from power.

Realizing that he must have enough time to build his power Thieu was forced to run on the same ticket with Nguyen Cao Ky in the presidential election of 1967. But unlike the situation of 1965, this time, Thieu would have full power after the election.

So, Nguyen Van Thieu had made his choice: coming from a peasant family, he could do only one of two things, become a revolutionary hero or make money through banditry rule. Becoming a revolutionary hero was beyond his capability, given his mercenary background. Besides, a revolutionary had to forget any material interest, while Thieu was permanently haunted by the miserable past of his family. South VN might collapse but until they collapse, Thieu would have at least time and means to get as much money as possible. His tactics were simple but effective: he corrupted every constitutional institution by terrible weapons: money, favor, position in the administration and terror.

After the inauguration of his first term of office, Thieu started necessary preparations for his long-term dictatorship. The first thing was to prevent vice-president Nguyen Cao Ky from doing anything. It was quite the reverse of the situation on 1965. Of course, Ky reacted but only defensively and weakly. Among Ky's supporters: one daily newspaper, one satirical weekly paper, one Air Force Division and some politicians. Ky had 16 months, from June 1965 to 1967, to carry out his program and his philosophy when he was Prime Minister. He could not make his choice. Having no valid philosophy to replace the Communist alternative, he adopted a vague anti-communist program. Having acquired some sence of political ethics, Ky could not promote banditry rule. Hesitating among these lines of thinking, Ky lost his political opportunities. From now on, his political career was finished.

Thieu did not have enough time to replace administrative and military commanders when the Communists launched their general offensive of Mau Than Lunar New Year (February 1968). The offensive lasted only three days (except in the old capital of Hue, where the battle ended only after nearly one month) but it did bring to the knowledge of everybody many interesting things about communism and about the War in Vietnam.

Before launching their big offensive, the Communists agreed with the Vietnamese-American High Command that they would observe seven days of a cease-fire on the occasion of the Lunar New Year. Observing the Vietnamese traditional way of life, many Vietnamese soldiers requested permission to celebrate the Lunar New Year with their families. At every military outpost or military base, there remained only about one third of the garrison. But this one third reacted heroically and effectively. This offensive was evidence that the communists never respected any agreement, any treaty if the observance of that agreement or of that treaty harms their interests.

The population reacted promptly, not in a positive way because civilian people did not have arm or weapon, but in a way that demonstrated a high sense of anti-communism: they fled to the government forces, abandoning everything.

The communists suffered heavy casualties. Most of the communist excellent cadres were killed and they were unable to control any provincial capital or any district capital. But they won a psychological victory: in spite of the presence of half a million GIs, in spite of many South Vietnamese divisions, they could launch an attack right into South Vietnam cities and province capitals.

Three months later, the communists launched another offensive but this time, it was crushed quickly. During this second big offensive, the communists began to use a new tactic, an inhuman but effective one: they deliberately shelled Russian made and Chinese made rockets (107MM and 122MM) on civilian houses and installations. Of course, the population was frightened and fear was exactly what the communists intended.

The offensive of 1968 revealed that South Vietnamese Armed Forces were outgunned and the communists were better armed, better equipped.

Formerly, South Vietnamese people did not know much about the way the communists behave. In the offensive of 1968, more than 5,000 people (most of them were civilian people) were killed by the communists. This massacre badly hurt the propaganda of the communists. And this massacre was a good opportunity for the Vietnamese government to improve its leadership and to deprive the communists of their propaganda themes. Unfortunately, Thieu's administration wanted only to build Thieu's personal power. Being a professional military man Thieu and his staff were thinking only about military solutions to every problem. Besides, by their nature, Thieu and his closest aides were the last people to think about improving the nationalist government in South Vietnam. Time was running out and the immediate effects of the 1968 offensive could not be wisely exploited by Thieu's administration.

In May 1968, when North Vietnam and the U.S. government started their negotiations in Paris, Thieu promulgated law No. 002/68 of general mobilization for South Vietnam. In fact, South Vietnam was in a state of partial mobilization since 1964. This country might be the only one in the world to maintain the reserve military men in the army indefinitely. Lacking an effective anti-communist doctrine, the successive governments in South Vietnam knew only one solution and that solution was the easiest, although not the best: mobilization of young people into the army. But once having placed young people in the army, the Saigon governments did not want to discharge them.

The general mobilization law was one of Thieu's dangerous weapons to practice blackmail. Many different classes of people could postpone their military service: apprentice priest, apprentice monk, student, family reason, etc. Those who wanted to enjoy this favor quickly became Thieu's debtors. It was a flourishing way to make money. Any civil servant and military man directly or indirectly related to the mobilization service could sell a certificate—valid or invalid—to anybody who would like to escape from military service. Thieu used that law to blackmail generals, religious leaders, politicians.

Because of the new general mobilization law, many tried to send their sons abroad. Those who could not get out of the country tried to "buy a safe place" either in some non-combat unit or in some supporting service which usually remained in rear areas. Those who did not have money, those who were not connected with any high-placed officials quietly went to the army. Of course, among them, many never came back. The Thieu war policy converted the armed forces into a strange organization: only those who were not rich would have to fight in the front line. The general mobilization law protected rich people.

The funniest story came from Cholon, a Chinese city close to Saigon. Because of a special law issued under the Diem administration, many Chinese automatically became Vietnamese. They had to serve in the Vietnamese Army. Somebody advised them to buy a safe position in the army. With VN$ 500,000 or 800,000, a Chinese was accepted as a new Navy crewman. He did not have to be permanently present at the Navy Headquarters. He continued his prosperous business and he could receive a phone call to report for inspection. Later, there were so many Chinese at some Navy units that the Navy Headquarters had to hire some interpreters to translate orders from Vietnamese officers to these Chinese Navy men.

According to the new general mobilization law, there would be a new armed organization named Popular Self Defense Service which included men from 16-17 years of age and from 43-50 years old. Theoretically, the PSD defend its own population areas. It was a good idea, but soon the PSD developed a new industry, rich people hired poor people to perform their service. Those who were in charge sent very optimistic reports to Thieu. Thieu claimed loudly that South Vietnam had more than two million PSD men.

Even at big unit level, the blood industry began to flourish. One of many striking examples: at Bong Son district (close to the coast about 80 miles from Qui Nhon seaport) a company commander asked his soldiers to pay if they wanted to be moved to Qui Nhon (a safer, more comfortable area). The soldiers gave him money which he sent (perhaps not all) to his boss at a higher level. A few days later, the entire company was replaced by another company, without any explanation.

In some provinces, young people reaching the age of military service simply purchased a military certificate and quietly continued to practice their private business. They did not receive their monthly army pay because they "delegated" it to their commanders. In periodical reports to the Ministry of National Defense, military commanders and province chiefs always wrote that they had full strength units. Theoretically, South Vietnam had the second largest army in Asia after Red China with 1,110,000 men. In fact, only half of that number could be counted on to fight.

Regarding the Vietnamese Congress and the Supreme court, Thieu used the same tactics: pharmacist Nguyen Cao Thang was in charge of buying the Representatives and Senators. He did not meet many difficulties in his job. Thieu succeeded in buying four of nine Supreme Justices shortly after his inauguration.

The mid-term election of the Senate was organized in October 1970. By a secret agreement between Thieu's government and An Quan Pagoda (South Vietnamese militant Buddhists) ten of An Quang's men were elected. There were still independent Senators in the Senate, but with the general mobilization law, it was easy for Thieu to blackmail many Senators who did not want their sons serving in the army.

It was the same thing with the South Vietnam Supreme Court. Thieu succeeded in buying almost all of the nine Supreme Justices. Only Justice Tran Minh Tiet continued to oppose Thieu's banditry rule.

As mentioned earlier, vice-president Nguyen Cao Ky was ousted by Thieu and in the strangest election that Southeast Asia has ever seen. Thieu won the one man contest in September 1971. He even won a much more important contest. From that point to the collapse of South Vietnam, Thieu and his gang would rule as absolute dictators.

Thieu's vice president in the election of 1971 was a former elementary teacher, Tran Van Huong. Thieu realized that he could not get popular support after he set up his banditry rule. But, he had to choose a vice president not among men of his gang. Tran Van Huong was a teacher. He had been born in South Vietnam. These were two advantageous elements but beyond these factors Huong meant nothing to the common people in South Vietnam. Huong's presence in the Thieu administration, of course, did not improve the seriously deteriorated situation in South Vietnam. He tried to explain to the South Vietnamese people that he ran with Thieu to "save" South Vietnam. Thieu did not expect any effective cooperation from Huong other than his image. Although he had once been prime minister, nobody in South Vietnam, except his immediate relatives, thought that Huong was a considerable leader. A minority of those people who were born in South Vietnam continued to maintain the strange slogan of "South Vietnam to the South Vietnamese." Having an inferiority complex (usually, Vietnamese leaders came from North Vietnam or from Central Vietnam and rarely from the South), this minority would like to see men born in the South become leaders of South Vietnam. Tran Van Huong was a third-rate politician—but he was born in the South. He actually succeeded in getting some contributors, but almost all of them were his relatives. And only a few months after the 1971 election, Thieu began to corrupt Tran Van Huong. From 1971 to the collapse of South Vietnam, there was another gang to compete with the Thieu gang: the Tran Van Huong gang.

The Governed in South Vietnam

Armed Forces

When the Geneva Agreement of July 1954, was signed there were only about 60,000 or 70,000 nationalist soldiers, not including French mercenaries. At first, it was a complicated army. But soon, there was evidence that this army could compete effectively with good leadership, qualified officers and above all, motivation and dedication.

Its officers came from either the ranks or from one of two Vietnamese military academies: the career military academy of Dalat and the Vietnamese reserve officer school of Thu Duc. After 1954, officers received American training. A South Vietnamese 2nd lieutenant graduated from one of these military academies received a standard training similar to that of any civilized nation.

Privates were trained at various military training centers scattered throughout the country. The most important centers were: Quang Trung Center, 10 miles from Saigon with a capacity of training of 10,000 new soldiers; Duc My Center close to Nha Trang Naval Base emphasizing special warfare and training for ranger units; Phu Bai Center, a center close to Vung Tau beach emphasized the training of armored units. New soldiers received eight week training and then were moved to combat units according to current needs of military regions. Of course, American training was required to use American weapons and American strategy.

At a higher level, there was first the Command and General Staff College. After 1968, the VN Defense College was established and then there was also the VN Political Warfare College. The birth of the latter was curious. It seemed a strange solution to revitalize the morale of South Vietnamese armed forces. Some of Thieu's assistants thought that if there were more military political schools, they would be to improve the morale of South Vietnamese troops. Poor and corrupt leadership of South VN was the morale destroyer. Yet, South Vietnamese leaders still persisted in denying that.

As for professional units, there were the Marines, the paratroopers and the rangers. They were hardcore soldiers and strongly anti-communist. Vietnamese paratroopers and Marines could be considered among the best soldiers in Asia. They were intensively trained and almost blindly obeyed their commanders as long as their commanders proved worthy. Since 1954, evidence demonstrates for each killed or wounded South Vietnamese paratrooper of Marine, the Communists lost from ten to fifteen soldiers.

But these elite troops did have shortcomings: they were proud and tended to be careless to a certain degree about properties of the population. From time to time, there was some sad stories about their behavior. But because they were elite, the critics were easily silenced. The South Vietnamese people just wanted to treat them tactfully.

The Vietnamese Air Force and Navy were also well-trained. They received training both in VN and in the United States. Through many bloody tests, nobody could deny that they really did want to defend non-communist South VN.

The biggest problem with the South Vietnamese Armed Forces was that they were trained to repel a conventional invasion like the North Korean invasion in

Korea in 1950. They became used to having air and artillery support. Their supply system relied heavily on motorized means of delivery. Later, they became more and more dependent on firing too much ammunition, on air and on artillery fire support. Finally, it was an American style Army in an underdeveloped nation. When the effectiveness of an underdeveloped nation depended heavily on foreign aid, that army would become endangered should that aid be reduced or be cut. In brief, South Vietnamese armed forces had received a remote training system cope with a revolutionary war.

From 1954 to 1963, living conditions of South Vietnamese armed forces were not too difficult. There was small difference between the material life of a civil servant and that of a soldier. But from 1954 to 1975 (21 years), South Vietnamese civil and military leaders were unable or were unwilling to find a practical solution to one of the most troublesome problems of South Vietnamese Army: housing and helping soldiers' families. Communists troops were forbidden to think about their family. It was understandable because of the inhumane policy of communist doctrine. But SouthVietnamese troops, on the contrary, had to constantly worry their families. Family spirit always occupied an important place in the soldiers' mind. The same family spirit was also a main factor accelerating the collapse of South VN in 1975. Each time a soldier changed his unit, he moved his family. It was a costly procedure. Of course, there was some help from Army transportation service but that help was slow and was generally inadequate. Some units organized dependent houses but soldiers' families could not stay permanently. If the head-of-the-house moved, his family moved accordingly. The government promised to take care of their families later, and rejected any solutions for that problem. There was no surprise about that line of thinking: once government men obtained a comfortable life, they really beacme selfish without thinking that one day, their selfishness would surely destroye their country. Besides, they did not want to change or to propose and change: they wanted their privileges at any price.

Much has been said about South Vietnamese high ranking officers. Those who achieved high rank by battle performance were really first-rate commanders. But many high ranking officers were political appointees from Diem's administration onward. When a big unit commander happened to be a political appointee officer, he became a criminal because he was not qualified to lead his men into battle. These political appointee officers were satisfied by their poor performance because of ignorance. Military ethics were quite strange to them. Each time they were assigned an important job, they tended to think about only one thing: get rich by any means in the shortest time.

South Vietnamese generals were generally poor leaders. The reason was that most of them were former French non-commissioned officers. They were trained in mercenary style. Most of them had only elementary military training and were almost completely ignorant of politics. The remarkable thing about those generals was that they did not want to improve their education. Each of the French trained generals had a small army to do his family work and to protect him. Out of touch with their soldiers, they treated inferiors as if they were their slaves. They became modern warlords.

It would be unfair not to write about Vietnamese qualified generals. These generals were highly esteemed by the South Vietnamese armed forces. Most of them were graduated from the first promotion of the VN military academy but were not former French mercenaries. At the top of the list were General Ngo

85

Quang Chuong and General Nguyen Van Hieu. Graduated from the Vietnamese reserve officer school of Thu Duc in 1953, Lieutenant Chuong quickly acquired a good reputation because of his courage and his honesty. He was among Vietnam's youngest corps commanders. Even his immediate relatives could not ask any favor from General Chuong. His presence in the South Vietnamese Army was an obstacle to less skillful generals. At times, it was rumored that Americans were thinking about General Chuong as a possible leader for South Vietnam. But General Chuong hastily denied that rumor.

Second in the honor list was General Nguyen Van Hieu. He was not so brilliant militarily as General Ngo Quang Chuong, but his official and private life were so virtuous that almost no one could criticize him. Three years before the collapse of Saigon, General Hieu was named General Secretary of the anticorruption committee presided over by vice-president Tran Van Huong. General Hieu met many obstacles when he wanted to carry out his mission seriously: most of the guilty were Thieu's, or Khiem's or personnel of Thieu's closest aids. There were also guilty men who were vice president Huong's relatives. (According to the wide family spirit of the Vietnamese society, we must understand the word relative in a very broad sense). General Hieu kept the files of any high ranking corrupt official (civilian and military). A few weeks before the collapse of South Vietnam, Hieu was killed at Bien Hoa, a province capital, with the approval of President Nguyen Van Thieu. At Orote Tent City on Guam in May 1975, the writer of this book met one of the immediate relatives of General Hieu and that relative confirmed the assassination of General Hieu. It was necessary to say that General Hieu had also the file of corrupt General Nguyen Van Thieu before he managed to become President.

Other qualified generals like Nguyen Duc Thang, former commander of artillery branch and Nguyen Viet Thanh were not appreciated by Thieu. General Thanh died in mysterious circumstances when he was IV Corps Commander. General Thang was fired by Thieu when he presented his conditions for cooperation. Thieu rejected his conditions.

The newly graduated lieutenants of the Dalat military academy at first were eager to do something to improve the quality of the South Vietnamese armed forces. But they were quickly disappointed.

In 1955, when Ngo Dinh Diem was attacked by French financed religious sects, South Vietnam had its first test of fighting capability. Commanded by qualified officers, that army fought well and won easily. Later, until 1959, that army had many other opportunities to prove its value.

From Ngo Dinh Diem to Nguyen Van Thieu, many people conceded that the South Vietnamese armed forces were the last anti-communist bastion to defend South VN. But at the same time, these armed forces were also the lowest income earners in South VN. Many lost motivation when they got few days leave to visit their families. Life on the battle front and life in the rear area were very different. Finally, many soldiers gave up the idea of visiting the rear area.

In their eagerness to criticize the war in VN but finding wrong only on the American side, many people (liberals, anti war, pro-communist, neutralists, etc. . . .) tended to conclude that these soldiers were really mercenaries.

It was an unfair conclusion. When one deliberately denied the real anti-communist fighting spirit of South Vietnamese soldiers, then it was a dishonest denial. And when one only criticized either the American involvement in VN or South Vietnamese armed forces, while deliberately forgetting the horrible and inhuman crimes of the communists, while deliberately forgetting massive aid from Russia and from Red China to North VN, it was truly unfair.

Normally, mercenaries are well-paid. The South Vietnamese soldiers were not. Their families were starving; their leaders were mostly unqualified or corrupted. Yet, they continued to fight year after year. The answer: they really did not want a communist regime in South VN. Thieu and his gang were clearly conscious of that psychological and ideological aspect. And the anti-communist spirit of South Vietnamese soldiers was exploited by Thieu as a blackmail weapon: either Thieu's corrupt regime or the communists.

As long as South Vietnamese soldiers saw their immediate commanders continuing the fight, they continued the fight, with the faint hope that maybe "some day," Thieu would be removed and a better administration would take power. When these soldiers knew that their commanders had abandoned them, they quit.

There could not be anything else to explain why, during 21 years, the communists were unable to take over South VN. It was impossible to deny the strong anti-communist spirit of the South Vietnamese armed forces.

South Vietnamese Intellectuals

In the old feudal Vietnamese society, there was a clear scale of value: Si, Nong, Cong, Thuong (Intellectual, Peasant, Businessman, Trader). If the intellectual was graduated, he would serve his country by serving his emperor. If he failed in his examination, he would retire not because of old age but according to the oriental philosophy about material glory, he would become a teacher. In his village, even the chief of village had to respect him, although he was only a poor teacher in terms of no money and no social position. He was consulted by the villagers if something wrong happened to them. The intellectual was really a leader of the population.

It is the same in most other societies—even socialism. Leaders of the socialist countries might boast that they came from proletarian class, but in fact, their society was led by intellectuals.

Unfortunately, this was not the case of South VN. Before the challenge of the communist alternative, the Vietnamese nationalist intellectuals were passive. Older intellectuals could not abandon their feudal way of thinking. The new generation had received a westernized education. But after they graduated, they became strangers to their native country. The knowledge they acquired abroad was quite remote from their own country. Vietnamese westernized intellectuals simply gave up before the challenge of the communists.

The majority of Vietnamese intellectuals complained about the corrupt South Vietnamese regime but they dared not do anything. The minority held a different view: they thought only of making money. To carry out their philosophy, they became Thieu's intellectual mercenaries.

The Silent Majority

The words silent majority did not have the same political meaning as in the United States. It indicated the common people who submitted to those who rule their country this way or that way. So many years frustrated by successive corrupt administrations made the silent majority passive and submissive. Living conditions under Thieu's administration became so precarious that common people hardly had time to earn their living. When the vital problem of the silent majority was daily survival, Thieu had no reason to fear an uprising of the population.

This silent majority had something in common with South Vietnamese soldiers: they did not want to live under communist rule. Each time fighting flared up, they thought only about fleeing. And as was the case of South Vietnamese soldiers, the silent majority faced Thieu's blackmail: either Thieu's corrupt regime or the communists.

Chapter Two
TOWARD THE FINAL AGONY

Some background is necessary to completely understand the collapse of South Vietnam.

First, there was the Watergate connection. It might be a surprise to many Americans that the Watergate scandal played a significant role in the course of the VN War. By their nature, the communists are liars and cheats. Over the years, the communists have kept only those agreements that worked in their favor. Only naive people or the pro-communists believed that the communists would respect agreements.

It became clear that the Paris ceasefire agreement would be only a respite for the communists while they readied themselves for the final assault. From January 27, 1973 to January 1975, North VN established an elaborate pipeline and all-weather paved road network through western Vienam and eastern Laos from the Demilitarized Zone. At the end of 1974, Hanoi was able to move military supply and reinforcements to the highlands in a matter of days . . . much faster than the Government could bring up its own troops from Saigon. As a result, Hanoi had better health, less fatigue, more ammunitions and more men in reserve. In this respect, North Vietnamese infringements had to be checked. Richard Nixon was a frightening adversary to the communists. His unpredictable reaction had made the communists reluctant many times before they dared launch any big offensive in South VN.

In April 1973, less than three months after the Paris Agreement was signed, it was evident that North VN had begun installing surface-to-air missiles around Khe Sanh. This was south of the DMZ and on National Highway No. 9 running from Savannakhet to Quang Tri province in South Vietnamese territory. Hanoi was also deliberately slow in freeing American prisoners and refused to supply information about U.S. personnel missing in action. Consequently, President Nixon and Secretary of State Henry Kissinger decided to resume bombing against Khey Sanh missiles (and possibly against Hanoi). The raids were more intense than the Christmas 1972 bombing.

However, after President Nixon had given his formal approval to resume the bombing, he learned that John Dean had begun to talk to the Watergate prosecutors. Nixon knew well that the renewal of the bombing would spur violent criticism in Congress, in the country, and also all over the world. He knew that John Dean's testimony was going to make life difficult for him. Later, to avoid dealing with severe criticism on two simultaneous major fronts, he rescinded his approval of the bombing. From then on, North Vietnamese infringements continued without check.

The second thing was the U.S. Congressional mood. The grand illusion of Vietnamization failed to take into account that South VN had become dependent on the United States not only materially but psychologically. Nowhere was it truer than in the leadership of South Vietnamese Armed Forces. They were trained, equipped and tested in battle as an integral part of the American military machine. It was natural that the military leaders of South VN would become deeply attached to the security blanket of American technology and support. Each time South Vietnamese Armed Forces fought back a big offensive, it had massive support of American tactical and strategic bombing. So even at the end of 1974, many South Vietnamese generals continued to harbor the illusion that U.S. B-52 bombers would fly again to stem the Communist offensive.

The third thing was the fighting spirit of South Vietnamese Armed Forces. How was it and how was it supported? After the U.S. Congress began to slash military aid in 1974, South Vietnamese air power had been largely grounded. Rising oil prices and shortages of foreign exchange forced sharp cutbacks in flying time. Combat losses were 350 aircrafts, i.e. one-seventh of South Vietnamese Air Force. From the second half of 1974, South Vietnamese pilots could fly less than a dozen of the 64 giant chinook helicopters and only five of 34 C-130 Hercules transport planes.

In January 1975 after Phuoc Long province fell, President Ford immediately asked Congress to approve $300 million in additional aid for South VN. One State Department official said "the best Nguyen van Thieu can hope for is a stalemate." The Ford Administration tried to blame Saigon's reverses on Congressional failure to appropriate the extra $300 million. To support Ford's request, White House Press Secretary Ron Nessen cited an article from the North Vietnamese journal *Hoc Tap* (Studies) that seemed to tie the offensive of the Communists to a decline in the fighting capability of South Vietnamese armed forces.

From one angle, it was logical to argue that a reduction in U.S. aid to Saigon would encourage Hanoi. But it was equally logical to argue that even in the days when the United States was spending $2 billion a month in VN, the Communists were mounting general and costly offensives throughout South VN. With the presence of 16 North Vietnamese divisions (about 325,000 men) on South VN territory, one could hardly say that a comparatively small amount of aid would stop the North Vietnamese final assault.

But the major military problem in South VN was its internal deterioration. Incompetent leadership, corruption, profiteering by officers and low pay for enlisted men sapped the strength and the fighting spirit of South Vietnamese armed forces.

The strategic concept of defense in south VN had been formulated according to the 20-year government policy: fight for every inch of South Vietnamese territory. After the Communist offensive of 1972 and after the Paris cease-fire agreement of January 27, 1973, it was almost impossible for South VN to maintain that concept. The balance of power had been shifted dangerously against the South VN side. Given the increases of Russian and Chinese aid to North VN; given the decrease of the U.S. aid to South VN; given the presence of almost the whole North Vietnamese armed forces on South Vietnamese territory, it was easy to conclude that South VN was moving toward its final agony.

The deployment of South Vietnamese forces was carried out according to the strategic concept previously mentioned: five divisions in Military Region I (the 1st, 2nd and 3rd Army Division plus the Marine Division and the Paratrooper Division). Two strategic forces, the Marine Division and the Paratrooper Division were pinned down at Quang Tri Province. That disposition deprived South VN of any strategic reserve force,—two infantry divisions in Military Region II (the 22nd and 23rd Division),—three divisions in Military Region III (protecting Saigon capital the 5th, 18th and 25th infantry Division) and three divisions in Military Region IV (the 9th, 7th and 21st Division—protecting the rice basket of South VN).

Under normal conditions, South Vietnamese supply system was already vulnerable: the Communists could blow up any bridge at any time. The air transportation supply system was also vulnerable because it depended upon available air fields and the Communists could shell mortar and rocket on airstrips at any time. In brief, South Vietnamese armed forces were overextended and facing a big offensive, it would be practically impossible for Saigon to supply these divisions. They would be surely isolated and would be no less surely destroyed.

Finally, the passive defense strategy of the South Vietnamese government made its armed forces even more vulnerable. Each division had a static defensive mission. They were waiting to be attacked. And when North Vietnamese succeeded in concentrating a temporary force larger than the government's, South Vietnamese troops needed massive firepower support, which was unlikely to be forthcoming.

About two weeks before the Vietnamese Lunar New Year (Vietnamese and Chinese people celebrate their Lunar New Year according to Asian calendar, i.e. one month after western New Year), and two weeks after Western New Year 1975, North Vietnamese forces attacked Phuoc Long province. It was a remote province and government forces of that province received their supply items almost exlusively by air.

Nguyen van Thieu had repeatedly said that the Communists would launch another big offensive after the cease fire agreement of January 27, 1973 but the more he said about this eventual offensive, the less attention he got from South Vietnamese people and from opinion abroad. His government was so tricky that when he talked about a general offensive, people tended to think that it was only a pretext for Thieu to be more repressive. Besides, after repeatedly saying that there would be a communist general offensive, Thieu's administration did not change the Saigon defense strategy.

Phuoc Long province fell after few days of resistance. It was the first province capital to be captured by the Communists since Quang Tri was held in the 1972 offensive. The pattern for the collapse has been set up. Lacking reinforcement and being isolated by the attacking forces, Phuoc Long province could not but surrender. Well-informed foreign observers in Saigon believed that Nguyen van Thieu simply gave up Phuoc Long to avoid sending reinforcements. He did not have any strategic reserve units in Saigon.

But the fall of Phuoc Long suggested matters of graver importance: the truth about the weakness of South Vietnamese after the cease fire agreement of 1973; the weak position of President Ford regarding his request for extra aid for South VN; and the comparative unconcern of the international community. The final assault would begin as soon as Hanoi obtained evidence that President Ford could do nothing more than request additional aid for Saigon.

Just a few days before March 10, 1975 (March 10 was the day North Vietnamese troops began to attack Ban Me Thuot, a highland province about 160 miles north of Saigon), U.S. Secretary of Defense, James Schlesinger, was still insisting that there would be no major Communist offensive until 1976, when it would neatly coincide with the U.S. Presidential elections. The fall of Phuoc Long province was a serious warning: Hanoi would not be satisfied with a remote province like Phuoc Long.

After Phuoc Long, Vietnamese Nationalists felt that the end would not be too far. They still wanted to save South VN from the Communist rule. But at the House of Representatives, more than two-thirds were simply Thieu's valets. The Speaker, Nguyen ba Can, originally a third rate clerk, was so servile that he agreed with general Nguyen khac Binh (Commander of South Vietnamese national police and Thieu's hangman) to beat and to torture any representative who acted against Thieu's hangman) to beat and to torture any representative who acted against Thieu, either by statement or by organizing opposition. Since, never had there been so many plainclothed policemen as there were under Thieu's rule. Before Nguyen Ba Can's own eyes, a group of oppositionist representatives were savagely beaten by Thieu's police. Finally, only the South Vietnamese private press raised a true oppositionist voice in South VN. Consequently, South Vietnamese journalists became Thieu's super-enemy. South Vietnamese people began to understand that these journalists did not fight only against a communist rule: they also fought for human rights in South VN. Until the end of December 1974, only the voice of South Vietnamese journalists still had influence. Even disciplined military and civilian servants in Thieu's Administration could not but admire and secretly cooperate with these journalists.

In Winter 1974, the scrap metal affair flared up into a national scandal: the foreign press, and especially the U.S. *Stars and Stripes Daily Paper,* even mentioned the names of Vietnamese generals involved in that scandal. Of course, the most guilty were General Nguyen Van Thieu and General Tran Thien Khien (ironically, one was President and the other was Prime Minister). Vietnamese daily newspapers reprinted these items and added more details provided by the men working in Thieu's and Khiem's Staff.

Thieu gave orders to spare nobody in the South Vietnamese press. The easiest way to hurt these journalists was to accuse them of being communist agents. On a TV show, Thieu's hangmen tried to make people think that all the Vietnamese journalists put in jail were communists. The funniest thing in this story was that most of these journalists had been on the communist "black list" for a long time. For instance Truong Cam Vinh, member of the Vietnam Quoc Dan Dang (the Vietnamese Kuomintang—and his father was killed by the Viet

Cong) was accused of being a communist or infiltrator into South Vietnamese press. One thing was sure: these journalists were fervent nationalists and also fervent anti-corruption fighters.

Evidence indicated this might be the last time that Thieu tortured South Vietnamese. The mood in the U.S. Congress was extremely critical of his rule. The U.S. Congress decided to send a six man delegation to Indochina. For the first time since the United States began to aid South VN in 1954, South Vietnamese people saw a truly uncompromising congressional delegation in Saigon. That delegation pointed out that it would visit any place at any time it liked, and would not accept any pre-planned program offered by the U.S. Embassy in Saigon. This visit might have been the ultimate balm after sufferings inflicted by the close cooperation between successive U.S. Administrations and successive South Vietnamese corrupt Administrations. The visit provided important evidence that since 1954, the American Congress and the American people had never been provided true and adequate information on the War in VN. Any South Vietnamese official delegation going abroad, either to the United States or to any other western country, parroted the result of a secret agreement between the U.S. Embassy in Saigon and the Saigon government. By this arrangement, the U.S. Congress and the American people would be contacted by delegations which knew only the unique song: praising the corrupt regime in Saigon. The arrangement offended any U.S. official delegation visiting Saigon.

But some U.S. Congressmen always managed to know the truth about VN. They had their own channels of information. And they knew the reality of the so-called South Vietnamese official delegations. So, at the end of February 1975, six U.S. Congressional members were in touch with members of the opposition force in South VN. Of course, Thieu's secret policemen used any means to prevent Vietnamese from meeting these U.S. Congressmen. Many persons were arrested after the departure of the U.S. delegation. Their crime was to tell the truth. The visit of the American delegation, was highlighted by the story of Madam Ngo Ba Thanh. She was one of the noisiest figures of the opposition in South VN and was often victimized by Thieu's repressive policy. The day the American delegation arrived in Saigon, Madame Thanh continued to be kept like a prisoner in her own house. But Thieu's administration told Mrs. Bella Abdzug (a U.S. representative) that Madame Thanh was as free as any free people in VN. When Mrs. Abdzug arrived at Madame Thanh's, she saw barbed wires clearly all around the house. Thieu continued to say that Madame Thanh was free.

Finally, the U.S. Congress knew the whole truth about VN. But it knew it too late. Still, the past had been prologue.

In the spring of 1972, when Richard Nixon began his summit meetings with the big Communist powers, North VN launched its biggest offensive in the South. This time from the 17th parrallel southward, 15 North Vietnamese divisions openly crossed the Demilitarized Zone and for the third time since 1968, South Vietnamese armed forces were outgunned. Many brand new Russian and Chinese weapons appeared for the first time in VN—extremely deadly. In their attempt to flee from Quang Tri province southward, many South Vietnamese civilicans died on National Highway No. I from Quang Tri to the old imperial capital of Hue called "Street without Joy." North Vietnamese artillery deliberately shelled these refugees. In other provinces, the situation was repeated.

For many reasons, and partly because of the new U.S. policy of detente, there was almost no reaction in world opinion. It was understandable: when the

United States of America, the world number one superpower and also the leader of the Free World—became so friendly to long time enemies like Russia and Red China, who would care about life and freedom in a small country in Southeast Asia—although the same small country had many times been given the romantic name of "outpost of the Free World"? Besides, the image of the Saigon Government had been so diminished through the years that many might have concluded that it was not worthwhile to save South VN.

The timing of the Communist offensive of 1972 had been wisely prepared. First, 1972 was an election year in the United States. For better or for worse, Nixon could not use daring tactics against North VN. More than anyone else, Nixon had to be aware of the war-weary mood of the American people. The most he could do to help South VN would be the renewal of bombing in North VN, but the experience of the Johnson administration showed that the United States could not expect North VN to surrender after the American bombing campaigns. Nixon would have to reduce even the air support for South Vietnamese troops. After the two invasions in Cambodia (April 1970) and in Laos (February 1971), Nixon could not do anything but comply at least partly with the will of the U.S. Congress. Any reduction of American air support to South Vietnamese armed forces would have serious effects on the morale of these troops. They had been trained to fight "all American." Now, once again, they found themselves obsolete before an enemy equipped with the most sophisticated weapons in the world. In fact, North VN had every kind of weapon, short of nuclear power.

On the other hand, South Vietnamese morale had been badly hurt after the invasions of Cambodia and Laos. It was difficult to imagine that South Vietnamese could fight effectively after suffering so many disadvantageous changes in South VN and from international politics.

Elated by the so called detente, the Western world believed that the Communist bloc would decrease tension in many parts of the world. The 1972 offensive demonstrated quite the contrary: Communist war by proxy continued even with increased violence: Political turmoil in Spain, Portugal and in Italy was only the prelude of the Second Cold War stirred up by International Communism.

The great offensive across the DMZ in March 1972 was a big decision from North Vietnamese leaders. Hanoi took a calculated risk to rub out the Demilitarized Zone. It was concerned with three things: American public opinion, world opinion and the fighting capacity of South Vietnamese armed forces. In early 1972, there was already some evidence that the U.S. Congress would use the power of the purse to stop the war, no matter what the result. The corrupt South Vietnamese government and the so called detente policy of the United States had deemphasized the war. Besides, world opinion would face a "fait accompli" after the crossing of the Demilitarized Zone. Finally, the self destructive nature of Thieu's banditry rule began to demoralize South Vietnamese armed forces.

Practically speaking, North VN could not hope to make a clean sweep of South VN at the first offensive wave. The most important thing was to launch a massive attack without significantly changing world public opinion. Therefore, North Vietnamese troops did not attack many objectives at the same time. World attention was diverted and the shock diluted. The next step would be a final assault. In fact, North Vietnamese tactics worked well: there was no longer a demilitarized zone between the two Vietnams.

After the shameful voting of the full power law in June 1972, the morale of South Vietnamese people was so low that a famous Vietnamese lawyer had to complain "Thieu's regime hurt our people so much that even a communist regime would be better for South VN." This complaint came from lawyer Do Nang An, member of the Saigon Bar Association.

In June of 1972, Nixon announced that the U.S. ground combat role had ended. At the same time, the South Vietnamese had learned about the "scrap metal affair." Scrap metal was surplus military hardware left behind by the U.S. troops. Its value was about four billion dollars. Of course, it was a big pie. Nguyen Van Thieu and his Prime Minister, Tran Thien Khiem, competed with each other. Many Vietnamese generals were involved in it. The South Vietnamese people realized that Thieu's gang was not satisfied with the incredible amount of money they had already gained by banditry rule. Now, the scrap metal affair further enriched them.

While Thieu and his gang continued to get richer and richer, South Vietnamese people witnessed the most tragic scene in Vietnamese history: wounded soldiers began to beg in Saigon streets. Desertion increased day after day: Deserters did not surrender to the communists, but stopped fighting for Thieu's banditry rule. Another warning that collapse was closer than one could imagine.

In the United States on the very eve of the election, Henry Kissinger declared "peace is at hand." Peace was at hand when almost the whole of North Vietnamese armed forces was already on South Vietnamese territory; when North VN had wiped out the demilitarized zone; when the closest North Vietnamese armored unit could reach Saigon within an hour and a half.

When the Paris cease fire agreement was signed in Paris on January 27, 1973, there were still theoretically more than 600,000 regular South Vietnamese troops, not including the nearly 400,000 regional armed forces. With such power (total 1,100,000 armed men) there was no reason to be alarmed about South Vietnam's political future, providing that these armed men received adequate arms, ammunition and supplies. And in early 1973, it was practically possible for Thieu to carry out a strategic withdrawal from some remote and almost unpopulated areas. After January 1973, a realistic strategist would think about abandoning some areas to avoid overextending South Vietnamese armed forces. Of course, this eventual withdrawal would not be the only measure needed to save South VN from collapse. But it might work, providing that South Vietnamese soldiers and civilians continued to maintain high morale. This would permit the American administration to request more aid for South Vietnam. And of course, this withdrawal would have serious significance only if South Vietnamese leaders could contemplate accepting the Viet Cong into South Vietnamese political life.

But to Richard Nixon, a withdrawal leading to a neutralist government in South VN was not compatible with his famous doctrine. Therefore, Thieu continued to promote his usual slogan: no concession of land or population to the communists, preserving both at any cost.

Only after the Paris Peace Agreement was signed did the whole truth about the strength of South Vietnamese armed forces become known. After 1965, the United States provided economic and military assistance to an army of 1,100,000 men in South VN. Now, it has become clear that since 1968, there had never been full strength in South Vietnamese forces. Only half of 600,000 regular troops really fought in battles. The remainder was simply ghost soldiers: their monthly salary was paid to their commander. Even when there were casualties, many commanders did not report them to superiors: they continued to receive the pay of those dead soldiers.

One of the most famous province chiefs under Thieu's banditry rule was Lt. Colonel Huynh Buu Son. He was proposed by Thieu's nephew as chief of Phuoc Tuy province. He remained in this position many months, despite a very strong press campaign sponsored by Lt. Colonel Vu Van Quy, representative of Phuoc Tuy Province at the house of representatives. Representative Quy was among some high ranking officers who were Thieu's debtors but who really wanted Thieu to carry out radical changes in South Vietnamese political life. He gathered proof about the crimes of the chief of Phuoc Tuy province. Examples are: one half of the regional forces of his province were ghost soldiers. The rest provided manpower to go into the jungle to get wood for the wife of this chief. Because Phuoc Tuy province was a forest land, it was also a communist stronghold. Many regional soldiers lost their lives while searching for wood. Colonel Huynh Buu Son did not report these strange casualties to the 3rd corps commander (his immediate chief). A 2nd lieutenant learned about this and informed Rep. Vu Van Quy. Shortly after, the 2nd Lt. was killed under mysterious conditions.

The prison of Phuoc Tuy province was permanently full of prisoners: this was the most flourishing business of any province chief. According to a Thieu decree, anybody could be put in jail without being charged providing that the province chief or the district chief thought this persons "could be a danger to national security." Of course, the suspect could be free again if he or she was ready to pay a certain sum of money. The ingenious Colonel Huynh Buu Son invented the most daring tactics of the Nguyen Van Thieu era: pretty women suspects had to become prostitutes to get money for the province chief. This writer was shocked and horrified when he read the file shown by respresentative Vu Van Quy in October 1974 in Saigon: 200 pages of documents, photos, complaints, witness declarations, etc. . . .

Representative Vu Van Quy sent a copy of that file to Nguyen Van Thieu but Nha did everything to prevent Thieu from interferring in his business. Representative Quy also received help from many Vietnamese newspapers which published the crimes of the chief of Phuoc Tuy province. Nha continued to defend his client until a few weeks before the collapse of South VN.

Among those Vietnamese criminals who played an important role in destroying South Vietnamese fighting power is listed General Khuyen. Three years before the collapse of South VN, he was assigned the vital role of chief of South Vietnamese armed forces supply service. Khuyen might be considered one of many extraordinary generals: he saw no action from the day he got the rank of second lieutenant to the day he was named three star general in charge of supplies for the whole South Vietnamese armed forces.

Khuyen's men made money in a quick manner. The tactics were simple: these men did not deliver enough supplies to every unit in the army. On the paper for example, unit B could receive one thousand gallons of gasoline. But Khuyen's men would deliver to that unit only 800 or 900 gallons. The supply officer of that unit had to sign a receipt for one thousand gallons. If he did not agree to sign, his unit would meet many difficulties in getting supply items the next time.

In the combat units many soldiers had to resort to a desperate solution to feed their families. They sold anything they could steal from the army: gasoline, weapons, equipment, hardware, etc. . . . . It was the last chapter in the history of non-communist South Vietnam: while Thieu's gang made money from the trades of blood, of power, and of justice, South Vietnamese soldiers sold weapons and supply items to prolong the agony of their families.

Along South Vietnamese borders, many province headmen quietly sold rice, gasoline and even weapons and ammunitions to the communists. The most flourishing province was Tay Ninh, close to the Cambodian border: the communists could buy any quantity of rice they wanted, providing they paid a high price. It was inhuman when one thought that these same province chiefs forced their soldiers to fight against communists.

But the most horrible crimes of Thieu's gang were committed by the national police and judges at all levels. As if they had the feeling that the end was near, policemen and judges cooperated closely to make money. Thanks to Thieu's decree laws, policemen and judges arrested the citizens at will. The palace of the supreme court was close to the Saigon court of appeals and it was convenient for policemen and judges to carry out their business. For any reason, a man or a woman could be put in jail. If that person had money, he could buy his freedom. If not, he or she might stay in jail indefinitely. The amount of money would decide which side was guilty. In this inhuman business, policemen and judges had the cooperation of many corrupt lawyers. Instead of using laws and procedures to defend their clients, these lawyers bargained with the policemen and with the judges. If the lawyer happened to be a young female, she could win easily, providing that she knew enough to be friendly to some judge. At county court level, judges were generally young and tended to be more corrupt than their older colleagues. The most effective way for a defendant to escape was to bargain at the highest level, at the Supreme Court. If the defendant paid enough money, he would surely win. The only supreme justice who preserved his integrity was Judge Tran Minh Tiet. He was elected Chief of the Supreme Court in 1969 and was praised by all honest Vietnamese lawyers in a decision Thieu's administration lost in a very important case: a citizen filed a suit against Thieu's government on the grounds that this government had "invented" an unconstitutional tax decree. The citizen won his case and Thieu's personal prestige was badly hurt. Shortly after, Thieu bought five of nine supreme judges and succeeded in ousting Judge Tran Minh Tiet from his position.

Before the collapse, there was one last battle between Thieu's gang and Vietnamese Nationalists. It occurred shortly before Nixon's resignation. Day after day, the South Vietnamese people's understanding grew that North VN was preparing to take over South VN. Immediately after the Paris cease fire agreement, North VN had modernized the Ho Chi Minh trail. At the end of 1974, intelligence sources reported that North VN was ready to launch its last assault in South VN at any time. In spite of the detente between the U.S. and Red China, and between the U.S. and Russia, North VN continued to receive more and more sophisticated weapons from the two communist giants.

The silent majority prepared for the worst. But true Nationalists wanted their revolution at the eleventh hour. By their nature, these Nationalists had chosen the moderate formula: they would protest without resorting to violence. Of course, this moderate course met the violent reaction of Thieu's gang. Even some of Thieu's agents recognized that his police force was more violent to the Vietnamese Nationalists than to the Communists. It was Thieu's permanent policy: he was more afraid of the Nationalists than of the Communists.

It was understandable that the Vietnamese Nationalists came to the revolution decision when they thought that Nixon would be impeached. As long as Nixon stayed in power, he would surely continue to support Nguyen Van Thieu. The Vietnamese Nationalists hoped that a new President of the United States would help South VN improve the Saigon government. They began to react openly after Nixon's resignation.

The popular anti-corruption movement, the struggle for freedom of the press and the activities of South Vietnamese politicans were the ultimate reaction of those who did not want to see a communist government in South VN. It was, of course, a desperate reaction: how could they save South VN from the collapse, when Thieu's banditry rule had been undermining South VN politically and militarily since 1967? Thieu's policy helped the communists much more than did Russian and Chinese aid to North VN.

Two weeks after the Vietnamese Lunar New Year (1975) the final North Vietnamese campaign began. This campaign was smaller in scale but far more devastating than the Tet offensive of 1968 and the spring offensive of 1972. At first, it seemed no more than the communist's usual harassment activities. But later, it turned into a display of classic communist tactics. They mounted spoiling attacks at the roads into the highlands. Then, they feinted an attack at Military Region II at Pleiku. By this feint attack, the communists drew the reserves of South Vietnamese 23rd infantry divison out of Ban Me Thuot provincial capital. Deprived of its garrison, Ban Me Thuot was overrun after a three-day siege.

In the wake of a determined North Vietnamese offensive, Thieu gathered with his four military region commanders. After several hours of discussion, they came to a conclusion: the highlands and the North were indefensible. After that grim meeting, Thieu himself flew to Pleiku to give his fatal order: retreat to the seacoast. But unfortunately for South Vietnamese people, Thieu did not give the commanders a chance to lay the complex plans necessary to keep such a risky military maneuver from turning into a tragic rout.

Thieu's strategy was clear: to cut off the central highlands and the northernmost provinces to save the body of South VN. The truncated map of South VN would include only most of military region III and IV, i.e. eleven provinces around Saigon and 15 provinces of the Mekong Delta farther in the south, along with some pockets of control at the seacoast as far north as the expected new line of defense at Da Nang.

Thieu's new defense strategy seemed plausible on paper: since the highland provinces were heavily infested with communist forces, the retreat should allow South VN to mass its units better in concentrated areas. In the north, Quang Tri and Thua Thien also had been outside of Saigon's control since spring 1972: five divisions (including the two strategic reserve forces) were wastefully deployed to protect the farthest area at the end of the supply line. It was a region that produced almost nothing and required importation of almost everything, including rice.

But on battlefields, one thing was clear: the strategic retreat ordered by Nguyen Van Thieu developed into a human tragedy of colossal proportions: a military collapse, a tragic political battle and a refugee disaster. Thieu's scheme had created a disastrous morale problem for his army and his people.

The North Vietnamese assault on Ban Me Thuot decimated the South Vietnamese 23rd Infantry Division. After the fall of Ban Me Thuot, Thieu realized that Pleiku and Kontum were also badly outgunned. In the coastal city of Nha Trang, Thieu met secretly on March 14 with General Pham Van Phu, commander of military region II. He decided to take the most dangerous step: strategic retreat. And during the evacuation of central highlands, Thieu made another crucial decision. He flew to Da Nang to meet General Ngo Quang Chuong, commander of military region I (and also South Vietnam's best field commander). He decided to pull back the main line of defense from Quang Tri and Thua Thien (Hue) down to the coastal city of Da Nang.

In military art and technique, strategic retreat was considered a most difficult action. The retreat of Napoleon and the retreat of Hitler in World War II were the most striking examples: morale and survival of the army were at stake. In South VN, it was national survival which was at stake.

From the time President Thieu met General Phu, commander of military region II to the time the retreat started, only six hours elapsed. Thieu did not consult with U.S. officials in either Saigon or Washington in advance of his daring decision. Perhaps it was because Ambassador Graham Martin was on home leave in North Crolina. Probably Thieu wished to show independence of Washington out of pique for not getting more military aid.

In ordering the retreat, Thieu deliberately overlooked the civilian population. And in doing that, he also forgot thousands of soldiers' families. Families left behind became a major factor in transforming the retreat into a rout. The lower level combat units in the highland provinces did not receive enough details for preparing the withdrawal. Some units did not receiv any orders at all. These cruel things exploded into an outburst of rage.

Frustrated by successive corrupt governments, South Vietnamese armed forces were waiting for a reason to give up their fight. The majority of South Vietnamese officers simply tried to look for safety in the rear area because they thought that now, more than ever, it was not worthwhile to die for Thieu's gang. Perhaps they didn't realize that their actions generated similar actions from their enlisted men.

The civilian population of the highland provinces was abandoned by Thieu but these people continued to flee to the government side, no matter how bloody and how deadly was their escape. They had no choice. Although there was the theory that "we should cease supporting the corrupt governments of Lon Nol and Thieu," thousands upon thousands of Cambodian and Vietnamese refugees preferred those corrupt governments to the alternative.

Rarely in human military history, could one find such a tragic mixed retreat. That retreat became more tragic when evidence showed the communists deliberately shelled rockets, mortars and every kind of their deadly weapons on civilians. The refugees preferred the death chosen by themselves than by the one imposed by the communist rulers.

In his office at Pleiku, General Pham Van Phu angrily wept after he received orders from Thieu to retreat by a phone call from Saigon Presidential Palace. On his shoulders, there was not only his prestige, there was also the prestige of the whole South Vietnamese armed forces. At least, Phu felt Thieu had to let them fight some decisive battles, to show their courage, their fighting spirit and their will to die if necessary to preserve a non-communist South VN. But Thieu bluntly told General Phu "You have to execute my orders."

Four ranger groups, each composed roughly of three battalions and a supporting unit defending Kontum were shifted to the coastal province of Tuy Hoa, to be followed shortly after by the 1200 truck refugee convoy from Pleiku.

General Phu moved his headquarters from Pleiku to Nha Trang, farther in the south. South Vietnamese air force men destroyed 68 aircraft in Kontum airfield to keep them from falling into enemy hands. These had been grounded earlier because of a lack of spare parts. South Vietnamese warplanes flew in and ARVN forces moved southward and bombed every bridge after the ground troops crossed. No one was planning to return.

In a short time, the population of Pleiku, rich and poor, scrambled aboard any means of transportation available. The rest simply grabbed their children and their portable belongings and trudged off on foot. In the week beginning March 16, 1975, a convoy of nearly 4000 vehicles and about 100,000 refugees left Pleiku for the coastal province of Tuy Hoa (Phu Yen). This convoy inched its way down National route number 7, a long abandoned route.

Most of the refugees carried little food and no water at all. They marched forward wearily but as fast as their legs could carry them. The convoy was led by a detachment of Vietnamese military engineers which patched the road and shored up bridges. At first, the evacuation went so smoothly that it raised the suspicion that President Thieu had a secret deal with the communists, a trade of territory for population. Soldiers and civilians in the convoy from Pleiku thought that President Thieu had agreed to surrender the central highlands to the communists in return for a guarantee of safe passage for all refugees to the coast. But as a way to deny that hope, about 45 miles down the road from Pleiku, the convoy was halted by a squad of communist troops. Because there were so many vehicles pressing from behind that the convoy could not stop, it was trapped in a blood bath. From the jungle, the communists showered the refugees with heavy artillery shells, mortar rounds and rockets. South Vietnamese soldiers opened a path, a bloody path. They were so angry when they saw civilians deliberately killed by the communists that they fought like angry tigers. They died and the civilians died with them. There were also South Vietnamese helicopter gun ships flying to their rescue but the convoy stretched out for at least 20 miles. These miserable people became easy targets to the communists. A horrified chopper pilot said that when he flew low, he could see human bodies scattered alongside the road, the line going back for miles.

Before the attack of Ban Me Thout, Communist cadres urged the local population to remain. The communists needed the local people to run tea and rubber plantations of the highland provinces. And if the local people chose to stay, it would be a signifiant propaganda victory for the communist side. Now, the massive exodus of so many people once again denied the communist. Thus, it was understandable when the communist artillery drew no distinction between military and civilians.

Many days after, the convoy limited into Tuy Hoa province. But the refugees found that this was only the beginning of their long and bloody exodus. From Hue, in the North to Saigon in the South, National Highway No. 1 swarmed with thousands of displaced people.

In Quang Tri and Hue, General Ngo Quang Chuoug had already lost the backbone of this defence. Thieu had ordered the Vietnamese paratroop division back to beef up the defence of the capital. The departure of this elite unit sent a shock wave through the streets of Hue. Without waiting for any order from Saigon, the mayor of Hue advised his people "leave as quickly as possible." The effect of such advice was disastrous to the military as well as for the civilians. In the evacuation from Pleiku, at least, South Vietnamese soldiers had the opportunity to withdraw together with their families. In Quang Tri and Hue, orders were so confused and the withdrawl so hasty, that many soldiers did not have time to warn their families. Incapable of taking revenge on Nguyen Van Thieu, these soldiers killed their commanders. Just as in Pleiku, many Vietnamese units did not receive an order southward. After the paratrooper division, the Marine division quit the Hue perimeter and boarded troopships at nearby Huong Dien District.

General Pham Van Phu (military region II) and General Ngo Quang Chuong (military region I) were victims of one of the greatest military routes of recent history. Thousands of their panicked troops threw down their weapons and joined an almost endless stream of refugees heading for Saigon, the end of the road.

In Military Region II, roughly half of 179,000 government troops were out of action. The 23rd division was decimated, with only 700 of its 9,000 troops able to regroup in Nha Trang coastal city. Five of seven ranger groups, two of four cavalry regiments and eight of twelve artillery battalions were out of action. Most simply fled, joining the civilian refugee stream. The same thing happened to about 10,000 of 152,000 troops in the five northern provinces constituting military region I.

The final chapter of Saigon government's route from the north began with the collapse of Da Nang. According to Thieu's scheme, the northern line of defense of South VN would be set up at Da Nang. To show his willingness to fight, General Ngo Quang Chuong moved his family from Saigon to Da Nang. They arrived only to witness the fall of this important seaport.

Using experience drawn from the evacuation of Pleiku, the communists changed their tactics. Instead of launching attacks, they simply infiltrated their men into the stream of the refugees in Da Nang. They did not need to attack. The city would fall by itself because of the collapse of public order.

In a matter of a few days, Da Nang's normal population had been tripled. The real source of trouble was not civilians but communists infiltrators and 100,000 government soldiers whose units disintegrated in the withdrawal from Hue, Quang Tri and the provincial capitals of Quang Tin and Quang Ngai in the south. In that extremely confused situation, Vietnamese military police were completely unable to control and to check who were South Vietnamese government soldiers, who were communist infiltrators. Later, when a part of the refugee stream arrived at Phu Quoc Island, government forces arrested 28 infiltrators and the refugees recognized them as the most wicked among those who roamed the streets robbing and shooting wildly. These infiltrators could not justify that they were real South Vietnamese Marines. They were shot on the shore of Phu Quoc Island witnessed by many refugees.

There are serious reasons to believe that the most horrible crimes had been committed by communist infiltrators. For instance, in the peninsula of Son Tra, five miles from Da Nang, there was a concentration of many soldiers of unknown units. Of course, at that time, nobody thought of checking each other to find out who were really South Vietnamese soldiers, who might be communist infiltrators. When a communist put on a South Vietnamese uniform, he became a government soldier and any horrible crime committed by him might be condemned by any observers as "crime committed by South Vietnamese government soldiers." Brigadier General Do Van Diem arrived at Son Tra peninsula when the confusion in Da Nang city was at its peak. He was escorted by some of his bodyguards sitting on a military jeep. When his jeep rode right into the military installation where there was the big concentration, his bodyguards were halted by an armed man in uniform (by night, it was difficult to check his uniform). This man said "don't enter . . . they are liquidating each other." Then, General Diem's bodyguards heard machine gun fire. When they asked about it, they got this answer "they killed General Diem. You better flee or else, you would be killed too." When the communists launched the offensive of 1972, General Diem was a colonel, brigade commander of the 1st infantry division. His soldiers loved him and it was difficult to believe that those who killed him were his former soldiers of the 1st infantry division.

The purpose of the communists was to create chaos and panic in that strategic coastal city, so that Da Nang would crumble from within. And their infiltrators succeeded in carrying out this mission.

In the three days between the beginning of disorder and the fall of Da Nang, many thousands of refugees swarmed aboard any means of evacuation. Even garbage barges were used to evacuate. As many as 90,000 refugees succeeded in escaping before the communists fired rockets at the ships to drive them away.

The trip south was a horrible nightmare. On one vessel, men in Vietnamese Marine uniform killed 25 civilians to win their place on the ship. On another, refugees were raped and robbed. Some barges spent many days at sea without food or water. When this unhappy armada finally landed at Nha Trang, a coastal city 280 miles to the south, there were at least 100 refugees (most of them were children) dead from thirst and exposure.

But worse was these refugees had endured the horrors vainly. Days after, major ports in South Vietnam collapsed one by one, and thousands of refugees from the north and from the central highlands, coupled with those who lived along coastal areas, fell into communist hands: Qui Nhon, Tuy Hoa and then Nha Trang. When Nha Trang was plunged into anarchy, the U.S. consul in Nha Trang ordered evacuation. One hundred Vietnamese employees and their families were left behind because the Americans brought in only one small C-47 transport. The lives of these Vietnamese were in jeopardy.

In Cam Ranh Bay, a once important U.S. strategic base, leaderless Marines went on a rampage when their evacuation ships arrived from Da Nang. They took over cars and military vehicles, robbed refugees and even fired on friendly helicopters and charter aircraft seeking to land to evacuate refugees.

About 200,000 refugees (many of them were soldiers) arrived in Nha Trang, doubling this city's population. To avoid the civilian panic, Nha Trang made an effort to seal itself off from the war. Newly arriving refugees were rerouted to another checkpoint, where they were promptly routed back to the one from which they had just arrived. At unthinkable sums of money, rich people managed to get out of Nha Trang by buying small fishing boats. They had seen the discreet departure of the Poles and Hungarians who were local representatives of the useless International Commission of Control and Supervision.

News of a desperate and heroic South Vietnamese armed forces action came from North of Qui Nhon port. Understrength, outgunned and getting only poor air and artillery support, for nearly two weeks, the ARVN 22nd infantry division held Binh Khe Pass against two reinforced North Vietnamese divisions. They paid a heavy price for their gallantry: nearly two thirds were killed or injured. Finally, that division had to give way, leaving open the route to Qui Nhon, the third largest port in South Vietnam. When Qui Nhon died, so did Nha Trang, 100 miles to the south.

The enemy was moving faster than people anticipated. Clearly, that latter city would fall. But many refugees began to realize further flight was no longer a guarantee of safety. And they bitterly thought that for all their fears of life under the communists, the Vietnamese who were left behind may have been more fortunate! Now, terrified soldiers hurriedly sought to shed their now incriminating identities. In spite of the evacuation of Nha Trang, it was an open city for days. Finally, the communists took charge of it, along with Cam Ranh Bay, where about 50,000 refugees were dumped before any preparation was made to receive them.

The rout did not end here. Dalat, the hill station that supplied a great part of Saigon's fresh vegetables fell. Then Phan Thiet and Phan Rang where Thieu had planned to establish the new line of defense capitulated. So, from March 10, 1975 to the first week of April 1975, the government had abandoned 17 of South VN's 44 provinces, two thirds of its land area and about half of its 18 million people. In military region III (area around Saigon), there were some skirmishes. There was even a speculation of an attack on Saigon by the beginning of the second week of April.

Incredibly, most cities and towns were given up with hardly a shot being fired. Even the communists were surprised these cities surrendered so quietly. Three days after the retreat from Nha Trang, a Vietnamese Lt. Colonel (artillery branch) who had fled down the coast, drove up to the military region II headquarters and found it empty. No communists troops. He called Saigon and got permission to take command of Nha Trang. Nobody knew what became of this officer when the communist troops moved in. Phan Thiet and Phan Rang were also evacuated before any communist combat unit was in sight. The communists were unprepared.

The real enemy of South VN then was not North Vietnamese divisions but spreading upheaval, fear and chaos among the South Vietnamese people and Armed Forces. The common people were resigned and they were preparing for the worst. For them, it was the loss of family and nation. None of them seemed to know what to do now. It was everyone for himself.

On March 26, 1975 claiming a plot against his government, Thieu's secret police arrested hordes of people in Saigon. Among them, there were those who had been in touch with former vice president Nguyen Cao Ky a few weeks before to try to convince Thieu to resign. It was strange that most of the arrested were strong nationalists. It was rumored that the U.S. ambassador in Saigon had advised Thieu to jail these nationalists to avoid trouble before the collapse of Saigon.

Another event seemed to reinforce the theory that the U.S. government was prepared for the collapse of Saigon. On March 27, 1975 after the fall of Da Nang, an American official working for the U.S. Department of State tried to communicate with a Vietnamese professional journalist in Saigon by telephone. The American was married to a Vietnamese woman and the journalist was his wife's brother-in-law. Twice on that morning of March 27, 1975, this American warned in their telephone conversation that "within four weeks, it would be completely finished for South VN. Nothing can save it. We will send you air tickets. Try to get necessary papers from the U.S. Embassy in Saigon to get out before it is too late." At the same time, it was rumored the Americans had accomplished necessary preparations to receive American citizens evacuated from Saigon and eventually some Vietnamese. Later, it was confirmed that this "Pacific Island" was Guam.

On the evening of April 4, 1975, Thieu delivered a radio and television broadcast speech in which he blamed the communists, the Americans, the Vietnamese commanders, the Vietnamese armed forces and the population for the chaos and for the panic. But he did not say anything about his responsibility when he gave his fatal orders for the great retreat that signaled the end of his government.

If South Vietnamese people were surprised not to see Thieu confess his guilt, they were much more surprised when they heard Thieu saying that he had accepted the resignation of the Tran Thien Khiem cabinet and that he had asked the speaker of the lower house Nguyen Ba Can to form a new government. Thieu said that it would not surrender to the communists. It would not accept a coalition government with the communists, but would be ready to negotiate with them on the basis of the Paris Peace Agreements. After Thieu's speech, among the foreign diplomatic circles in Saigon, there was this unanimous remark: "Nobody knows who Nguyen Ba Can is. This is Thieu's last funny show."

On April 5, 1975, at least seven people, including the top aide of former vice president Nguyen Cao Ky, were arrested in Saigon for "plotting a military coup d'etat against Mr. Thieu," according to Thieu's spokesman. It was the second crackdown on anti-Thieu leaders in nine days. U.S. officials in Washington were reported to feel increasingly that government forces, under present circumstances would fail to defend Saigon.

Thieu's presidential palace was turned into a veritable fortress. A formidable arsenal (sandbag fortifications, machine guns, anti aircraft guns, etc. . . .) was set up to defend against a communist attack on Saigon. But it was also Thieu's line of defense against his rapidly growing political opposition.

Pressures mounted on Thieu to resign. The South Vietnamese Senate, long a puppet body controlled by Thieu's lieutenants, unanimously approved a resolution equivalent to a no-confidence vote. The resolution blamed Thieu for the current debacle, charging him with "counting exclusively on military solutions" to solve "a war with many political characteristics." The resolution said Thieu was guilty of power abuse, corruption and social injustice. More than 20 of 41 senators voted for the resolution and called for Thieu's resignation. The moderate Archibishop Nguyen Van Binh agreed with the Senate and he even prayed aloud that Thieu would resign. Days later, the top VN ranking Buddhist, venerable Thich Tam Chau (who got many Thieu favors in the past), joined the resolution and said that Thieu should have to resign for the national interests.

Formerly, Thieu's opponents were far from united in a strong block. But this time, the danger was so imminent and so great that they succeeded to a certain degree in coordinating their campaigns against Thieu. Roman Catholic priest Tran Huu Thanh, leader of the Popular Anti-Corruption Movement was the principal liaison. High ranking officers in the army and high officials in the administration began to act against Thieu as if they would like to do something to redeem themselves. Secret orders were issued by Thieu and by his hangmen, Generals Dang Van Quang and Nguyen Khac Binh, to assassinate Father Tran Huu Thanh and some of his staff members. These orders were almost immediately reprinted by some secret officials and sent to Father Thanh.

None of Thieu's major opponents talked publicly of a military coup. Nguyen Cao Ky said "A coup is not the best way, for it only benefits the communists. We must have a smooth transition of power." But in a semi-secret meeting with prominent Vietnamese politicians at the office of Chinh Luan, the only political daily newspaper in Saigon, Nguyen Cao Ky promoted the bombing of Thieu's presidential palace. Of course, it was not the first time that Nguyen Cao Ky had changed his mind, even on serious matters. Besides, the opposition needed troops to mount a coup. Throughout many years, Vietnamese soldiers had been so frustrated that they became completely passive on political matters. There remained in their minds only two things: anti-communism and traditional obedience to their commanders as long as these commanders stayed with them to fight. To prevent a military coup Thieu hastily moved to reinforce his personal security. General Toan, one of the most corrupt Vietnamese generals, sacked in November 1974 for corruption, was named military region III commander including 13 provinces around Saigon.

Shortly, after Toan was named, General Hieu was killed under mysterious circumstances. General Hieu was one of the few clean generals, a former general secretary of the anti-corruption committee presided by vice-president Tran Van Huong. General Hieu had in his hands the files of high ranking corrupt men in military and civilian services.

The special military region of Saigon capital then received a new governor: General Nguyen Van Minh, a man able to do many things, except to command an important military operation.

In Saigon, after the fall of 17 of 44 provinces of South VN, the military, the religious leaders and the prominent politicians agreed that Thieu must go. But they seemed too passive or too shy to make a move. They could console themselves that they had discovered a truth a few days before the collapse of their country: that fear of bloodshed, amateurish politics and selfishness never pay off in a developing country endangered by a revolutionary war. They had to accept either a corrupt non-communist regime or communist rule since they had failed to change radically their line of thinking.

After the heroic battle of Binh Khe Pass in military region II another valiant action took place at the provincial capital of Xuan Loc, 40 miles northeast of Saigon. And just as in the battle of Binh Khe Pass, the South Vietnamese 18th infantry division was outgunned and outnumbered, but it held firm for two weeks. And for two weeks, South Vietnamese people hoped the ultimate hope: if the 18th division could hold on, then a new line of defense for South VN could be set up. The new map would include only the territories of military region III and military region IV. And if a new line of defense could hold on firmly, then South VN could negotiate an honorable agreement which would permit them at least to coexist peacefully with the communists.

The 18th infantry division was reinforced by many regional forces under the command of Colonel Pham Van Phuc, a former chief of the province of Binh Long. Shortly after the fall of Nha Trang, Colonel Phuc was named chief of province of Xuan Loc. About 44 years old, Colonel Phuc looked older than his age, because of bloody experiences with the communists. In 1954, as a company commander in a Vietnamese infantry battalion, he had participated in the great exodus of nearly one million North Vietnamese people southward after the Geneva Agreement of July 1954 was signed. His theory and his philosophy were simple: either he or the communists would win. No problem or coexistence. His military leadership was also simple. As long as you (the commander) stand firm and fight side-by-side with your soldiers, there would never be question of defeat.

In Xuan Loc Province, Colonel Phuc continued to carry out his philosophy. As soon as he took command, he met his officers and said simply "I am here to defend this province and to protect its population. I'll die right here to carry out my mission. No problem of surrender or defeatism. If you see me fleeing, kill me. On the contrary, if I see you trying to stop fighting, I'll kill you too." Xuan Loc province stood firm. For each soldier of this province killed in action, North Vietnamese troops lost from 10 to 15 men.

From Saigon and from many other parts in South VN, people sent congratulations to Colonel Phuc and to the 18th division. The Chinh Luan daily newspaper even received bottles of whiskey, money and gifts from the Saigonese to give to "the valiant Colonel Phuc and his men and to the 18th division who are fighting for the survival of South VN." People requested to visit the battle area. They were denied this trip for safety's sake.

This euphoria did not last long. The North Vietnamese brought more and more fresh troops to replace their extremely heavy casualties. Finally, they overran Xuan Loc Province. In the withdrawal, Colonel Phuc was the last man to leave and also the last man in the retreat column. Because he paid so much attention to his soldiers' welfare and so little attention to enemy fire, Colonel Phuc was killed as his column left the town.

The battle of Xuan Loc, the death of Colonel Pham Van Phuc and the death of so many South Vietnamese soldiers during the last days of non-communist South VN were an emotional and pathetic farewell dirge. These deaths did not prevent North VN from taking over South VN, but they were not wasted. They proved two things: in spite of successive corrupt regimes in South VN since 1954, millions of Vietnamese still preferred that regime to the communist alternative; and South Vietnamese soldiers with qualified commanders could defy any good army in Asia even in their most desperate hours.

When the remnants of Xuan Loc's defenders arrived in Saigon in mid-April 1975, it was plain that the military initiative now lay entirely with the communists. They effortlessly knocked off another provincial capital: Ham Tan. After the fall of Xuan Loc, there were 130,000 communist troops surrounding Saigon against just 60,000 ARVN troops. It was a disadvantageous ratio to the South Vietnamese. But what was more dangerous was the replacement problem. While it was almost impossible for South Vietnamese armed forces to replace their casualties, the North Vietnamese forces kept growing. They poured into South VN at least 1,000 fresh troops every day. For South VN, practically, the battle was lost.

For the time being, the communists spurned the military option. They wanted to blackmail the Saigonese for the last time: the surrender of the City or its destruction. In fact, an intact Saigon after the surrender would add more prestige to the communist victory because they could develop their propaganda theme: they conquered that city by docile surrender.

For two days, U.S. ambassador Graham Martin tried to get through President Nguyen Van Thieu to carry out a bitter task. He was conveying a message from the Viet Cong representatives in Paris. Beginning midnight Sunday, April 20, 1975, Thieu had exactly 48 hours to resign or Saigon would be leveled. (For months, Graham Martin, as did former ambassador Ellsworth Bunker, blindly supported Nguyen Van Thieu.)

At the same time, a delegation of South Vietnamese generals met with Thieu at his palace and presented their ultimate message. Thieu's resignation was the only way to avoid a disastrous military showdown. Thieu accepted the proposition immediately.

On Monday, April 21, 1975, the iron gates of Thieu's palace were opened and black limousines rolled up, carrying deputies, senators, justices and generals. They had only two hours notice. Having completely lost his credibility as a leader, Thieu announced his resignation.

In a hastily prepared 90 minute speech, he denounced Henry Kissinger and the U.S. by name and denounced the U.S. Congress by implication. He said that it was the loss of U.S. aid that had caused defeats and collapse of many cities in just six weeks. At times, his language was like that of a housewife counting money for shopping. He recalled the amount of American aid in the past and said that even if the U.S. Congress voted $300 million, it would prolong the fight of South VN for only 30 days. He emphasized that Washington failed to fulfill promises made when the Paris accords were signed. In Thieu's words, Washington promised that the U.S. would "immediately and vigorously supply South VN" in the event of a full-scale communist offensive. Before announcing his resignation he asked his countrymen to forgive him his past mistakes.

Vice-president Tran Van Huong was introduced by Thieu as the new president of South VN and Huong took the oath on the spot.

For North VN, Thieu's departure represented their great triumph after nearly 30 years fighting French, fellow Vietnamese and American soldiers. For South Vietnam, Thieu's departure had an extremely painful and bitter significance. Had it not been for the invasion of the communists, South VN might never have been able to get rid of Thieu's rule. It was much more painful when one thought that his banditry rule was strongly supported by successive American administrations from 1967. One thing was clear after Thieu's resignation: hundreds of billions of American aid could not help South Vietnamese people caught between the communists and Thieu's banditry rule. In his infinite stupidity, Thieu could not understand that his resignation speech damaged South Vietnamese as much or more than his disastrous orders for strategic retreat. In his words, South Vietnamese did not have their own sacred cause to fight for and the efficiency of South Vietnamese armed forces changed according to the level of the American aid.

Even at the very minute of his resignation, Thieu could not get rid of his innate dishonesty. Four and a half tons of gold that he took with him to Taiwan Island on April 26, 1975 proved his corruption.

With the fall of Xuan Loc, Bien Hoa air base (about 20 miles north of Saigon) was within the deadly range of the sophisticated 130 MM Russian-made guns of the North Vietnamese. Now, Saigon became the front line of defense of South Vietnam before the final assault. It is interesting to write about Saigon under siege in its last days.

For the first time since the communist offensive of 1968, Saigon was imperiled and its 3 million people knew it. This time, pressures were building slowly but surely. There was no overt panic, partly because the raging panic had not yet spread to the capital, and partly because the government was trying very hard to keep out refugees, deserters and saboteurs. Anyway, the old insouciance was disappearing. Residents and refugees were shaken, afraid and even desperate. The government abruptly moved the curfew from 10:00 P.M. to 8:00

P.M. and set up roadblocks on approaches to the city. The Saigonese interpreted these measures as a signal that serious trouble was on the way.

In appearance, Saigon retained almost an unreal normality. Food was no problem. There were plenty of vegetables and raw meat. Streets were filled with every kind of vehicle and were as noisy as usual. Every morning, the Mini-Rex Theater was crowded with teenagers. In fact, the Saigonese paid very little attention to the departure of Nguyen Van Thieu. Twenty-four hours after his resignation, people forgot him and their hope focused on a political settlement, which for better or for worse, could preserve Saigon from the destruction.

The 6,000 Americans in Saigon planned their departure hastily but quietly because they feared that the Americans who remained behind would become scapegoats for the anger and frustration of the Vietnamese. But most Vietnamese were still treating Americans with their traditional politeness.

Yet, there was a mood of desperation in the air. Advertising columns in the newspapers were full of notices reading "car for sale" and "house for sale." Cars and houses were selling at one fifth or one sixth of their former value, but there were almost no takers. Hundreds of troops strolled through the city and many men in camouflaged fatigues begged cigarettes from passersby.

Rumors came and sometimes were printed in some Saigon newspapers as though editors and readers wished they could be true. For instance, the rumor of Chinese invasion in North VN, a military coup in Hanoi and Vo Nguyen Giap (North Vietnamese defense minister) was killed by Truong Chinh (leader of North Vietnamese pro Chinese tendency), necessitating the withdrawal of many North Vietnamese divisions. Another rumor said that many U.S. Marine units had landed at Vung Tau, Da Nang and Cam Ranh ready to counterattack the communists.

Ironically, Thieu's banners still proclaimed military victories in the province of Xuan Loc though the province was lost. And not less ironically, life went on in many parts of Saigon as if the North Vietnamese divisions were thousands miles away. Members of Cercle Sportif Saigonnais continued to drink French Champagne as usual. In a tennis party within the Cercle Sportif Saigonnais, a Vietnamese lawyer happened to hear a conversation between the Hungarian Chief of Delegation in the ICCS in Saigon (International Commission of Control and Supervision) and Mr. Price, Australian ambassador in Saigon: (Price) "Do you think that Thieu's departure will make the political situation in Saigon better"? "I think yes, if it not too late, of course."

Many foreign embassies were closed from the beginning of April 1975, after the fall of Da Nang. At the end of March 1975, the West German Embassy in Saigon was closed "temporarily." But one week later, all German personnel were gone, and all Vietnamese personnel received one month's salary in advance, with the vague promise "we'll be back when Saigon gets a better government."

On Saigon streets, people were selling their precious belongings to raise money for tickets abroad. Many Chinese closed their shops and slipped away to Vung Tau or Rach Gia, where they would find ships to take them to Malaysia and Singapore. Almost all the banks in Saigon were besieged by hordes of Saigonese who wanted to withdraw their life savings. Many Indians and many bar girls had switched to money changing. At the end of March, the Vietnamese piaster fell to 2000 to $1, while the rate was 800 to $1 only a few days earlier. In mid April, before Thieu's resignation, the rate was 3000 to $1 and near the collapse, it was 4500 or 5000 to $1.

At dinner parties, at social gatherings, conversations turned only to questions about how to get out of VN. At times, trials at the Saigon County Court and the Saigon Court of Appeal were postponed because "the presiding judge was gone, because the prosecutor was gone."

To avert a mass exodus, the government had banned travel abroad and had banned any news in Vietnamese newspapers related to evacuation. A bribe of $2000 or even more was needed to get a passport and the passport office was crammed with applicants. The French Embassy and the Australian Embassy were besieged by a massive crowd looking for a visa. Each day some Vietnamese lost some friends, either Vietnamese or foreigners. If you did not receive the usual phone call from such or such friend within 24 hours, that meant he was gone. Officials at the U.S. Embassy were literally overwhelmed by applications. Many Americans in Saigon were hastily marrying their girlfriends so that their new wife would qualify for the preferential treatment accorded to an American citizen's wife.

By means of an affidavit, an American working for the Defense Attache Office could sponsor as many as 70 or 80 Vietnamese. Of course, it was not so simple to get out of Saigon. At the gate of Tan Son Nhat airport, you had to seek "understanding" with policemen, military policemen: if you gave them a tip of 5,000 VN$ or more, you could get into the airstrip. Many other people found another way to get in the airport. They gave some money to some Vietnamese air force men and these men would house them in their house at night. In the morning, they would take these people to the airstrip. Even without being sponsored by some American, people could get aboard if they gave at least $1000 to the men in charge of the manifest of each flight.

Many rich people tried to get out by ship. Each family subscribed a big sum of money to a family leader to buy or to hire a ship. The smallest ship was sold 60 millions VN$ after April 5, 1975. Those who could not buy a ship went to Vung Tau and waited for the collapse of Saigon. As long as Saigon stood, secret police and military policemen arrested anybody seeking way to get out of Saigon. While staying at Vung Tau, many rich people were robbed, and even killed mysteriously. Other people paid in advance, but when they were going to get aboard, the shipowner would not let them go because his ship had been "invaded by many strange people."

From the beginning of April 1975, there were hundreds who could not find a way to get out. There was one thing that many observers and many rich people could not understand: even the poor were worried about and feared communism. The odds against a Vietnamese escaping were 50 to 1 if he did not have an American connection (a relative who was American citizen or an American willing to guarantee a job or guarantee financial support).

The procedures were so difficult that many Vietnamese, even the rich, were resigned to stay. Some were preparing a so-called safe place for their families in case Saigon was shelled. Others were preparing their surrender.

Others desperately considered suicide. Some Vietnamese medical students were asked by their parents to bring home large quantities of sleeping pills. Others considered poison. Even some Catholics spoke of "suicide." The manager of a Vietnamese daily newspaper told the writer of this book the day after Thieu's resignation: "I'm getting old. I don't care about staying or getting out of VN. I'm only anxious about my children. They are too young to die. I'll try to ask some of my friends to take some of my children out of this country. I'll try to live as many other people. If they want to kill me, some sleeping pills will be my savior."

The evacuation got under way on an emergency basis in the wake of Nguyen Van Thieu's resignation, when the Ford administration belatedly accepted the truth: Saigon was in danger of complete military collapse. For weeks, the U.S. Defense Department wanted to step up the pace of the evaucation. But the Pentagon was stymied by the U.S. Ambassador, Graham Martin. In the end, tens of thousands of Vietnamese who had worked for the Americans and could have been saved, were left behind.

After the Thieu resignation, support for General Duong Van Minh (Big Minh) became almost unanimous. Most of Saigon's leaders urged that Big Minh become Premier in full charge of the government, with President Tran Van Huong as only a symbolic head. But from the very beginning, Minh insisted that he be Chief-of-State with real power.

In the meantime, Nguyen Van Thieu and his family, Tran Thien Khiem (his former Prime Minister) and his family left Saigon for Taipeh (island of Taiwan). Most of the Saigonese did not know of that departure. Later, they learned through foreign radio that on April 26, 1975, in the afternoon, Taipeh airport closed for four hours to unload Thieu's ten tons of baggage including four and one half tons of gold.

After a vain two-day search for a substitute, the Vietnamese generals accepted Minh's conditions. But the asthmatic and nearly blind Tran Van Huong wanted to play a historic role at the eleventh hour by stubbornly insisting that he remained the legitimate president of South VN. Then, after more than a day of vacilating, he finally gave in when the communists began shelling rockets on Saigon itself.

Saigon's death throes began when communist troops camped outside of Saigon grew tired of waiting for the installation of Big Minh. They fired a salvo of 122 MM rockets into Saigon and struck on all four sides of the capital.

The last battle of South Vietnamese armed forces took place at Cu Chi, 20 miles from Saigon. Cu Chi was the base of the 25th South Vietnamese infantry division, guarding Saigon from the Northwest. Generally Tong Ba, the division commander, ordered his men to fight to the end. He was not a brilliant officer and was also among Vietnamese dirty generals. But he did want to fight heroically, even when there was no hope for the survival of Saigon. In the morning of April 29, 1975, the communists laid down 4,000 shells on the base of the 25th division with a tank column pushing inside. Estimated losses of the 25th division were 2,000 killed and wounded.

On Monday, April 28, 1975, as Big Minh arrived at the presidential palace to be sworn in as president, four U.S. made A-37 attack jets flown by defector pilots took off from an unknown airfield bombed Tan Son Nhat airport when Big Minh had hardly finished exhorting the army to fight. Later, under the cover of darkness, the communists moved in and by dawn of April 29, 1975, they were entranched on the edges of Tan Son Nhat airport. Soon, the airfield was rendered useless. That sealed Saigon's fate.

Throughout the collapse, Big Minh tenaciously held the hope that the communists might be enticed into a coalition with the Vietnamese neutralists he claimed to represent. But with about 16 North Vietnamese divisions massed outside of Saigon, it was plain that the communists no longer would make concessions.

Big Minh's Prime Minister, professor and Senator Vu Van Mau did not have even time to form a new cabinet. Nguyen Ba Can (prime minister just for a week) fled without giving any notice to Big Minh. At last, with parts of Saigon in flames and all hope gone, Big Minh gave up. He recorded a surrender message and sent it to Radio Saigon at 10:00 A.M. on Wednesday, April 30, 1975. Then, dressed in a tan safari suit, he sat down in the palace with his aides (about 30 men) to await the end.

Almost immediately after the broadcast of Big Minh's surrender message, on every street leading to the Saigon waterfront, hundreds poured down to the river bank. Each one tried esperately to find out a means to get out of Saigon as quickly as possible. Only a few days earlier, it would have cost them hundreds of thousands of VN$. to pay for a place on a small ship. But now, finally, nobody cared about making money. Vietnamese Navy ships, civilian boats, barges, etc. . . . tried to take the maximum number of refugees. Some boats and some navy ships were betrayed by communist infiltrators. They were navy men bought by the communists. After sailing for a while, these infiltrators turned their ship back to Saigon and delivered the unlucky refugees to the communists.

On the other hand, tens of thousands of Vietnamese were still putting out to sea, truly a picture of despair. For two days, many of the U.S. armada ships lingered off the coast of South VN, picking up men, women and children from rafts, sampans and fishing boats. The U.S. armada received this radioed message from a Vietnamese vessel: "About 200 children will die of hunger and exhaustion if no help is forthcoming." Reports from U.S. command and field centers said tens of thousands of South Vietnamese were trying to flee through the port of Vung Tau, which was being mortared and shelled by the communists. Others were on boats on the Mkong River heading for the open sea, hoping to be picked up by bigger vessels. Some ships standing off Vung Tau, 45 miles southeast of Saigon, said thousands of small craft were putting to sea, crammed with refugees.

The final agony of South VN lasted fifty days, beginning March 10, 1975 and ended on April 30, 1975.

Chapter Three
ANATOMY OF A DEBACLE

There are many approaches to understanding the anatomy of the South Vietnamese debacle.

Viewed from the Paris accords of January 1973, three points should be considered: failure of the Paris accords, American aid to South VN and the absence of leadership in South VN.

Only naive people believed that the communists would respect the Paris accords of 1973. To Hanoi, the whole agreement was simply another means to fulfill the Ho Chi Minh line of thinking: "Fight until the Americans are gone, then fight again until the puppet government is overthrown."

The agreement did not require North VN to withdraw about 150,000 troops from South VN. Besides, Hanoi moved more and more new troops into the South and the overall communist strength had grown to 220,000 combat troops at the start of the March 1975 offensive (Viet Cong combat units comprised only a small part of the communist forces). The Ho Chi Minh Trail was turned into paved all weather highway and North Vietnamese troops began to receive more sophisticated weapons. This build-up had been accurately recorded by U.S. intelligence agents and by satellite photos.

U.S. officials assumed that the next general offensive of North VN would not come until 1976, election year in the United States. The assumption was based on the past. The previous communist offensive came during 1968 and 1972 (two election years in the U.S.). It is also assumed that Hanoi did not originally intend the drive of March 1975 to be an all-out offensive until South Vietnamese armed forces began disintegrating so quickly. It was not the first time that the Americans were wrong in their assumptions.

In VN, many observers believed that Hanoi really intended on an all-out offensive. All internal and external factors were favorable. Under such conditions, why should they hesitate when victory was at hand?

The International Commission of Control and Supervision was paralyzed at the very start. Its two communists members, Poland and Hungary never planned to investigate violations by Hanoi. That made the Canadians so disgusted with the impotence of the ICCS that Canada resigned in August 1973.

After the debacle, in an unusually candid "mea culpa," Secretary of Defense James Schlesinger admitted, "It is obvious in retrospect that the strength, resiliency and steadfastness of those (Saigon) forces were more highly valued than they should have been." That means the illusions about the Vietnamization were shattered. Washington may have been fooling itself about the capabilities of South Vietnamese forces. Under the Nixon administration, Nixon tried to make the American people believe that the fighting ability of South Vietnamese armed forces had been so improved that South VN no longer needed the assistance of U.S. troops. It was not illusion, it was the intention of the Nixon administration when it overestimated the fighting ability of South Vietnamese forces. When the Americans wanted to withdraw, they overestimated that fighting ability.

About the U.S. aid to South VN, controversy surrounds the question of how far cutbacks in U.S. military aid undermined SVN armed forces confidence. One line of argument claims these cutbacks fatally undermined that confidence. Ceilings placed on the number of shells, cutbacks in helicopter and warplane missions to save fuel, and lack of spare parts all wore away confidence. Thus, South Vietnamese armed forces were reduced to a passive role, and they could only respond to an enemy attack when it was too late.

Once the Paris accords were negotiated, the South Vietnamese received assurances from almost every level of U.S. Government that after the GI withdrawal, aid would definitely not diminish. In fact, despite the U.S. administration's critics, Capitol Hill had approved generous aid bills for South VN after the Paris accords. In fiscal 1973 there was $3.8 billion in aid of which, $3.3 billion was military. In fiscal 1974, the administration got $700 million, and later, Congress voted $300 million in supplementary aid.

But while the United States reduced military aid to South VN to fulfill the one-to-one replacement provision of the Paris Accords, there was no reduction in Russian and Chinese aid to Hanoi of assistance totaling $1,57 billion.

It may be true that reduction in aid to South VN and corresponding increases in aid to North VN fatally undermined the fighting ability of South Vietnamese Armed Forces. But it is impossible to deny the fact that Hue, Da Nang and many other provinces were abandoned not because of a lack of ammunition and equipment, but because of disastrous failure in leadership and a loss of will to fight to the end.

Regarding the American military aid to South VN, high ranking U.S. officials tended to deny another sad truth: some communist weapons were more sophisticated than American weapons: 130 mm gun, anti-aircraft missile SA-7, 122 mm gun etc. . . . The 130 mm gun had a firing range two times more than the firing range of the biggest gun provided for South Vietnamese armed forces (155 mm gun), plus the 130 mm gun can fire faster. The South Vietnamese did not have any individual weapon as deadly as the B-40 of the Communists. The M-16 rifle was among the best ones in the world, but it did have a serious disadvantage: its maintenance is much more difficult than the maintenance of the Communist

AK-47, AK-50 submachine gun. Russian made and Chinese made 107 or 122 mm rockets were extremely dangerous and the Communists quietly could move their rocket launchers close to the target. At times, Communist artillery used only two bamboo sticks instead of a launcher for their rockets. Of course, a bamboo stick was never as accurate as a real launcher, but it was not a problem to the Communists. From 1965 to 1975, Saigon and the Pentagon were unalbe or unwilling to invent an effective tactic to negate the deadly effect of Communist rockets. Normally, small South Vietnamese units could rarely get fire support from artillery or from warplanes. Communist small units used rockets as a very mobile artillery, and therefore, even a small unit could use rockets to prepare their attacks.

Compounding endemic problems of South Vietnamese armed forces was the failure of leadership by President Thieu. Apparently, after consulting only two close aides, Thieu ordered his army to abandon three central highland provinces and the province of Quan Tri (northernmost). He gave his officers only six hours notice before the withdrawal. Many units did not even have time to fuel their military vehicles. According to a U.S. expert, it was even worse at Hue: First, Thieu gave the order to pull back and defend Da Nang. Then, he countermanded it and ordered that Hue be held. Then he changed his mind again and told the troops to withdraw. A reasonably orderly withdrawal turned into a rout. On June 15, 1975, author Lloyd Shearer wrote in Parade Magazine: "The reason they refused to fight the Communists, several Army of the Republic of Vietnam (ARVN) soldiers explained, was because of President Thieu. According to their account, "We had many excellent infantry divisions who would have defended our country to the end. It was General Thieu who was indecisive. He ran around like a headless chicken. He didn't know what to do. When our men were defeated at Ban-me-thuot in March, President Thieu issued different orders every hour. First, we were to stand and fight, then we were to retreat only to attack again. In the end, our officers decided to save their own skins . . . Once that happened, panic took over. It became every man for himself . . . The objective was to escape to the coast . . . The fault of the ARVN was that it was rotten on top, starting with Thieu . . ."

In one respect, the Paris Accords were not completely a failure. The withdrawal of all U.S. personnel from South VN and the return of American prisoners of war were really the American objectives when Henry Kissinger negotiated the cease fire agreement. Once Kissinger attained the goals, he provided a cloak of respectiability under which the United States could get out of VN. In that light, there was some serious reason to believe that the U.S. commitment to South Vietnam's government had been intentionally ambiguous. Kissinger wanted only to buy a "decent interval" for the U.S. troop withdrawal and leave Saigon strong enough to survive some time in the future. Thus, when the collapse came, the world would not view it as a setback for the United States.

This approach provided an overall view of the war in VN since the Paris Accords of January 1973. Since the war in VN has been a very complicated war, the Paris Accords approach did not satisfy those who want to know much more about that war.

A second approach was developed by Ira C. Eaker, a Lt. General U.S. Air Force (retired) and published in the San Diego Union on July 26, 1975. It is based on a document released by Hanoi early in July 1975. It was a 20,000 word account of the reasons for Hanoi's South VN victory. This document was authored by Vo Nguyen Giap, North VN defense minister, assisted by his deputy, General Van Tien Dung.

For the victory, first, Giap pays tribute to the communist party and system. It inspires (or compels) dedication to one plan, supported by all the people. Next, the document credits the support of the rear area (the home front) which provided logistical support for combat troops in the field, with efficiency and dedication. Then, it pays tribute to the courage and skill of the troops, regular and guerilla. General Giap modestly reserves his final accolade for the leadership (the party's and his own) and its brilliant war plan. General Giap reveals that the decision was made in March 1975, when the South Vietnamese withdrawal became a rout, to go for broke and press on to Saigon, which fell on April 30, at least a year earlier than anticipated.

But General Giap reflects the usual tricky and dishonest line of thinking of any communist leader. Therefore, General Eacker wrote "For example: nowhere is credit given to the Russians and Red Chinese for providing the weapons, equipment and supplies which were vital to their success. Mention is not made of the fact that this essential support was doubled after the Paris peace agreement was supposed to have halted further U.S. and Red aid to the belligerents . . . Nowhere, does he credit the South Vietnamese rout in March to the fact the U.S. aid stopped, destroying morale and paralyzing South VN's military capability . . . He does not refer to the anti-war agitation in the U.S., which eventually resulted in cutting off vital support for Saigon. All anti-war protest groups in the U.S. should complain about this lack of recognition, this base ingratitude. In fact, General Giap defeated the U.S. in the same way and for the same reasons he defeated the French. When Paris failed to support French troops in the field, Dien Bien Phu fell. When Washington discontinued adequate support, Saigon's defeat became inevitable . . . Giap's boastful, self serving summary contains one ominous warning. The reds demand and compel unanimous support from all their people. For lack of such unity, democracies become dangerously vulnerable."

Neither of the approaches mentioned here is complete. They complement each other. In that light, the historical approach to the anatomy of the debacle would help. The war in VN must rank as the bloodiest and costliest war ever to be waged within one small country: a war of independence by the Vietnamese against foreign armies, a civil war among the Vietnamese themselves and an international ideological war between communism and capitalism.

After the 1920s, the French rule brought the three parts of the country together, North VN, Central VN and South VN. By its repressive nature, the French rule facilitated leadership for the Vietnamese Communists in the struggle for independence. The communist dominated resistance consolidated in North VN. After World War II, the British and some American leaders allowed the French back in Indochina. The resistance against Japan merged into an armed resistance to French rule.

The Geneva Accords of July 1954 brought into existence the de facto two Vietnams along the 17th parallel. Indigenousauthorities in North and in South VN were to hold elections within two years leading to reunification under one Vietnam. For political reasons, the general elections between the two Vietnams could not be organized in 1956.

The great exodus of nearly one million refugees from the North to the South reminded the outside world that North VN was not a promised land. With Ngo

Dinh Diem, South VN became the last rallying point provided to the non-communist Vietnamese. The United States quickly came to help this new country.

But after his four successful first years, Ngo Dinh Diem proved inadequate as the challenger to Ho Chi Minh. Diem's first error was to refuse North VN's request to normalize trade and communication between the two Vietnams. This resulted in North VN depending more heavily upon Russian and Chinese aid. The second error was that Diem and his family not only sought to liquidate communists but also the non-communist elements whose support he should have courted and who for some reason did not agree with Diem's policies. So, by this home policy, Diem destroyed the confidence of the South Vietnamese which he had won during the early years and practically drove them into desperation and revolt.

The communists naturally fought on. The war began again and the Geneva accords were recognized as abandoned. U.S. support for Diem grew and grew. But Diem was a difficult ally and he did not like to take Americans' advice. In the coup of November 1963, Diem and his brother Ngo Dinh Nhu were killed unmercifully. The Americans evidently had some responsibility in his deposition.

Since then, South VN has been governed by many who proved to be only pirates or bandits in uniform. They were by no means united among themselves and they were always unwilling to give true nationalist politicians a share of power.

Of course, it was not the first time that the U.S. aided a friendly country. During World War I, World War II and even after, American aid was provided to many countries. Right now, more than 300,000 U.S. troops are still in Europe and 26 years after the Korean War, a U.S. Army is still stationed in South Korea to deter aggressive North Korea from renewing the Korean war. The motives were honorable in these areas, and the U.S. achieved the desired result with the means chosen.

Unfortunately, this was not the case in the Vietnam War. The U.S. realized too late that the reality of the Vietnam War differed from the American perception.

Throughout the war, Hanoi permanently simulated the role of an indigenous civil insurrection. North Vietnam continually refused to acknowledge that it had any forces in South Vietnam, Laos and Cambodia. This subtle subterfuge denied the world a specific target for criticism.

To cope with these strategies, the U.S. exercised restraint. Its desire was to maintain the facade of the Geneva Agreement on Indochina in 1954 and the Geneva Accords on Laos in 1962 for future use. They did not realize that the Accords on Laos were vital instruments in Hanoi's long range campaign to take over South Vietnam. In terms of military strategy, Laos was a deadly gun that Hanoi pointed at the heart of South Vietnam.

Moreover, because of its restraint, the U.S. never did permit South Vietnam to mount operations to close the Laos routes of infiltration.

Up to 1968, the U.S. was imprecise in its perception of the nature of the Vietnam war. Hanoi infiltrated aggression was treated as the insurgency it pretended to be. Its external origins were only treated as secondary, resulting in a misapplication of the doctrine of counter-insurgency. With the concept of "advisors," the U.S. forces were progressively committed to fight in South Vietnam and not against the external attack. Hanoi steadily mounted its external

116

input in response.

When the U.S. could no longer tolerate the North Vietnamese buildup, it deployed the U.S. Air Force slowly in Laos and in North Vietnam. But it did not follow the bombings with ground exploitation to close or to destroy the infiltration routes in Laos.

Another strategic error was the application of the concept of "measured response." When applied in the Vietnam war, this concept became "gradual escalation." Those who promoted it believed that it would minimize the danger of provoking dangerous reaction from Red China and Russia. Therefore, "gradualism" was aimed at testing Hanoi's endurance without achieving American ends. Gradualism reduced the war to a contest of political attrition. In that seemingly endless war, the winner would be the side capable of sustaining the costs longer.

In that strange contest, the U.S. was obviously stronger in military terms but it was not as strong politically. America is the most democratic country in the world. Nobody can deny this reality: American citizens do enjoy more freedom and more human rights than any other people on this planet. Faced with a permanent threat from international communism, it seems that American citizens have had even too much freedom regarding such touchy areas as freedom of information on national defense.

Successive administrations in Washington faced a tragic dilemma. Each time the White House had to discuss its foreign policy with Capitol Hill, American citizens were almost immediately informed by the media. It is constitutional that they be informed on national affairs, but this freedom provided classified information to the outside world. The Communists took advantage of this constitutional weakness to reassert their strategy for their ultimate objective in Indochina.

Democracy required that U.S. citizens must be informed about any national affair. However, from 1954 to 1975, American people knew little about the Vietnam where 56,000 GIs died and more than $150 billion were spent. Five successive American administrations were unable or unwilling to provide answers to two basic questions: What precisely were the U.S. national interests in Thailand, Cambodia, Vietnam and Laos? To what lengths was America prepared to go in support of these interests?

The war in VN was never portrayed accurately to the American public. In their eagerness to provide latest news and living documents on the war in VN, American reporters damaged the American cause. For some secret reason, some reporters exaggerated civilian casualties from U.S. bombing. Other American reporters warmly praised the communists while GIs died every day in battle. And almost every day, American citizens saw the GIs in action. These American citizens never saw the communist killing. It was one-sided reporting of a war in a remote and underdeveloped nation. And because America is the first super power in the world, the American people felt guilty. The more truth asked for, the less they were given adequate information. And these American citizens were right: they had the right to know why their sons were sent to VN. American people came from many parts of this planet. They knew better than any other people what democracy means, freedom and human rights. And they were and are generous people. But they must know before they give. American administrations failed to justify the U.S. military involvement. The American people had the impression that they were crushing a small nation. The communist invaders were praised and the GIs who helped the South Vietnamese preserve their free society were condemned. It seemed that North VN was victim of the American involvement in VN while in reality, it was the U.S. which became victim of the dirtiest blackmail in the history of ideological warfare.

On the other hand, from the very beginning, American policy-makers have considered South VN essentially as a creation of the U.S. Therefore, they thought of Vietnamese generals and presidents as instruments of the American policy. Consequently, these generals and presidents were easily tempted. They knew however corrupt they might be, they would be blessed by the American government, providing that they demonstrated their anti-communism, if only verbally. Take the case of Nguyen Van Thieu. American people were cheated when they did not receive adequate information and justification on the U.S. involvement in VN. And they were cheated for the second time when they learned that American aid, while supporting an anti-communist regime in South VN, was really used to defend and to preserve a banditry rule. That was more than enough to create a credibility crisis.

Theoretically, the U.S. should not have become involved in a land war in Asia. But once involved whatever was necessary should have been considered. U.S. policymakers made a tragic mistake by allowing U.S. troops to be in VN with their hands tied. A truly successful strategy can never be efficient based on purely defensive tactics. VN is the most striking example.

The first rule of successful guerilla warfare is to have sanctuaries. And the first rule of successful anti-guerilla warfare is to eliminate sanctuaries. In VN, the strategic sanctuaries consisted of Laos, Cambodia and North Vietnam. Over the years, the U.S. attempted to help South VN defend itself from aggression. But the communists were granted the perfect access route for aggression in Laos and in Cambodia, while the chief center of aggression, North VN, was guaranteed from counter attack. Because of these tragic errors the communist butchers killed Vietnamese people at will. They are considered national heroes while U.S. troops were accused of genocide because they helped South Vietnamese people preserve their free society. This is the most sorrowful aspect of the VN War.

The sending of U.S. troops in VN from 1965 onward has been most opposed by the war critics. It is unfair criticism because this is not the first time the U.S. sent American soldiers abroad to defend western civilization. It is impossible to deny war critics' charges that there were conflicts of interest, racism, cowardice, intellectual dishonesty and spiritual wickedness. One thing is certain: At least the noble sacrifice of so many American soldiers and the noble gesture of the American people prevented South VN from the communist takeover for a decade. Only the communists and dishonest people could deny that fact.

The United States could not win the war in VN because it is too powerful as a nation, because American leaders are too decent to face inhuman strategy and tactics of international communism and because American society is too democratic, having too much freedom and too many human rights to confront a revolutionary war waged by a monolithic, closed and tightly controlled political system. Democracy is a good thing but in the U.S., individualism goes too far and deprives the U.S. of its necessary unity. That individualism makes American democracy dangerously vulnerable in the present struggle for survival between capitalism and communism.

Responsibilities from the South Vietnamese side are not so complicated for

118

the simple reason that South VN is a small country with modest expectations.

Unlike people in advanced countries, the Vietnamese wanted only such small things as a little land, a little rice, and a little peace. They suffered so much for so many years without getting these small things that they finally became terribly passive. They simply accepted any regime able to assure them a little peace.

Although it did have hundreds of intellectuals trained in many famous foreign schools and universities, South VN remains an agricultural country. The common people in South VN used to obey the government and left public affairs entirely in the hands of an educated elite. It is a strong Vietnamese tradition.

Vietnam is a stagnant society. A radical change in such a society is necessary to improve life. While the communists promoted marxism as a means for that change, South VN had an opportunity in 1954 to promote an alternative. Democracy is not incompatible with governmental authority. It needs a young, strong and dynamic leader with a clear vision the public can share. It also needs a government able to decentralize and involve the people more directly in their regional and local administration.

Unfortunately, the educated elite of South VN proved to be unable to lead the South Vietnamese common people. Intellectuals could not abandon their feudal ways of thinking. The new generation had been educated in western universities but they simply could not adapt their knowledge to local conditions.

Instead of trying to build a new society in South VN, the educated elite had chosen the easiest way to compete with the communist alternative: a western style consumer society. Physically, this pattern of society provided better living conditions to South Vietnamese than the communist alternative but its affluence relied almost completely on foreign aid.

Material interest always attract dishonest people and when dishonest people took power, this consumer society quickly became a flourishing monopoly for the minority ruling that society. If one could blame the U.S. for supporting such banditry rule as the Thieu regime, one could also blame those who remained passive during his ruling years. While a minority of the educated elite thought only of making money and accepted their role as Thieu's intellectual mercenaries, the majority complained about the corrupt regime but dared not do anything to change it. They wanted to fight against the communist alternative but they feared bloodshed and they feared any radical change in their stagnant and feudal society. This majority of the educated elite was the most guilty when one looked for those who were responsible for the fall of South VN. Their guilt was even greater because they were natural leaders of the common people in South Vietnamese society.

The western style consumer society deprived South VN of its opportunity to seek a compromise with the communists and more dangerously it provided the illusion that American aid would be available forever. And when the U.S. reduced its assistance, South Vietnamese people were so disillusioned, including the armed forces, that the fighting will collapsed from within an unthinkable short time.

From 1954 to 1975, there were many opportunities for the Vietnamese nationalists to design and implement an alternative to vie with the communist alternative. But passive and selfish by essence, they missed these opportunities. The American responsibilities in the fall of South VN are only of secondary importance. Primary responsibilities must be the ones of South Vietnamese people. When freedom for 17 million people is at stake, the fight can not be won

119

at a cheap price. Passivity, pusillanimity and selfishness never pay off in ideological warfare against communism.

About the Vietnamese responsibilities, the key question was what made South Vietnam stand firm from 1954 to 1975?

It cost North Vietnam 21 years and millions of human lives to take over South Vietnam.

Neither of the two great and decisive offensives of 1972 and 1975 could be considered revolutionary techniques. Nowhere on South Vietnam territories did people cheer or welcome the "liberators," except in those meetings organized by armed Communists after April 30, 1975. Nowhere did people revolt against the non-communist government or against South Vietnamese armed forces, although many communist radio stations urged people to do so. South Vietnamese people simply and unanimously fled when the invaders came. When it was no longer possible for them to flee, they accepted their new rulers with indifference and contempt.

It was the North Vietnamese Army, modernized by Russia, which overcame the defense of South Vietnam. Russian economic and military aid was decisive. Obviously, North Vietnam had taken advantage of the American defection and of the surplus of arms provided by Russia to mount the last offensive. For 1974, Russia alone had provided to North Vietnam 1,500 T-54, T-55 and T-59 tanks, 600 guns (heavy artillery), 1,700 Sam missiles, 246,000 tons of ammunition and many torpedo boats.

Economic aid to Hanoi was evaluated at 1,200 millions of dollars in 1973 and 1,700 millions in 1974. Eighty-five percent of economic and military aid to Hanoi came from Russia. An impartial observer could reasonably perceive that it was the Soviet weaponry which entered Saigon in late April 1975.

From 1965 to 1969, while the presence of GIs did prevent a collapse, South Vietnam was demoralized by dollars. The cost of living was suddenly skyrocketing. Dollars had destroyed traditional moral structures of Vietnamese society and undermined the economy of South Vietnam. A pedicab driver earned more money than the principal of a university.

A horn of plenty poured out in South Vietnam and of course, undermined the traditional morality of that war-torn country. All government employees, including soldiers, received a poor monthly salary. A monthly salary for an American soldier was many times more than the amount paid every month to a Vietnamese three star general.

Corruption in South Vietnam became so dangerous that it badly weakened the country. The high morale necessary for defense became blunt. And when a number of honest people who served the fatherland were bypassed by dishonest people, when those who worked hard and whose sacrifice was the biggest were not the best paid, the Vietnamese people became demoralized.

Ideas, political parties and the war only served dishonest and individual interests and no longer served interests of the nation. It was the same with the administration and the armed forces. People did not know whom to trust.

Evidently, there were honest people. But they were not numerous enough and their actions were too timid to preserve for South Vietnam a sense of effort and faith, or an appeal for sacrifice in war time. Individual interests overcame the interests of the nation. How could South Vietnam survive under these miserable conditions? And how could the South Vietnamese armed forces maintain their high morale to continue their ungrateful but sacred mission?

Free World countries did not care about the situation in South Vietnam. Instead of realizing that South Vietnam, their defensive bastion, was clearly in danger, they only locked themselves in their own national problems.

In this tragic situation, South Vietnamese armed forces collapsed because they were betrayed:

• By their American friends who had assured them of a continued aid in arms and equipment withou which, Vietnamese weapons became useless;

• By the South Vietnamese government which was so corrupt and so weak that it could not impose the necessary discipline and necessary efforts to support them in the battles;

• By the people of South Vietnam who were enfeebled by their taste of pleasure and by their excessive search of selfish individual interests;

• By the Vietnamese intelligentsia which devoted more time to discussing rhetoric and stupid disputes than to serving the nation. Their behavior undermined the morale of South Vietnamese armed forces;

• Finally by the Vietnamese people who did not participate directly in the common fight and who decided to flee in a visceral fear which turned up to panic.

The South VN collapse was not unique in the history of war. In 1940, within 60 days, the French Armed Forces surrendered and nearly all French territories were occupied by Germans.

There was the retreat of French troops from Lang Son in North Vietnam in 1950 after the disaster of Cao Bang, where, in spite of the heroism of some units, most French troops withdrew in panicky conditions along the colonial highway 4 without fighting, without instructions from higher commanders and worse, without seeing any enemy.

It is necessary to remind the Americans that in Korea in 1951, 16 Red Chinese divisions of Lin Pao had swept the Korean peninsula and inflicted on the United Nations troops the most cruel defeat that they had ever had.

It may be unfair to conclude that the South Vietnamese soldiers refused to fight. From 1954 to 1975, they were the only courageous and disciplined forces to successfully defend South Vietnam against the infiltrated aggression from North Vietnam. They were trained according to the American military doctrine. They relied heavily upon firepower, whether in offensive or in defensive action. This doctrine required tremendous quantities of armor, artillery and ships that only the American armed forces could afford to provide to their own soldiers. When the U.S. reduced its aid to South Vietnam, it tragically deprived South Vietnamese troops of such vital firepower.

Finally, there was the weariness of 30 years of continuous endurance and sufferings.

Before the insane order of retreat from the highlands issued by Nguyen Van Thieu early in March 1975, South Vietnamese soldiers did not refuse to fight. After the cease fire accords signed in Paris on January 27, 1973, South Vietnam continued to order 3,000 coffins every month. But the military strength of the enemy was increasing day by day. More new and sophisticated weapons from Russia were shipped every day to North Vietnam. It was impossible for South Vietnamese army to replace the best who died in battlefield, whereas, the enemy was continuously reinforced. The South Vietnamese had to realize they were outgunned. When their weapons became useless in their hands, only one alternative was left to these soldiers: give up the fighting.

—0—

In the first Indochina War (1946-1954), the real and decisive battle which decided the outcome of the war did not take place in Hanoi, Vientiane and Pnom Penh. It took place in Paris.

In the second Indochina War (1954-1975), the real and decisive battle took place in Washington. In fact, there were Nixon's two battles: the first in the living rooms of Kleber Avenue in Paris (France) to sign the peace accords and the second in Watergate, Nixon's Waterloo, where all he probably gained in the first battle was destroyed.

To get the Paris Accords which stopped the North Vietnamese marching south, Nixon gave orders to invade Cambodia to cut the routes in neutral territory by which the Communists supplied with impunity their invading troops.

Nixon crushed the economy of North Vietnam with U.S. bombers and blocked Hanoi's supply in cereals without which, North Vietnam could not survive. Nixon's blockade in all major ports of North Vietnam made the economy of North Vietnam worse.

Finally, by a sensational reversal, he went to Peking to shake hands with Mao, to attack North Vietnam from its rear and to convince the world that he really wanted to take all GIs home.

Nixon did all this against the U.S. Congress, against the U.S. media, against the opinion of the left. And he did all this to give what Congress, media and public opinion were asking: no more GIs in Saigon.

To the world, Nixon looked to be a redoubtable poker player who ruled international affairs as a supreme master. Brezhnev admired him and said so. Mao kept Nixon's hands long in his own during their televised show. The President of the United States won. But only briefly. He lost the battle and he did not know it yet.

At the White House, in his fortress, with his aides, his advisors, Nixon had been besieged during the whole battle because he did not have, according to American traditions and Constitution, absolute and discretionary powers. His adversaries did have these powers and could decide on their citizens' matters of life and death. Nixon and his staff tried to get the same powers in order to defeat the Communists. By their own means, Nixon and his men had created something like an illegal secret service, other than the secret service authorized by the American Contitution. With this new secret service, he tried to counter attack the offensive from the opposition.

The real and ultimate battle did not happen in the Mekong delta of South Vietnam, in the Highlands or in the Plain of Jars in Laos. It took place when illegal secret agents of the White House broke into the office of Ellsberg's psychiatrist. The same battle went on when the offices of the Democratic Party were taped.

To fight better against the enemy, Nixon tacitly accepted that his men crossed the Rubicon of constitutional legality. That mistake lost the White House and Indochina.

Only Nixon could deter Hanoi from going too far in the South. If they did so, Hanoi's leaders might think that Nixon would come back to Peking or send back the U.S. bombers to North Vietnam. His name and his presence in

Washington, in the Oval Office, would be able to prevent the collapse of South Vietnamese Armed Forces.

Saigon fell because of Watergate. As Montesquieu indicated, democracy can be perpetuated by no other means than virtue. Nixon missed this necessary virtue when he violated the American Constitution. Thieu and his hangmen were completely short of virtue when they sold in the black market pieces of military aircraft, military fuel, weapons, rice, supplies to get rich.

Westerners must convince themselves that Montesquieu is not getting old and that only by virtue can they safeguard their freedom against the Communist tyranny whose motive power is fear.

The last chapter of the human tragedy in VN was definitely closed on April 30, 1975. As in any war of human society, there must be winners and losers or victims. North Vietnamese leaders can enjoy their victory enormously. They won the long contest with the most powerful country in the world. In human history, the war in VN was the best example of the communist strategy. Being good and decent, American policy makers under successive American administrations could not use nuclear weapons, particularly against a small nation. Because they were good and decent, they became victims of communist blackmail. While they restrained their use of weaponry, the communists blatantly used more sophisticated weapons, short of nuclear power, to carry out their monopoly of killing Vietnamese, Laotians and Cambodians.

Anyway, the Americans are not losers because Henry Kissinger said when he negotiated the Paris Accords of January 1973 that it would be an honorable peace. The withdrawal of all American personnel and the return by Hanoi of American prisoners of war were accomplished without difficulty.

After the fall of South VN, President Ford said: "The surrender in Saigon is not the beginning of the end in Asia. The U.S. is still a Pacific power and we must demonstrate with our knowledge and feeling."

Nor were the banditry rulers in South VN losers. Nguyen Van Thieu and his hangmen are now living in privileged exile. Their banditry rule policy paid off: tons of gold for Thieu and for his former prime minister Tran Thien Khiem, hundreds of thousands of dollars were rewards for their hangmen.

Losers in the VN war were the non-communist Vietnamese. In North VN before 1954, the tacit consent of western powers has made many victims among the Vietnamese nationalists. The result was the great exodus of nearly one million of Vietnamese from North VN to the South. In South VN after 1954, these refugees and the South Vietnamese people have had really modest needs. They wanted so little: a little land, a little rice and above all, a little peace. Instead of giving them these little things, they were given a grandiose name and a more grandiose mission. It was some American administration which elevated the VN conflict to such strategic important for the Free World. The poor and modest South Vietnamese people became defenders of South VN, the anti-communist bastion of the Free World in Southeast Asia. It was too much honor to too modest people. For reasons which have been explained, these people were equipped with a feudal, remote and family rule from 1954 to 1963 and with a banditry rule from 1967 to 1975 to defend that bastion.

After April 30, 1975 for some 140,000 Viet refugees who succeeded in coming to the U.S. and for thousands of other Viet refugees who are living in some non-communist countries in Southeast Asia, it would be a rebirth. To those who can adapt themselves to the new life, it will be a promising future. A slow death to those who can't.

For millions of Vietnamese people who are living under the new communist regime in South VN, the light at the end of the tunnel was extinguished forever, as it was for the Vietnamese who were living in North VN since 1954.

PART III
Chapter One

THE REFUGEES AND SOME COMMUNIST TACTICS

They came by tens of thousands, by any means of transportation, sampans, helicopters, troop ships and transport planes. They fled their homeland for the refuge of the United States. After losing their freedom, they look now for freedom in the most democratic country in the world.

Who are they? They are the Vietnamese refugees and they include those who bribed their way out (mostly rich people and those who became rich thanks to the business of war: trade of blood, trade of power and trade of justice); those who made quick marriages to any American to get out of the country; those who mastered English and those who had technical knowledge and worked for foreign enterprises; those who are trained medical doctors or pharmacists; those who had made themselves early enemies of the new regime because of their religious belief or their political conviction; Vietnamese officials South Vietnamese servicemen, etc. . . . They also include fishermen and low income people.

Like most immigrants before them, the Vietnamese refugees were sad about the life they left behind and apprehensive about what lies ahead in America. But with or without a proper, binding legal commitment, they have trusted the United States for many years. About 150,000 succeeded in escaping South Vietnam under extremely difficult conditions. 25,000 were evacuated by the U.S. Embassy in Saigon and 125,000 by their own means and later, recued by U.S. Navy or merchants ships. Among them, nearly 5,000 are living in some non-communist countries in Southeast Asia and looking very eagerly for some help to take them to the United States.

From Camp Pendleton, South California, author Lloyd Shearer wrote: "In 1956, the Voice of America and other U.S. quasi-intelligence agencies helped stimulate a revolt against Hungarian Communism. The Soviets sent in troops

125

while the Hungarians vainly pleaded for U.S. arms. Khrushchev's men brutally quelled the insurgency. Eventually, the U.S. welcomed 40,000 Hungarian immigrants to these shores.

"In 1960 and 1961, the CIA recruited and trained a group of Cuban exiles in Florida, Louisiana, Panama and Guatemala to invade Cuba and defeat Cuban Communism. The Castroists entrapped the invaders in the Bay of Pigs and defeated them. Today, the U.S. is home of some 600,000 Cuban immigrants.

"In the 1970's, the Americans, after training, financing, and supplying the South Vietnamese to beat North Vietnam Communism, pulled out their troops. Under Richard Nixon, we instituted a Vietnamization program designed to make the South Vietnamese militarily self-sufficient. A few months ago, the army of South Vietnam collapsed. Now, approximately 130,000 Vietnamese refugees reside on American territory."

But the problem of these Viet refugees is not so simple as that of 1956 or of 1960 and 1961. In April and May 1975, the Vietnamese refugees were greeted with initial hostility. There was an outpouring of ugly protest across the nation, demonstrating that the U.S. was not yet free of the rancor that the Vietnam war had spawned.

There was in the United States a growing controversy over how far U.S. obligation to Vietnamese refugees extended. Most Americans were torn between a natural desire to help the war victims and fear . . . the often exaggerated fear that these refugees would add to U.S. economic and social problems. There were also those Americans who worried about the political alignment of the refugees: they may become very active in right-wing politics.

But opposition dwindled as Americans learned more about the refugees and after they were assured that the refugees will be scattered throughout the country. And eventually goodwill and public relations combined to soften the bitterness that had festered the first week. Resentful attitudes dissipated American traditional hospitality began contributing blankets, clothing and food for refugees. Some Americans even recognized that there are temporary economic benefits from the refugees. Aides to Arkansas Senator Dale Bumpey reported that the resettlement programs would pump about $10 per refugee per day into the Fort Chaffee area economy.

In the end, most Americans seemed to agree that for moral reasons, the United States had no choice but to help the refugees. Political scientist Wesley Fishel said: "If we lose our compassionate touch with helping mankind, we'll lose a part of our tradition."

Because of the rapid exodus, the U.S. government was caught almost unprepared. There were frantic preparations at three military bases designated as refugee centers. Refugees began to be airlifted from Guan, Philippines (and later, from Wake Island), to the Marine's Camp Pendleton in Southern California, Fort Chaffee in Arkasas and Eglin Air Force Base in Florida. At Pendleton, hundreds of tents were erected by U.S. Marines in an incredible time as they worked around the clock. In a very short time, there were enough comfortable facilities for their Vietnamese guests. The U.S. Marines at Camp Pendleton were quite friendly, courteous and helpful to the refugees. Most of the refugees warmly welcomed the wise handling of General Paul Graham, the commander of Camp Pendleton and they were truly grateful to him.

At two other refugee centers (Fort Chaffee and Eglin Air Base), U.S. servicemen also went out of their way to help their South Vietnamese guests. The refugees themselves were praised for their amiability, courage, optimism, self-discipline and cheerful gratitude for the help they received.

Of course, there were many things that happened at these camps that helpful U.S. Servicemen were not prepared to deal with. Guam was the most complicated staging and processing center.

Because of thousands of refugees who began streaming into Guam by Navy ships, merchant ships, by airlift, U.S. Government officials fell behind in the processing. Procedures changed almost every day and confused the refugees. But from mid May, procedures clearly improved as U.S. officials in refugee centers were reinforced by volunteer people from the United States.

With thousands of refugees arriving in Guam day after day, sad stories arrived too. One former Vietnamese Minister of Economy used a tricky tactic to get out of Saigon and by his tactic, not only the Dean of The Law School of Saigon University but many other distinguished people in Saigon were left behind.

"Equal opportunity and justice for all," are beautiful words which reflected the democratic and generous spirit of the United States. But to the Vietnamese refugees who arrived in Guam, they had a bitter significance. There were ten camps in Guam, and the refugees were supposed to be sent to any of these camps as they arrived. It didn't happen that way. Orote Tent City was the staging area for the common Viet refugee and, at times, this camp had to receive more than 18,000 refugees. Those who had an acquaintance with some Americans, civilian or military, might be sent to other camps which were much more comfortable and much less crowded. There were many reasons behind that story. Among the refugees, many corrupt figures in Saigon appeared, including the most wicked butchers of Nguyen Van Thieu: Nguyen Khac Binh, Hoang Duc Nha, Trang Si Tan, Do Kien Nhieu . . . Some groups of refugees attempted to beat these butchers, but the U.S. responsible servicemen succeeded in preventing that punishment. The butchers were quickly allowed to leave camp under special conditions. One refugee said synically, "The same old story." The story was spread and other butchers tried to be moved to other safe camps like C and J, Barrigada, Anderson, etc. . . . At Andersen camp, former minister of interior Le Cong Chat and his assistant colonel Huynh Ngoc Diep hid themselves behind their barracks at each meal to eat their food like outlaws. In fact, they and many other corrupt servants of Thieu's regime were considered by most refugees to be war criminals. The refugees bitterness increased when they found out that these butchers received special protection measures from U.S. officials at various camps in Guam and in other camps (Pendleton, Fort Chaffee).

Almost all ships or boats were overcrowded when they arrived in Guam, but there were one or two ships hired by corrupt officials and corrupt generals. These war profit people had to throw away food when they left Saigon, because there was too much food on board. There was a tragic food shortage on many other ships. For instance, the U.S. steamship American Challenge planned to take only 1,000 refugees when it left Phu Quoc island on May 1, 1975. Shortly after, the ship received orders to take many refugees offshore from Vung Tau province. Finally, when this ship sailed to Guam, there were more than 6,000 refugees and of course, food shortages and health conditions were frightful problems.

Processing was another nightmare for the refugees. Many refugees slept on the ground all night in front of the processing tent. Remnants of corrupt Saigon life prevailed at the refugee camps. Some rich refugees too eager to come to the

U.S., gave money to some Vietnamese working for the processing office. Of course, thanks to money, these rich people were processed first. Fortunately, the American military authorities were immediately informed and at least, two Vietnamese working at the processing center of Orote Tent City were arrested and kept in custody at an unknown place.

The same story was repeated with some voluntary agencies. Some refugees gave money to the Vietnamese clerks working for these agencies to obtain a sponsor quickly. Naturally, American authorities could not deny or confirm that story. People knew that there was corruption but nobody could prove it. There was, at least, some evidence about the way some voluntary agencies handled their job. On July 18, 1975, the San Diego Union newspaper published the statements of Mr. Mario Obledo, Secretary of Health and Welfare of California State on refugee aid plans. He said: "Most of the Federal money allocated for Vietnamese refugee assistance is being absorbed by the sponsor-finding agencies. Most of the money is kept by volunteer organizations and very little gets to the refugees." And on July 19, 1975, the same paper related another story about one volunteer agency. The story was written by Mr. Donald H. Harrison on 32 Cambodian refugees who asked to drop ties with an agency. When the petition was presented to this agency, members of their families were frightened by threats that the petitioners would be arrested.

Among these unhappy stories, there was encouraging news for the refugees: on July 8, 1975, the Canadian Government said it would deport Dang Van Quang, former South Vietnamese general alleged to have been involved in heroin smuggling in Saigon. Canadian Immigration Minister Rober Andras said that Quang would be deported "as soon as he can arrange for his admission to another country." Later, there was also news that the U.S. refused to admit Quang. The Vietnamese refugees' attitude was these war criminals should be denied entry into the U.S. One Vietnamese intellectual at Camp Pendleton told the writer of this book: "I feel extremely ashamed to live together in this camp with these criminals."

Another aspect of the refugee problem is the desire of the Vietnamese communists to infiltrate and to make propaganda. Of course, the U.S. immigration and naturalization service sent the names of all refugees seeking to settle in the U.S. to five federal agencies, including the Central Intelligence Agency. Up to June 26, 1975, 209 out of about 60,000 refugees checked for immigration clearance were identified as possibly undesirable because of alleged criminal activities or communist affiliations in their former home. Yet, the problem of security clearance for the Vietnamese refugees is far from resolved.

It was easy for the communists to infiltrate their agents into the streams of refugees leaving South VN. The most difficult problem for U.S. security agencies is that the communist agents look exactly like normal Vietnamese refugees in appearance. And because of the exodus, it is difficult for the U.S. Government to maintain its strict current regulations on immigration.

From Saigon to the U.S., through various refugee camps, secret communist agents are exploiting these popular themes: American responsibilities in the collapse of South VN, living conditions while moving from VN to the U.S., living conditions at refugee camps on U.S. territories, family spirit, home sickness and patriotism. These agents were reinforced by other communists agents living in the U.S. even before the collapse of South VN.

Information and cross checked information among many refugees arriving in Guam by navy or merchant ships seemed to confirm that there might be more than one communist agent in the flow of refugees seeking refuge in the U.S. Food shortage and unsatisfactory health conditions aboard were subjects used by the communist infiltrators to create resentment and division between Vietnamese and Americans. In fact, there were some refugees who did not intend to go as far as the U.S. When the collapse came, they had been told by their spiritual leaders that they would be evacuated only temporarily out of VN. Most of these people did not speak English and were not involved in anti-communist political beliefs. They became easy targets for communist propaganda. Of course, on these ships communist agents failed because the majority of the refugees have made up their own minds since they left South VN.

Communist propaganda efforts increased dramatically when the refugees touched down on Guam and at other refugee camps in the U.S. This time, homesick and waiting period were the topics. At these camps, some refugees are desperately homesick and some worry about an uncertain future to the point of suicide. They are anxious about everything. They have no future at all while waiting to be cleared to settle in other areas. They are anxious about their status, anxious about jobs. They are anxious about losing their identities. Resentment among some refugees about their former Saigon leaders combined with worry over fragmented families and the uncertain future may lead some to suicide.

In Arkansas, Fort Chaffee, American authorities did not forbid the distribution of a Vietnamese so called non-profit newspaper Doi Dien published by a group of pro-communist Vietnamese students residing in and around Washington, D.C. This paper only praised the communist regime in South VN and promoted the return to the fatherland among the refugees. At Camp Pendleton, another mysterious group distributed a Vietnamese newspaper, the Thai Binh, exploiting the same pro-communist theme as the Doi Dien. There was also some discussion between these mysterious messengers and the refugees at Camp Pendleton. The refugees realized one day that many of this group were Vietnamese students who had been living in the U.S. for a long time. After listening to their pro-communist propaganda, some Vietnamese refugees asked them a question "If you say that it is not worth it to stay in the U.S., why did you live here for so long?" The propagandists tried to escape the answer for that question. Did they belong to the communists or did they belong to some American intelligence agency to detect pro-communists among the refugees? The answer has to be seen. One thing is clear: a great majority of the refugees did not pay any attention to these propagandists.

The problem is more complicated with those who came singly to the U.S. Most of them were South Vietnamese air force pilots and they were the staunchest anti-communists during the last months of non-communist South VN. Until the last days, they were so busy trying to destroy the communist attacking forces that many of them simply did not have time to evacuate their families. In Guam and at various refugee camps in the U.S., they were really badly homesick. For some reason, some other civilians also did not have time to evacuate their relatives. These people are targets for the communist propaganda.

One of the many aspects of the refugee problem largely exploited by the communists is the repatriation. According to a report released by UPI on June 24, 1975, as of June 15, 1975, 131,399 refugees had entered the U.S. system of control, including camps on Guam and 32,321 of them had joined their families or sponsors in the U.S. As of June 15, 1975, 3,756 refugees had been relocated in

18 countries other than the U.S., a majority of them in Canada. An additional 4,000 refugees had indicated their desire to resettle in other countries. 1,927 refugees indicated a desire to return to Indochina and the U.S. government will pay the cost of transportation if repatriation can be arranged with authorities in Saigon and Pnom Penh.

As one probes further into the problem of repatriation, it is obvious that the communist agents are making increasing efforts to turn the problem into an international scandal to hurt the prestige of the U.S. and to attempt to gain international sympathy for the new regime in Saigon.

Two repeated themes appeared in the refugees' requests: a wish to rejoin other family members and a desire to take part in the country's reconstruction. Refugees who wanted to return to their country have to fill out a form containing questions prepared by the communist government in Saigon. Among other things, they are asked why they left and why they want to return.

Requests for repatriation hurt the political cause of the evacuation. Pro-communist people tended to claim that the refugees were forced by the U.S. to come to the U.S. But the tactics used by the requesters up to now proved that they are very much like the political struggle tactics of the communists. At first they asked to be repatriated and they knew quite well that there must be some time before the U.S. could reach an arrangement with the new regime in Saigon through some international organization, for instance the United Nations. Meanwhile, they continued to harass the U.S. government for having deliberately delayed their repatriation. On June 21, 1975, the United Nations representatives had processed 76 applications from Vietnamese refugees seeking to return to their homeland but had no response from the Provisional Revolutionary Government. In mid August 1975, the new regime in Saigon declared that it refused the intermediary of the United Nations. The delay will give more ground to the requesters to become noisier in their anti-American claims.

A brief anatomy of their claim can help observers to understand better the communist tactics. At Fort Chaffee (Arkansas) on June 20, 1975, about 80 of the refugees who wanted to return to VN demonstrated for eight hours in hopes of speeding up their repatriation. Other refugees who do not want to go home planned a counter demonstration. Late in that day, camp administrators assured the repatriates they would be moved to Camp Pendleton, California the following week. The demonstration was ended and plans for a hunger strike on June 21 and violence on the 22nd were delayed. Le Minh Tan, 44, a spokesman for the demonstrating refugees said if the group was not flown to Pendleton on June 24, 1975 they would demonstrate again.

The transfer of the repatriates was delayed because the planes were being used to transfer other refugees from Guam to the U.S. Nguyen My, a spokesman for the second group of refugees had called the demonstrators Viet Cong agents and urged they be separated from other refugees at the post. Nguyen My said "They do not represent the majority of the refugees in this camp. We fear their action has affected our future relocation and we don't accept their actions. In my opinion, they are Viet Cong agents."

Le Minh Tan denied the demonstrators were communists. He said: "If we were communists, we would never come to the U.S. or if we were communists, we would stay in the U.S. and send information back to VN. We are not communists. We just love our country and want to return." Nguyen My said that some of the refugees who want to return to VN have coerced other refugees into filling out repatriation forms by threatening the safety of their relatives in VN.

Le Minh Tan was former fire inspector for the U.S. defense attache office in Saigon. He must understand at least as much as many other refugees that he fled South VN because of the communist inhuman policies. He must understand also that the communists never forgive those who have cooperated with the Americans. He could not harbor any illusion about his fate if he returns to Saigon, unless he has received some assurance from somebody. His argument was not a convincing one, because the communists did not need to send information agents to the U.S. The Vietnamese students residing here for long periods were their active agents. And to those who understood the policies of the Vietnamese communists, they must remember that for many years Hanoi did not urge their students to come back to VN. They just wanted them to stay abroad to act as propagandists and as lobbyists, if necessary. A former employee of an American agency, in Saigon, Le Minh Tan will be a good subject of propaganda for the new Saigon government. The familiar communist song will be heard again, for instance, "here is a former enemy of our people. Now, he confesses his sins and wants to redeem himself by coming back to our Fatherland and contribute to the reconstruction of our beloved country." Le Minh Tan may become a kind of hero in Saigon for a while. And after a few months, his story will fade away. One day, the people of South VN will learn that Hero Le Minh Tan has volunteered as hero of reconstruction at some railway public works. And consequently he will quietly disappear shortly after. It was the usual communist tactic to exterminate their former enemies. In a communist regime, nobody dares ask any question on such or such person when this person has secretly disappeared.

At the end of July 1975, there was another demonstration of the repatriates in Guam. On July 24, 1975, an estimated 200 Vietnamese waiting to return to their homeland marched on the Guam governor's residence to demand immediate repatriation. U.S. Marshalls arrested them and jailed them in a stockade. Officials said the demonstrators had been warned not to leave their camps, but did so and entered a U.S. Navy communications station. Witnesses said that no one was injured. The United Nations Representative in Guam, Mr. George Gordon Lennoz, said that the government in Saigon has been provided with detailed background information on each of the repatriates but the Saigon government told UN officials it will be "another several weeks" before Saigon would be ready to receive those seeking repatriation. This time, Le Minh Tan was assisted by another refugee named Nhu Van Uy. About 32 or 33 years of age, Nhu Van Uy was a former reporter of Chinh Luan, the only one anti-communist political newspaper in Saigon. When he was still a reporter, he used to criticize President Nguyen Van Thieu and his government in an uncivilized manner. His criticism gained him a reputation. In 1971 at the election for a new house of representatives for South VN, Nhu Van Uy managed to become a strong supporter of Nguyen Van Thieu. And he was elected very easily after signing some secret document pledging blind support to Thieu. The irony in this story was that he became even more verbally anti-communist than Thieu and liked to prove this anti-communism. Shortly after the election, there was the great communist offensive of 1972. Thieu's lieutenants in the house of representatives managed to carry a motion aiming at supporting Thieu and blaming the communists. After the ceremony for this motion, Nhu Van Uy stood in front of the house and shot three pistol bullets at the communist effigy, swearing that he would fight to destroy the communists until his last breath. Of course, his noisy tactics have been used by the Saigonese to make fun but Nguyen Van Thieu did like him.

Now, Nhu Van Uy left his family behind. He did not speak English and because he came from a peasant family, he may think that he can never start all over again in the U.S. He was back to his noisy tactics and when U.S. newspapers wrote about him, he was satisfied. Much noise to get attention from public opinion was his usual tactic. Nhu Van Uy has proved to be able to make a U-turn early in 1971 and this time, he may be able to make another U-turn in Saigon, if he can ever make himself accepted by the communists. However in Guam, Nhu Van Uy changed his mind another time when he said in the end of July 1975 that he did not think the UN would be able to take him home. Instead, he would seek the intermediary of the North Vietnamese Embassy in Paris (France).

In the future, some refugees resettled in the U.S. may be blackmailed to become some kind of communist lobbyists. The repatriation, noisy as it was, is only of secondary importance. Next step will be more important: to make propaganda to convince U.S. Congress and to convince Americans to provide aid for the communist regime in South VN. If they carry out that important objective, the Vietnamese communists will accomplish another remarkable victory, after the collapse of the nationalist regime in Saigon.

To counter that eventuality, nationalist refugees may be helpful to the anti-communist cause if they can develop a clever leadership right in the U.S. Unfortunately, there is no such bright prospect in a foreseeable future. After ten years of banditry rule, now, the Vietnamese refugees become leaderless. Someone may suggest some familiar names as Nguyen Cao Ky (former vice president), Nguyen Chanh Thi (former two star general, commander of I corps in South VN) but they were and are a painful disappointment to the refugees. Being an ex-sergeant in the French army and having a weak intellectual background, Nguyen Chanh Thi left South VN in 1966 and nobody can hope anything from him now. The era of the ex-French sergeant is really ended. After 1971, the South Vietnamese people have had some sympathy for Nguyen Cao Ky for the simple reason that at least, he did not participate in Thieu's gang. But with time running out, he still preserved his careless language. Sometime after August 1974, when the Catholic anti-corruption movement and the struggle of the Vietnamese journalists in Saigon began to get true sympathy from the common people in South VN, many thought that Ky would make history this time. But they realized that from 1967 to 1975, there was no serious change in his language, and in his political belief. He continued to be eloquent but South VN needed much more than words and promises.

Ky was among the men who left Saigon at the eleventh hour. Soon after the first Vietnamese refugees touched down on Guam, Ky discouraged his sympathizers with his usual sickness: his words are never followed by his actions. The refugees could hardly believe he intended to stay in Guam to help his compatriots (he loudly declared that intention to the journalists). Then they learned that he already left Guam for Camp Pendleton in South California. At Camp Pendleton, too, he promised to stay and share sorrow and happiness with other Viet refugees. But once again, after some patriotic and anti-communist declaration, he flew to meet his family in Washington, D.C. At the end of July 1975, he came back to Fullerton (close to Camp Pendleton) to deliver a speech. He said that he would rather return to South VN and fight side by side with more than 12,000 diehard nationalist soldiers, than stay here and that he was old enough to die now. This kind of unrealistic statement hurt him in Vietnamese eyes and destroyed his political career, if he did have one in the past.

For other refugees, it may be a long time before they can recover from the political and psychological shock of the collapse of South VN. Nobody can predict how long it will be before they will be able to unite and rid themselves of their disastrous passivity.

In April 1975, the airlift began and ended before Congress ever got around to granting Ford the authority to use U.S. troops to evacuate the South Vietnamese, but that did not deter President Ford. Pressed to defend his action, he replied "I took them out because they would be killed. I am proud of it." (Report from Newsweek, May 12, 1975)

Not only President Ford but the American people could be proud, too, for helping the Vietnamese refugees. The United States had a history of immigration, Irish, Hungarian and Cuban. But they came when the U.S. economy was good, unemployment was low. Now, when the U.S. economy is not so good and unemployment is high, the American people continue to honor their generous tradition. It is interesting to quote the noble statement of Senator Daniel K. Inouye, Hawaii, on May 23, 1975 to answering criticism of U.S. policy to welcome Vietnamese evacuees. ". . . Added to this is another element that these refugees for many reasons serve as reminder of a very bleak chapter in our history and there are those who don't want to remember and this is understandable. There is another element, which I hope is not too profound, and that is racism. I think we should openly acknowledge this . . . There are some who may not be openly antagonistic to a Hungarian refugee, but may be a bit more dismayed with someone who we recently referred to as a gook . . . To those who oppose our refugee program, I'd like to ask them what options do we have? Do we shove them back into the ocean or do we knowingly force them back into Saigon knowing that their lives might be in jeopardy?"

It is also interesting to recall that the U.S. government spent more than $1 billion in 1975 for Cuban refugees who left their country fifteen years ago.

But there were many countries which benefited greatly from the Indochina Wars and which failed to come to the aid of refugees from VN. Recently, the Americans have been able to find justification for their intervention in VN in the belated expressions of support from the non-communist states. Most of these resent the American presence in Asia, but they are also aware that America is their last available source of external help in the event of any future communist putsch. The American thwarting of communist plans in VN has indeed bought time for these non-communist countries without the distraction of external threats. The Indian, Burmese, Singapore, Malaysian, Thai and Philippines have all made this clear, in private if not in public, to Washington.

At least, these countries acted civilized when they accepted some Vietnamese refugees in their country: Thailand, Singapore, Hong Kong, Taiwan. There were, as of August 1975 about 5,000 refugees, scattered throughout these countries. But in the future, nobody knows what will be the lot of these refugees because of changing foreign policy in these countries. It is understandable that these refugees are now looking eagerly for the generosity of the American people.

Japan was one country which made large profits from the Indochina Wars. They made U.S. uniforms and some U.S. armaments. The Japanese sold over

800,000 Hondas, transistor radios, and television sets. But the Japanese government did not want to share in the human project and did not offer refugees aid. Canada which did not benefit from Indochina wars, has volunteered to take in 3,000 refugees. Next, in the western world, came France and Australia. Of course, the United States had the heaviest burden in this human project. What the U.S. is looking for is a civilized, although symbolic action from western countries and from all countries in the Free World to prove in humanitarian fashion at least there is a unity and solidarity among those countries which do not want to live under communist rule. Some countries did not respond. And now, they may become victims of their political selfishness. In ideological warfare, selfishness and intellectual cowardice never pay off: look at Portugal and Italy after 1974. The communists began to demonstrate that their frontier will not stop at Saigon, Pnom Penh and Vientiane.

Chapter Two

FROM WAR TO SLAVERY

Why had Vietnam suffered so much in 30 years of war and why will it no longer enjoy freedom?

Many factors led to the rivalry between North and South Vietnam. Two capitols—Hanoi and Saigon—were competitive. Poor and overpopulated, North Vietnam envied the wealthier South Vietnam. Northerners, sometimes being described as "proud and arrogant," gave themselves the idea that they had the sacred mission to look after the destiny of all Vietnamese people, because the southerners were supposed to be nonchalant and light-minded.

In 20 years, these two societies evolved into their own caricatures, the pastiche of the universe where we are living. The flame of war and its smoke had accelerated the decantation: rottenness of the South due to the exploitation of the dollar, puritanism in the North due to the excitement of virtue. In Hanoi, the sacrifices, in Saigon, the benefits, each one found there its satisfaction. The North was preaching and the South was amusing itself.

The Americans went home. Entangled in the tapes of Watergate, the foreign policy of Washington crumbled. That was the end. Hanoi watched America. It would never have the same opportunity: a demystified Kissinger, a confused foreign policy after Nixon's resignation, a power hungry Congress . . . North Vietnam launched its last great offensive under the cover of the so-called National Liberation Front. And the imperfections of the South, carelessness, indiscipline, confusion broke out. Then, it was the exodus, the debacle.

It was against this 30-year backdrop that millions of Vietnamese and 56,000 GIs died. The stubborn people of South Vietnam endured, supported and resisted. Finally, 20 million Northerners overwhelmed 20 million Southerners, thanks to military art and to a ceaseless flow of arms and equipment from Russia and Red China.

In spring 1975, the world witnessed a striking demonstration: in defiance of the most elementary human laws, violence and only violence of weapons decided the fate of a whole nation.

For years, the imperialist marxists, disguised as pacifists, promoted the necessity of a political solution for the Vietnam War. They achieved the conference of Paris which helped the U.S. to get out of Vietnam and which brought face-to-face two Vietnamese delegations at La Celle-Saint-Cloud without talking to each other for months.

The media however, announced every week the latest proposition from North Vietnam for "peace and democracy" in Vietnam: it would be a Third Force and the present government had to draw aside to be replaced by a government in which three political tendencies would put an end to the war and would rule democratically.

The entrance of Soviet tanks in Saigon on April 30, 1975 terminated that famous propaganda machine and nobody would hear again about the Third Force in Vietnam.

In invading South Vietnam, North Vietnamese soldiers took over all levels of command and the poor puppets of the PRG (Provisional Revolutionary Government) disappeared as if caught in a whirlpool.

Discipline, spirit of Sacrifice, absolute obedience and total submission to a simple catechism brought victory to the armed forces of North Vietnam. Now the leaders of North Vietnam became supreme masters of 50 million people in Indochina. At the price of millions of dead, they were victors on the military front and imposed their system on a nation which did not want their system.

Although Thieu's regime was hateful, it succeeded in motivating thousands of men to die in battle for the sake of freedom. It was probably a freedom with black spots on its robe but it was for that freedom that millions of South Vietnamese fought from 1954 to 1975.

All foreign newsmen, including the leftist journalists, (a total of 150) who were in Saigon the last days of the siege and the first days of victory, were unanimous on this point: the PRG (Viet Cong's government), so-called spontaneous movement of liberation of South Vietnam to fight against imperialism, was in reality non existant. Of course, there was a unit, only one, of militant women but its role was very small in the last campaign to take over South Vietnam. It was the army of soldiers in green uniform coming from North Vietnam which did everything and which began to impose everything on everybody.

—0—

The biggest question to the international public after April 30, 1975 was what would be the communist policy regarding their enemies (presumably the former officials, former servicemen, politicians etc. . . .) Would there be a bloodbath? As yet, was there anything foreign observers could conclude about the Saigon behavior?

If foreign observers were easily satisfied with the appearance, they would hastily conclude that there has been nothing substantial in terms of a bloodbath. Because these observers were looking only for quick results, they became natural victims of the most ingenious tactics of the Vietnamese Communists regarding millions of people connected to the old regime.

Even before the fall of South Vietnam, the Communists knew that the world opinion was waiting for a bloodbath in South Vietnam. Professor J.P. Honey, a British expert on Asian affairs predicted that at least, one million South Vietnamese would die and from four to five million would be sent to concentration camps.

So, drawing experience from the past, the Vietnamese Communists did not want to shock the world, particularly when they still hoped to get some kind of help from non-communist countries.

In North VN, after the communist takeover beginning July 1954, there was also the big question of how would the communists behave. Of course, among foreign observers and Indochina-watchers, there were those who jumped to the premature conclusion that there would be no blood bath in the coming months or years. North VN leaders waited two years and launched their bloodbath at the end of 1956. Half a million landlords and their family members were killed during the land reform movement in 1956. These landlords were put on trial at different courts called mass courts or courts of the people where arguments were presented and decisions were made by people who did not even have elementary knowledge about law and legal matters. The victims were accused of dishonestly gathering properties, of maltreating and over exploiting the peasants. But the truth is that most of these landlords had been hard working peasants before they became landowners. One year later, realizing that the land reform movement had been a terrible shock and a terror to North Vietnamese people (or perhaps because North Vietnamese leaders found out that enough killing had been done) the communists declared that the land reform movement had been a mistake. They decided to stop the killing and to readjust their peasant policies.

With time and experience, the Vietnamese in the North and in the South have become masters in the art of torture and in the art of killing people. Chinese domination, French colonialists, Japanese imperialists taught them the most inhuman art of torture. Unlike the Khmer Rouge, the Vietnamese communists were much more sophisticated. They did not kill hastily and openly as did the Khmer Rouge.

After April 30, 1975, some foreign reporters remained in Saigon. The bloodbath will not begin until the new regime in Saigon gets undesirable witnesses out. Presumably, "undesirable witnesses" include non-communist reporters and the foreigners. So, as long as the so-called undesirable witnesses stay in Saigon, the outside world still has some hope of getting true information on the new regime's behavior.

Associated Press was the first foreign news agency to release the report about the fighting that went on in at least eight provinces. At first, the Viet Cong radio said that "eight provinces to the south and west of Saigon were not yet liberated." It named these provinces: Can Tho, Vinh Long, Rach Gia, Soc Trang, Tra Vinh, Bac Lieu, Ca Mau and Long Chau Ha (including three former provinces of Long Xuyen, Chau Doc and Ha Tien). But later maybe the new rulers of Saigon realized that this report would be dispatched by foreign news agencies and that the news would be disadvantageous to the communists. Therefore the Viet Cong radio stopped talking about the fighting in any province in South VN after their takeover. Still, the U.S. intelligence establishment has good evidence that "lots of ex ARVN (Army of the Republic of VN) troops" are still fighting hold out actions. Small bands are operating in the Saigon area and occasionally for example they will toss grenades at groups of North Vietnamese soldiers. Larger bands are operating in the highlands waging guerilla war against the experts in guerilla warfare." On June 16, 1975, the Associated Press reported from Bangkok, Thailand that the Viet Cong avowed that isolated pockets of military resistance have been reported since Saigon fell on April 30, 1975.

Realizing the danger from foreign reporters, the new regime in Saigon began to expel non-communist reporters in July 1975. But Saigon could not prevent these reporters from dispatching many interesting news items about the secret bloodbath which is quietly carried out in Saigon and in many other areas in South VN. The first and serious evidence came from writer Paul Scott (The San Diego Union morning newspaper, July 1975). The article was entitled "Phu Quoc The final chapter" and this author wrote: "the final chapter of this tragic story of Phu Quoc is now being written in blood, tears, and internment in VN and largely indifference from the outside world. Approximately half of the 40,000 refugees taken to the island 50 miles from the coast of South VN, during the communist offensive on the mainland early this year have been returned and placed in special internment camps set up near Saigon by their communist captors. From these reeducation and indoctrination centers, many of these Phu Quoc refugees have literally disappeared. Officials of the United Nations international refugee office have been told by communist authorities in Saigon that the refugees are being returned to areas in VN from where they originally lived. Since most of these refugees fled originally from communist North VN in the 1950s, this report could mean that these refugees have been returned to internment camps in the North or have been killed.

"A number of killings are believed to have taken place shortly after the refugees arrived in the internment camps near Saigon. Dozens of refugees were last seen being forced aboard trucks at the Saigon camps and taken into the countryside. The trucks returned empty except for the guards and drivers.

"At the time of this writing, an estimated 15,000 refugees are still being held on Phu Quoc in two old prison camps on the southern part of the island. They sail nightly in small boats to international waters in hopes that passing ships will rescue them. When none appear, they return to their hiding place in the mountains. An estimated 300 have been picked up in the past 10 weeks by foreign vessels passing near Phu Quoc. The rescued refugees stressed that there are literally thousands of Vietnamese floating in the waters off the southern and western coasts of South VN and surrounding islands seeking to be rescued.

"When in Washington recently, Alexander Solzhenitsyn the exiled Soviet writer, forecast that more than one million persons will be killed in South VN by the communists and another two to three million placed in internment camps over the next five years. As far as those refugees from Phu Quoc are concerned, the killing and internment already has begun. The question each American must begin asking: can we as a people, who cherish freedom stand by and let all of South VN become a Phu Quoc?"

The second important evidence came from author Russel Firk when he wrote on July 29, 1975 in the San Diego Union daily newspaper ". . . American doves have mocked the Domino theory that if South VN should fall to the communists, many more states would fall successively. Well, South VN fell and the domino states are tumbling everywhere.

"Cambodia has fallen hideously into the hands of the Marxists so has Laos; Malaysia already is seriously troubled again by communist guerilas. Thailand is severing its ties with the U.S., perceiving the writing on the wall. The Philippines have gone neutralist . . .

"There remain American Doves who think that if a domino is knocked over why, it may be more comfortable prone. Those doves, like the United Nations, ignore the continuing extirpation of half Cambodia's population by the Khmer Rouge. No mass slaughter has occurred yet in South VN, the doves say: so, why don't the Vietnamese exiles go home?

"One thinks of how the communist regimes of eastern Europe shortly after the end of World War II, pretended to be merciful and persuaded some eminent fugitives to return. In Poland, even though the exiles went to Warsaw for discussion at the urging of Winston Churchill, they never were seen again. What we see just now in South VN probably is similar grisly communist strategy: profess moderation, entice the refugees back and then liquidate thoroughly.

"My wife and I are doing what we can to provide for some of the Vietnamese fugitives now in American camps. Two Vietnamese families, broken families, probably will come to live with us soon. Through the relief organizations, we obtain ghastly accounts of what already is occurring in Saigon.

"There is the narration, for instance, of a South Vietnamese soldier who contrived to escape about a fortnight after the mass flight from Saigon. The communists put him to work as a driver of the dead. He says that many officials, military officers and other opponents of the communists were sent to hospitals but not for the pretended "reeducation" that Radio Hanoi and Radio Saigon propagandized about.

"In those Saigon hospitals, our informant continues, the captives 'give' blood for a grand blood plasma bank thus atoning for their former ways by contributing to the communist medical arts. But they are bled excessively. In a few days, they are bled to death, deliberately. Then the bodies are disposed of, after this form of Chinese torture, and our informant was driving a truck loaded with bloodless corpses until he escaped.

"Perhaps you doubt that such atrocities could be perpetrated. But then, a good many Americans doubted that the Nazi concentration camps could be all that horrible, until American troops took the camps. In the lines of T.S. Elliot, It is hard for those who live near a police station to believe in the triumph of violence.

"Just now, America would like to forget about the fallen dominoes. But the ideologues who toppled those dominoes do not mean to forget about America . . . As Hilaire Belloc wrote once, those of us in seemingly secure and comfortable circumstances sit round a cheerful campfire and laugh at the Barbarian. But from the shadows beyond the firelight, great grim faces stare at us. And on these faces there is no smile."

—0—

At first, Hanoi leaders decided to move South Vietnam slowly and cautiously along the road to socialism. But the outside world was caught in a surprise when it was announced that the general election would be held in the North and in the South as well in late April 1976. What made Hanoi change its speed to socialism? There must be many serious reasons behind that change.

After a year in which the entire South Vietnamese population has gone through an astonishing process of reeducation and in which the beginnings of a new social organization have been painfully created, the boat to socialism is gathering speed.

Indeed there is evidence that this change follows a largely secret debate in Hanoi.

The basis for that change is fourfold. First, the gigantic and tricky management of the re-education which touched every social class, every occupational group and virtually every individual in the South Vietnamese society. Second, the creation of a vast network and hierarchy of committees and associations from the "solidarity cells" of 10 households to province and city councils, trade unions and left-wing pressure groups within the Church and the Buddhists sects. Third, the "new economic areas," mutual aid teams, worker's control in factories which pave the way for later collectivization. Finally, the formal political basis with an election scheduled.

Of course, the word "re-education" is an umbrella covering many things. It is an euphemism for the isolation of former army officers and government officials in permanent labour camps. Re-education can be a name for the new centres for drug addicts, beggars and prostitutes in Saigon. It has ranged from three day courses for waiters to endless sessions for the intellectuals.

There were various ad hoc meetings of street groups and workers in the cities, and villages in the countryside to speed the election of officials. They were guided by communist cadres. These elections have created a complicated array of committees. It would be naive to suppose that these committees represent a popular democracy. But we have to recognize that such committees represent more participation in decision-making at low levels than South Vietnamese have had before.

The "new economic areas" are like "re-education camps." In appearance, they may be state farms in embryo. According to some officials of the new regime, the new economic areas are aimed at correcting the distorted distribution of population that had swollen the cities, particularly Saigon. These areas are also a basis to prepare for later collectivization.

But as in the case of the re-education camps, the new economic areas are also an umbrella covering many things. They are a euphemism to isolate those people who were relatives of former servicemen or former officials. During the war years, South Vietnam had an army of 1,100,000 men, not including a police force of 300,000. An army of officials was composed of nearly another 300,000 men and women. Including dependents and relatives, there were about five million people in the South who were directly or indirectly connected with the old regime.

From the beginning, the Vietnamese Communists knew that it would be impossible for them to "re-educate" those people. Had it not been for the early warnings of the outside world about an eventual bloodbath, the Vietnamese communists would simply exterminate them. World opinion had at least made the Communists reluctant in planning for bloody revenge.

Of course, communist regimes do not care about world opinion. All they needed was a facade to deny international opinion a target for criticism. Re-education camps and new economic areas are therefore two good facades for that purpose.

The outside world has received only contradictory, emotional reports on the re-education camps and new economic areas. People had only a vague idea that life in South Vietnam must be harder than life under former non-communist regime but nobody can be sure how hard this life is.

In late November 1976, an important and reliable report from South Vietnam written by Father Andre Gelinas was received. Published by the French magazine L'Express on November 28, 1976, Father Gelinas gave a first-hand report after spending 15 months in South Vietnam after the Communist takeover. He is 52 years of age and spent the last thirty years in the Far East region. Born Canadian, he speaks fluent French, Chinese and Vietnamese. In December 1948, a month before Mao Tse Tung took over power in Peking, he left mainland China for Vietnam. Twenty-eight years later, he was expelled from Saigon together with the last religious people by the Communist government. His report is living testimony and deeply documented because he had a broad knowledge of Vietnam. Besides other horrible stories, he confirms that re-education camps and the new economic areas are really terrible punishment centers. Each camp contains from 3,000 to 5,000 people and nobody knows exactly where these camps are situated.

Ex-officers and important ex-officials were put in special camps where discipline is harder than in other camps. No Marxist lectures and only ditch digging. The status of the prisoners varies according to the importance of the "mistakes committed in the past." In the camp of ex paratroop-special forces, the Communists shoot five or six people every day. In one of many ex-policemen camps, situated at Long Giao not far from Saigon, Father Gelinas wrote that on April 24, 1976, the Communists sent military airplanes to bomb and to machine-gun the camp. The camp was completely destroyed, including the ex-policemen. It was a pure and simple extermination.

The new regime can kill the prisoners by other means: no medicine for sick people, malnutrition for everybody. Of course, there are many medical doctors among those confined in re-education camps but they can do nothing because of the terrible shortages of medicines.

The new government does not need high barbed wire fences around these camps. Those who want to escape will surely fail. Without identity papers, they will be captured within 24 hours because the whole country is tightly controlled by communist cadres and agents. With no ID card to explain movement, it is virtually impossible for a prisoner to escape. If their attempt fails, they will be sent to harder work, like clearing minefields in jungle areas. Everybody knows well what that kind of work means.

On the grounds that such or such social class did not produce, the new regime is sending the relatives of former servicemen and former officials to the new economic areas. Living conditions in those areas are not much different from those of the re-education camps. Sooner or later, sickness, malnutrition and many other things will destroy these people. And the communists continue to deny any killing, any massacre. This is the new tactic to "remove those directly or indirectly connected with the old regime." The tactics work well and deny world criticism. In a year or more, the busy daily life of the outside world will make everybody forget these huge prisons, forget these miserable people. This selfish attitude from most of the international community will provide something tantamount to a blessing for the new form of bloodbath in South Vietnam. The same attitude portends many Vietnams in the future.

So, every class and group in South Vietnam has found itself subject to some kind of redirection or coercion. This will continue. Two groups are already on their way to total destruction—the old upper class of top officers and officials and the war-induced service class of non-productive city dwellers. Perhaps half of all urban dwellers face the unpalatable prospect of a return to the countryside. And the Communists have plans which represent a threat to virtually every class or group in the South.

For better or for worse, after the so-called general election of April 25, 1976, the two Vietnams now have a single undivided assembly and a new unified government. However, there is serious reason to believe that even after the general election and after the birth of a unified government, the speed of change in the South is bound to continue after the formal reunification. Broad sectors of southern society are potentially hostile. Mishandling, bullying or economic problems could turn that potential hostility into conflict. Already the treatment of the officer corps and of some thnic and religious minorities has produced an active armed resistance. In November 1975, Radio Saigon spoke of "thousands of remnant enemy troops still operating surreptitiously in the jungle."

For the time being (20 months after the Communist takeover), the resistance does not represent a major problem for the Communists. This resistance is still in the form of small scale, unorganized groups and eventually, it may run out of ammunition and/or equipment, let alone morale. But it is a pointer to the way in which things could go wrong in the South on a broader scale if, in spite of the new and formidable political organization set up by the Communists recently, the people were pushed too hard or too fast. Then the Communists might face an enlarged armed resistance. More important, they might find they had alienated large sections of the population, encouraging cynicism, apathy and shirking when what they need desperately is trust, enthusiasm and hard work.

—0—

To close this gloomy chapter, readers should be reminded of something regarding the attitude of the Viet war critics.

Columnist John P. Roche wrote on June 15, 1976:

"Ten years ago, the academy was full of Southeast Asian experts who confidently asserted that in Vietnam, the United States was interfering in a civil war, that the people of South Vietnam, down in their hearts, were supporting the National Liberation Front against the repressive, unrepresentative Saigon clique.

"As the so-called peace negotiations proceeded, a number of variations on this theme surfaced, the most popular of which was that we should dump Thieu, replace him with General Big Minh, and watch the love feast as all the South Vietnamese rallied around a coalition government."(1)

The so-called Southeast Asian experts received their answer directly from Hanoi in the form of a report of 40,000 words published by Hanoi's official newspaper, the Nhan Dan, at the end of April 1976. General Van Tien Dung, Chief of Staff, North Vietnamese armed forces is supposed to be the author of this lengthy account under the title Great Spring Victory. It was a candid account and a cynical confession about how Hanoi planned and achieved its final victory in South Vietnam in 1975. After more than twenty years denying that it never had any troops fighting in South Vietnam, now, it was Hanoi itself which loudly issued the account in which, North Vietnam proudly confessed its planning from the headquarters of the Politburo in Hanoi.

Most of the western newspapers published General Dung's account and these papers were inclined to forget that it was Hanoi which started the war years ago. The naivity of western people served well the interests of international communism. The western world apparently accepted the "fait accompli" in Vietnam. And now, the same world (namely Free World) did not even care when Hanoi confessed the invasion in South Vietnam.

In Vietnam, people who loved liberty as much as the Free World were cruelly betrayed by a guilty silence. This world pledged to help them achieve democracy, then the same world stood aside as they were enslaved by the Vietnamese Communists. The silence of the Free World as Hanoi avowed its crimes is infamy. It will be impossible for any country of the Free World to deny this unfortunate truth: the silence of the Free World not only became tacit complicity of all war crimes committed by the Communists in Vietnam but the blessing for the Communist invasion in South Vietnam.

Fortunately, there are still those people who realize that General Dung's account was quite an outrageous act to defy the international community. From many cities in the world, people began to analyze this shameful account.

Finally, Hanoi gave orders in October 1976 to withdraw the account entitled The Great Spring Victory.

Throughout two decades of the war in Vietnam, world opinion was so poisoned that even now, it is still quiet. "Where are Viet War critics now?" Was the title of an article signed Smith Hempstone and published on November 21, 1976. Mr. Hempstone wrote:

"Back in those bad old days when Nguyen Van Thieu was running South Vietnam, Lon Nol was in charge in Cambodia and Souvanna Phouma was the boss of Laos, not a single sparrow fell without arousing the horror and anger of a goodly claque of American politicians, folksingers and pundits.

"Not a Buddhist monk could immolate himself, not a truncheon could fall without drawing a pack of journalists eager to make the repressive nature of these pro-Western regimes known to the world.

"And that was, of course, as it should be: the press has a duty to report injustice.

"But things are going on now in South Vietnam, Cambodia and Laos that would make a statue weep. And we hear nary a peep about them.

"The North Vietnamese who are a little smarter than those who believed that Ho Chi Minh was just a grandfatherly nationalist who wanted to reunite his country, waited until May of this year to launch a bloodbath that liberals told us was just a figment of the conservative imagination.

"All Western journalists, missionaries and diplomats were expelled from South Vietnam in that month. And the absence of witnesses makes it ever so much more convenient for Ho's boys to get about their bloody work . . . It is not known how many people have died or been summarily murdered by kangaroo courts as the ultimate act of their 're-education.' But escapees report that prisoners are kept on a near starvation diet, and that many thousands have died of malnutrition, malaria, beriberi and dysentery.

"So harsh are conditions in South Vietnam that more than 100,000 have risked their lives to flee, sailing in small boats to Thailand (where they are wanted) or escaping overland to that country through Cambodia. Many thousands have drowned, died of thirst or been shot in the attempt . . . All this of course, is taking place far from the prying eyes of Western journalists since neither they nor non-Communist diplomats are admitted in those countries."(2)

143

A year ago, Hanoi sensed that the coming of peace was a great victory but the joy has evaporated quickly with the passing months.

Peace has not yet brought about many of the material improvements that people hoped it would. Moreover, the fighting spirit that dominated the North during war time has faded. The North Vietnamese are now asking for more comfort, more goods. They see no reason why they should continue to make sacrifices.

In South Vietnam, the false wealth of the past is disappearing. People have to adapt themselves to the hard conditions under the new regime.

In the North and in the South, they do have independence and peace. The war is over but the price of that peace is Vietnamese poverty . . .

The new unified government in Vietnam is facing immense problems: the South, accustomed to living on wealth, can no longer afford hard life under the present regime. The North is thirsty for consumer goods it could not get during the war. But the economy of the unified Vietnam has only a narrow industrial base.

Therefore, the new authorities in Hanoi and Saigon have adopted an economic strategy that relies on foreign aid. But this strategy is more difficult now that peace was restored.

While the Red Chinese maintain only a low profile in terms of economic aid, Russia did offer more than Hanoi asked for. Hanoi sees danger in the Soviet offer and decides therefore to offer diplomatic relations to the United States. Hanoi hopes that the U.S. will help Vietnam with the reconstruction and prevent Vietnam from becoming a Soviet economic dependency.

With a new president who will take office on January 20, 1977, U.S. foreign policy will be kept open.

From the present situation, the U.S. is in the best position to give the Vietnamese Communists the lesson they need: in recent guerilla warfare history, winning a war is one thing but building a viable nation is quite another.

In the past, for reasons which have been explained in this book, American aid to South Vietnam had damaged more than helped because it did not reach the majority of Vietnamese people. In the future, it may be hard for anybody to say that the U.S. should not aid Vietnam. On humanitarian and pragmatic grounds, postwar reconstruction aid seems a policy worth considering because it will be another way to look at Vietnam besides the ideological ways.

But on the other hand, American aid should not be provided to South Vietnam if the American taxpayers are not assured that it helps to improve the living conditions of Vietnamese people in terms of a society in which every citizen must enjoy basic human rights.

Of course, the Communists will be reluctant to receive any kind of aid tied to some pre-condition. The Russians had the same attitude when they started their negotiations with the U. S. on the problem of Jewish-Russians.

Regarding U.S. aid to Vietnam, it will not be realistic of the U.S. to negotiate the evacuation of the Vietnamese people. Negotiation, if any, will seek assurances that this time, American aid will put people, and not just government, into the foreign aid equation.

In considering any form of aid to Vietnam, the U.S. should not forget thousands of South Vietnamese who are living under unthinkable conditions in the so-called re-education camps or in the so-called new economic areas. Because these people believed in a non-communist South Vietnam created, supported and defended by the U.S., they are becoming victims of the fanatic and primitive marxists in Vietnam.

To forget those miserable victims is immoral.

Chapter Three
ON POST-VIETNAM U.S. FOREIGN POLICY

The fruits of the Vietnam War are sour. In one sense, it was an ignominious defeat for the greatest military power on earth.

The sour taste will not only be for America, but also for many other countries which have or thought they had an American "commitment." Will the American people, at least in this generation, rush to honor other commitments after Vietnam? Will the war in Vietnam lead to a new form of American isolationism? In light of South Vietnam's experience, will other threatened small nations seek American protection, or will they prefer to passively succumb to communist pressure? Answers to these questions will shed light on the role and destiny of the U.S. over the next decade and perhaps beyond.

The American involvement in the Vietnam War has provided successive Administrations in Washington with these ingredients: great power confrontation, national interests and national prestige. Since 1954, the problem faced by each U.S. President in Vietnam has been to reduce the dangers of confrontation with Russia and with Red China, while pursuing what were perceived to be American interests (containment of Communism in Asia by helping and preserving non-communist countries).

Complicating this problem has been a need to preserve the "National prestige." The question of prestige has had a significant influence on decisions to move step by step up the ladder, increasing military activities, and it has substantially complicated any attempt of disengagement.

The post-Vietnam dilemma for American strategists is to relate such considerations as strategic importance to the expansion of American industrial and military technology and to the mood of American people. The present mood is one that forces any Administration to take a hard new look. For this result at least, the American people have to thank the involvement in the Vietnam War.

For Americans, the U.S. involvement in Vietnam may well be the last crusade. Americans of the post-Vietnam era have become wiser and more realistic about the world. Future U.S. foreign policy will have to be based more on an appeal to reason and self-interest than to emotion and righteousness.

What does this portend for America's friends and foes? According to one line of thought, the fall of pro-western governments in Indochina was in reality the result of replacing the policy of containing China with the policies of the Nixon doctrine. These shifts could have a considerable influence on the future U.S. foreign policy as the U.S. is trying to balance the interests of security against growing demands for further reduction of American overseas commitments.

Having abandoned containment as a policy, the U.S. has established friendlier ties with Russia and Red China, thereby creating a new world order.

The same reasoning does not think it is wise of the Americans to be alarmed at the new geopolitical configuration in East Asia after the fall of South Vietnam. The realignment of Asian countries is not necessarily detrimental to the U.S. interests, meaning that U.S. policy should be based on actions of other countries rather than on any abstract political ideologies they might embrace. In other words, the U.S. will establish diplomatic relations with a nation, irrespective of its political leanings, if such relationship will further U.S. national interests.

Is this approach inconsistent with the Nixon doctrine and the detente the U.S. is seeking to establish with major Communist powers? It seems that if it wants to achieve detente, the U.S. must establish a working relationship with all nations having a capacity to shift either regional or international power balances.

This approach also advocates that the U.S. refrain from social and political experimentation in its dealings with other nations. It implies that if this approach includes temporary alignment with communism as a means, then the U.S. policy must be flexible to accommodate regional political realities. It implies, too, that the U.S. cannot stem the tide of communism in Asia if there are Asian nations which are bent on accommodation with or abdication to some form of communism.

The reasoning mentioned above seemed to be reinforced by a survey on the political situation in Asia one year after the Communist takeover in Indochina. The fall of South Vietnam did not mean, at least for the time being, hostile forces leaping from Southeast Asia to the Middle East, swarming down across the whole of Africa and again leaping an ocean to spread across Latin America.

So, today, the U.S. does not dominate Southeast Asia but no one else does either. Great powers are rivals for influence in Southeast Asia. Meanwhile, Southeast Asian countries are playing one off against the other and even trying to use the U.S. as a counterweight against either Russia or Red China, depending on which seems to be the more intrusive. America apparently is sought rather than feared.

Such reasoning is quite logical if it is based on the premise that future U.S. foreign policy will be characterized by three options:

- Maintain leadership, at least militarily with respect to Europe, some partnership with Russia and set up something to the Third World;
- Interdependence option—avoid arms race with Russia, set up limits to any intervention, partnership with Europe and Japan, realistic way of aid, not necessarily that the recipient countries must be non-communist, no more concept of foreign aid to buy friends; and

147

• Disengagement in Asia and in Africa.

This premise is plausible if the international communism really wants the detente and if the Communists stop their expansion in the world. In other words, security and peace for the Free World can be negotiated with the Communists.

But when we face reality, things are not so rosy. After the fall of Indochina, there was Angola. By sending an expeditionary force of 12,000 Cubans almost openly to Angola and by supplying sophisticated weapons, Moscow demonstrated that American passivity undoubtedly strengthened the long-standing Soviet belief that the U.S. was forced into detente by its own weakness and indecision. Such conclusion doubtless will result in stronger Soviet pressures on far-flung revolutions—forms of ideological warfare which Moscow specifically reserved the right to accelerate.

The Far East is now the part of the world where, in the wake of the Communist victories in Indochina, American influence has most rapidly declined. Thailand and Malaysia are threatened by domestic insurgency and far-reaching economic problems. Neither can count today on either America or Britain to guarantee their security. Each of them has to juggle the sometimes conflicting, sometimes competitive ambitions of three major communist powers: Russia, China and the unified Vietnam.

The overriding question for Thailand and Malaysia is whether they can exploit the Chinese-Soviet dispute to protect their own identity and to contain the potential threat from Vietnam. If the Chinese abandon their present moderation—possibly as a result of some future rapproachement with Russia—then Thailand and Malaysia could find themselves up against an inter-communist competition to support the guerillas who threaten them.

In 1941, Mr. Herbert Hoover declared that "If we stand aside and do not help the Soviet government, the time will come when we can bring lasting peace to the world. The result of our assistance to the Russians would be to spread Communism over the world." A generation later, Mr. Solzhenitsyn tells the U.S. the same story.

And so it goes. American allies are shaken because they saw the U.S. fail in steadfast leadership. Asian countries are finding their way out simply by surrendering to the Communists.

To Western Europe, surrender to the Communists is not a suitable solution. Europe was and is the heartland of the Western world. The peace and prosperity of the U.S. is tied closely to the peace and prosperity of Western European countries. The deep concern of Western Europe is that the U.S. may not see it the same way.

Why do the warnings of the voices of experience go regularly unheeded and unechoed in their home countries? Peace is never in greater danger when a generation arrives at maturity without any knowledge of war. It is the case of more than half of Europe now.

In the U.S., the causes of complacency may be different but the result is the same. Fewer and fewer Americans place national defense and the Communist threat among their interests of concern. One of those causes can be traced to the Vietnam War. American politicians, sensing the new isolationist trend at home bred by the war in Vietnam, seized on the opportunity to bury American swords for their own political gains.

More dangerous is the complacency caused by the detente with the Soviet Union. Kissinger himself has contributed to the public mood of complacency in

148

the U.S. Today, the U.S. defense budget has the smallest share of the gross national product and the federal budget since the Korean War. The grim realities that must shape the U.S. investment in defense in the next decade cannot be wished away. Such grimness will be felt the most by those people still clinging to the illusion that the end of the Vietnam War would produce a peace dividend for U.S. domestic programs.

There is nothing obscure in the message of Hoover and Solzhenitsyn. They said that 30 years ago, the U.S. began to lose a simple perception of what a foreign policy is. The strong survive, while the weak are destined for mediocrity or slavery. Strength is not confined to military means alone.

In its dealings with other nations, the U.S. cannot impose its own standards and it must accept nations as they are. But at the same time, there must be a moral component in American foreign policy. The U.S. must stand for something, especially in a world where democracy seems to be in retreat and repression on the ascendant.

There is nothing wrong with American foreign policy if its goal is to build a better alliance in the West, to reach an understanding with the Communist powers and establish a better relationship with the Third World.

Unfortunately, the consequences of the Vietnam War for the U.S. are likely to be grave: an over-reaction on the part of the Administration to other international crisis (the *Mayaguez* affair, May 1975) in an effort to "prove" itself. A sense of general disillusionment and malaise leading to a popular revulsion against any international commitments, even those involving foreign economic assistance.

We are living under the permanent threat from International Communism. The malaise of the post-Vietnam period may lead to a new trend of isolationism. In one sense, the new geopolitical reconfiguration in Asia may be considered by the new trend of isolationism as not necessarily detrimental to U.S. interests. But what will be the reaction of the American people if there is another new geopolitical reconfiguration in Europe—for instance the Communists entering the Italian government through an election? Will the same mood of malaise prevail in case of the domino theory in Europe?

When we looked back to the post World War II era, we could realize clearly the strategy of the International Communism. Always on the offensive, the Communists invented strategy according to a new international political situation. The War in Korea in 1950 was the first model to test the will of the Free World. It was the unity of the Free World rather than sophisticated weapons which repulsed the Communist invasion in South Korea.

After the Korean War, the Communists changed their strategy. This time, their strategy would deny any intervention by international organization. The War in Vietnam was proclaimed by the leaders of the Kremlin as a model "War of Liberation" and it would be strongly supported by the whole international communist movement.

Now, once again, the Communists change their strategy in the conquest of Europe. This time, the Communists will have a "human face" by seeking their way into European political life through the elections.

The Western World seems satisfied that NATO had its unity renewed and that no danger lurks. Kissinger once referred to America's relationships in the Atlantic area as "the absolute core element of American foreign policy." What would happen to this relationship should the Communists succeed in taking power in Italy, in France and/or in Portugal by elections?

NATO is a military organization. Can this organization prevent a communist takeover by peaceful means: election, referendum?

Many Western European countries are experiencing serious economic difficulties. Some of these countries are not yet completely recovered from the oil crisis of 1973. People in those countries began to think of the Communists as an alternative to a democratic government when they saw their form of government incapable of solving internal economic problems.

Facing the Communist new strategy in Europe, it is doubtful that the U.S. could intervene with its nuclear arsenal.

America is a highly developed country. Most people in that country do not like to look directly at the danger from the Communists, because they are living in an affluent society. This society is satisfied in itself and does not want to sacrifice its present affluence. It explains the difficulties encountered by successive U.S. Administrations each time they had to request funds for military spending.

The Communists do not want to attack directly in the U.S. territories because it is suicidal. They continue to attack America's allies by peaceful means, while they continue to build up their military forces. They did not get in trouble because their leaders did not have to report to any congress.

Unless the Free World tries to break this encircling strategy of the Communists, America may find itself some day completely isolated and surrounded by a hostile world.

—0—

EPILOG

In the Vietnam War, a South Vietnamese soldier died in the battles every 8 minutes.

After the cease-fire accords were signed in Paris on January 27, 1973, South Vietnam lost 150,000 more on battlefields and 700,000 joined the army of 6 million refugees.

After the fall of South Vietnam on April 30, 1975, about 5 million people were living in unthinkable conditions either in re-education camps or in the new economic areas.

Almost every day, more and more South Vietnamese are fleeing in flimsy fishing boats. Officials in Australia which has taken in many of the refugees, think that while hundreds arrive safely, many others perish during the dangerous voyage. Despite all this, the flow of refugees continues.

But the Free World does not care. More than ever, countries in the Free World care only about their economic problems and about immediate pleasure.

Selfishness and material life make them forget that when it takes power, a totalitarian regime can never become humanized and that liberty, which is the most precious property, is vulnerable.

The fall of South Vietnam is only a stage of the retreat route of the Free World. This retreat looks like the retreat of Napoleon from Russia: scattered with corpses. Right now, there are already more corpses on the retreat routes of the Free World than on Napoleon's. And there will be many more corpses in the coming years if the Free World continues its present complacency regarding detente, material life and divisiveness.

For those Vietnamese who were lucky enough to seek refuge abroad, it will be a new life. Whether their new life will be good or bad, depends largely on their will and their capacity to start all over again. They may discover new human freedom after losing their freedom in South VN. But for those who remain in South VN, because of passivity or because they were unable to flee, they will have the taste of what was happening to the North Vietnamese since 1954. From now on, a smile will be an extreme luxury.

That is the story of the fall of South VN, a remote country in a remote continent of the third world. To those people who simplify everything related to the Vietnam War, the conclusion is easy: the fall occurred because of the corrupt regime in the South and because of the determination of the North. Besides, South VN is still far from any other advanced country of the Free World. It is still time to contain the international communism.

For those who are really worrying about the survival of free and open societies, the writer proposes the conclusion of Alexander Solzhenitsyn. Thirty days after the fall of South VN, Solzhenitsyn wrote an article published in the French daily newspaper Le Monde, "The Third World War has ended." The article said: "The third world war began at the end of second world war, in 1945 at Yalta. We have not understood that the third world war came about differently from its predecessors. It began, not with a thundering declaration of war, not with attacks by thousands of airplanes, but invisibly, stealthily boring into the flabby body of the world. It used a variety of pseudonyms, cold war, peaceful coexistence, normalization, Realpolitk, detente, trade which serves only to strengthen the aggressor.

"When we study the course of these last 30 years, we see it as a long, sinuous descent toward enfeeblement and decadence. The powerful western states having emerged victorious from two previous world wars have, in the course of these 30 years of peace, lost their real and potential allies, ruined their credibility in the eyes of the world, and abandoned to an implacable enemy whole territories and populations.

"The victorious nations have transformed themselves into the vanquished, having totally ceded more countries and peoples than have even been ceded in any surrender in any war in history. And that is why it is not speaking metaphorically to say: The Third World War has taken place and has ended in defeat for the West.

"In the 30 years of the Third World War, 20 nations lost their freedom: Estonia, Latvia, Lithuania, Moldavia, Mongolia, Yugoslavia, Albania, Poland, Bulgaria, Romania, Czechoslovakia, Hungary, East Germany, China, North Korea, Cuba, North VN, South VN, Cambodia and Laos. In addition, Thailand, South Korea and Israel are in danger, Portugal is throwing herself irretrievably into the abyss, Finland and Austria are resigned to their fate, powerless to defend themselves.

"There were three temporary victories for the west in the Third World War: Greece in 1947, West Berlin in 1948 and South Korea in 1950. These victories inspired hope and faith in the west. But take a look at these names today. Which of these three places now has the power to resist enslavement? Who will defend them when they are threatened? What senate will approve the sending of arms and aid? Who will not prefer his own peace and quiet to their liberty? When valiant Israel was defending herself to the death, Europe was capitulating, country after country, before the threat of a reduction in its Sunday driving.

"It is too late to worry about how to avoid the Third World War. But we must have the courage and clearheadedness to stop the Fourth. To stop it, not grovel on our knees."

152

PART I

Chapter I

Notes

1. U.S. Senate, Committee on Foreign Relations, Hearings: Nomination of Philip Jessup 82:1 (Washington, 1951), 603.
2. Chester L. Cooper 'The Lost Crusade': *America in Vietnam,* (Fawcett Premier, 1970-1972) p. 67.
3. *Charles de Gaulle:* tr. by Richard Howard 'The War Memoirs', Salvation 1944-1946 (New York: Simon and Schuster, 1960) p. 242.
4. Charles de Gaulle, *Ibid,* p. 258.
5. Chester L. Cooper, *Ibid,* p. 68.
6. Chester L. Cooper, *Ibid,* p. 69-70.
7. Ellen J. Hammer *The Struggle for Indochina* (Stanford, California: Stanford University Press, 1954) p. 13.
8. Edgar Snow *The other side of the river: Red China today* (New York, Random House 1961) p. 686.
9. The New York Times Book Review, Oct. 12, 1969 p. 30.
10. Marvin E. Gettlemen, ed. *Vietnam History, Documents and Opinions on a major world crisis* (New York 1965) p. 79.
11. U.S. Senate, Committee on Foreign Relations *Hearings: Nomination of Philip Jessup:* 82:1 (Washington 1951), 603.
12. Dept. of State Bulletin, Feb. 13, 1950, p. 244.
13. Dept. of State Bulletin, April 10, 1950, p. 565.
14. U.S. Senate, Committee on Foreign Relations, Hearings: *U.S. foreign aid programs in Europe* 82:1 (Washington, 1951), 208.
15. J.F. Dulles, *War or Peace* (New York: The McMillan Co., 1950) p. 231.
16. Hammer-op. cit. p. 312.
17. and 18. Eisenhower, *Mandate for change,* p. 168 and p. 337.
19. Eisenhower, *Mandate for change,* p. 345.
20. Dept. of State *American Foreign Policy II,* 2389-90.
21. New York Times, June 27, 1954, p. 1E.
22. Dept. of State Bulletin, May 24, 1954, p. 781.
23. Wall Street Journal, July 23, 1954.

Chapter II

Notes

1. Bernard Fall, *The Two Vietnams,* Second revised Edition, 1966, Praeger Publishers, New York.
2. and 3. The Pentagon Papers, Chapter 2.
4. The Pentagon Papers, Chapter 2.

Chapter III

Notes

1. The Pentagon Papers, Chapter 1.
2. The Pentagon Papers, Chapter 5.

PART III

Chapter II

Notes

1. The San Diego Union, June 15, 1976.
2. The San Diego Union, November 21, 1976.